PRAISE FOR BILL RE

FALL RIVER DREAMS: A Team's Quest for Glory — A Town's Search for Its Soul (St. Martin's Press, 1994)

"Reynolds uncovers, in a moving and sensitive book, the desperate values of a city whose only dream is basketball glory."
—Newsday

"A marvelous book."
—The Boston Globe

"Poignant."
—USA Today

"Reynolds does a fine job…Fall River Dreams illustrates that sports can provide marvelous highs, but the joy of achievement can be supplanted by the desperate need to win — again and again and again."
—The New York Times

LOST SUMMER: The '67 Red Sox and the Impossible Dream (Warner Books, 1992)

"A treasure…written with such grace and humanity that it reads like a novel."
—Doris Kearns Goodwin, author of The Fitzgeralds and the Kennedys

"A terrific book."
—Leigh Montville, Sports Illustrated

COUSY: His Life, Career and the Birth of Big-Time Basketball
(Simon & Schuster, 2005)

"(an) insightful, well-written biography...Reynolds does a remarkable job illuminating the sport's early days in the 1940's... But the book's best parts are those in which Reynolds illuminates how Cousy's impoverished 1930's youth...created in him a drive to succeed..."
—PUBLISHERS' WEEKLY

"Voluble, basketball-savvy tour of Boston Celtic great Bob Cousy's life...Reynolds does a beautiful job of painting Cousy, right down to his French lisp...Not only an insightful biography, but a shining history of the early NBA as well."
—KIRKUS REVIEWS

'78: The Boston Red Sox, a Historic Game, and a Divided City
(New American Library, 2009)

"Reynolds does a superb job of stitching this baseball story into the larger tapestry of racial unrest that had Boston seething thirty years ago."
—DAYTON DAILY NEWS

"(A) wide-ranging, zeitgeist-laden account of the terrible year that saw the Red Sox in first place in the American League East by a wide margin in July and humbled by the despised Yankees in October."
—THE BOSTON GLOBE

OUR GAME: The Story of New England Basketball (Hall of Fame Press, 2006)

"Where some describe what they see or capture
what they've learned, Reynolds is the rare scribe who did it
himself and feels every bit of it. This is a basketball player with
the gift of observation. The thrill of the race up-court or the
last-second jumper comes back to anyone who ever played
the game when they read OUR GAME."
—DORIS BURKE, ESPN BASKETBALL ANALYST

"Bill Reynolds is a man who has great feeling for the game of
basketball. In OUR GAME, he dedicates himself to capturing all
of the golden moments and characters of New England basketball.
Trust me, Bill Reynolds is a winner!"
—DICK VITALE, ESPN/ABC TV COMMENTATOR

OTHER TITLES BY BILL REYNOLDS

BIG HOOPS: A Season in the Big East Conference
(New American Library)

GLORY DAYS: On Sports, Men, and Dreams that Don't Die
(St. Martin's Press)

RISE OF A DYNASTY: The '57 Celtics, the First Banner,
and the Dawning of a New America
(New American Library, 2010)

HOPE: A School, a Team, a Dream
(St. Martin's Press)

BASKETBALL JUNKIE, a Memoir with Chris Herren
(St. Martin's Press)

Story Days

HIGHLIGHTS FROM FOUR DECADES
COVERING SPORTS

BILL REYNOLDS

STORY DAYS

CONTENTS

FOREWORD

For decades, Bill Reynolds indulged an abiding passion by playing basketball several times a week. He would pull up to the gym and pick out a shirt, a pair of shorts, and athletic socks from a pile of clothes in his locker, which also happened to be the trunk of his car. After all, you never know when a game might break out.

Well into his 60s, Bill had game. A standout player for Brown University back in the day, he had refined a turnaround jump shot from the corner that I can attest was impossible to block. But he was also *the* game, the one who had assembled the ever-changing collection of characters taking the court with him. There were lawyers and ex-cons and computer whizzes and problem gamblers and journalists and grad students and guys whose sources of income were left best unspoken — a diverse and sometimes contentious bunch who seemed to play less for the competition than for the chance to be in Bill's orbit.

And everyone wanted to be on Team Reynolds.

Looking back, I see now how those games — and the people he gathered around him — were integral to Bill's other passions. Opening himself up to all walks of life. Choosing empathy over judgment. Listening, truly listening, to the stories of others, and then sharing those stories with the exact right words.

You could be a self-assured college basketball coach well on your way to national fame and success. Or you could be a young man whose bad choices had ruined your chance at glory, leaving you staring at a rim without a net on some outdoor court, haunted by the what-ifs. Bill treated both of you the same — with respect.

There are sports journalists who only see the world that exists between the lines that determine fair or foul, in-bounds or out. Then, retreating to their keyboards, they surrender to sports cliches

dating to the Olympics of ancient Greece, glorifying feats of athlet-
icism in ways that only diminish what it means to be truly heroic.

Then there are the journalists who see beyond the lines; who rec-
ognize that sports provide a means by which to explore the human
condition. They understand how naturally the words of the Irish
playwright Samuel Becket — "Ever tried. Ever failed. No matter.
Try again. Fail again. Fail better." — apply to what they see on and
off the field.

These are the journalists who instinctively separate from the pack
and go the other way. Murray Kempton, heading to the locker of
the losing pitcher, Sal Maglie, when Don Larsen of the New York
Yankees pitched a perfect game against the Brooklyn Dodgers in
the 1956 World Series. Jimmy Breslin, the only reporter watching
the gravedigger Clifton Pollard dig the resting place for John F.
Kennedy at Arlington National Cemetery in 1963. Bill Reynolds.

Read the selections in this volume and you will understand what
I mean. Bill can be silly at times, as when he imagined a therapy session centering on the sudden national obsession with Doug Flutie.
More often, though, his stories are driven by a rare compassion. His
reporting instincts and writing skills are superior, of course, but it is
his empathy that truly elevates the work.

In 1988, for example, a professional basketball player quietly
ended his career. This was Billy Donovan, a tough-nosed guard
who had stunned the college basketball world a year earlier by leading a gritty Providence College basketball team to the Final Four of
the N.C.A.A. tournament. For many he personified the rewards that
can come from perseverance.

His 44 appearances with the New York Knicks had been the
realization of a boy's dream, but they were behind him, and now
here he was, cut from yet another NBA team. All that hard work —
the training, the weightlifting, the 500 jump shots a day — hadn't
been enough. His playing career officially over, Donovan returned
to his home on Long Island.

Right away, Bill Reynolds was on the phone with Donovan. He saw the operatic humanity in a moment that might otherwise be recorded only in the small-type "transactions" column at the back of the sports section — this pivotal first move in a young man's reinvention. And Donovan – who would go on to extraordinary success as a head coach in college and the NBA — knew that he could trust Bill to get it right.

So many other pieces in this collection reflect Bill's value system, especially his resolve to honor people who endure tragedy, grapple with private demons, struggle to succeed. Time and again, he swept away the statistics and preconceived notions to better understand the person behind the sports-figure facade.

Here is Bill, glimpsing major league baseball's racist past in the fraught relationship between the Boston Red Sox pitcher Dennis "Oil Can" Boyd and his father, who had been a barnstorming ballplayer in the segregated South. Bill talked to the father as he prepared to watch his son pitch for the first time in a major league game — in the World Series, no less.

Here he is, talking to the runner Kathy Switzer a quarter-century after she broke up the boys-only gambol that was the Boston Marathon and emerged as a trailblazing icon. Switzer was clearly at ease with Bill, and at one point she shared something so tender and wonderful that it took my breath. She recalled that a few years earlier, she had been depressed at the thought of never having children.

"Don't be," her mother told her, "because you have all those women who got into running because of you. You have 100,000 women."

Here he is, in Maryland, in the fresh wake of the drug-related death of its favored son, the 22-year-old college basketball star Len Bias, who had been expected to be the future of the Boston Celtics franchise. Even now, some aggrieved Celtics fans will refer to the tragic death of Bias only in terms of its impact on their team. But Bill immediately recognized its more profound meaning, and traveled to Bias's old neighborhood — to an outdoor basketball court where some boys are shooting around. Let's pause to consider the potential awkwardness of this moment: A tall stranger from New England just shows up in a Maryland playground to ask some questions about the recent death of a local hero. But these boys clearly sensed his understanding of their loss, his lack of condescension, his interest in what they had to say — his authenticity. They could tell: He got it. And they opened up.

This story, and every story contained in this volume, is a timeless moment of journalistic grace, written with words as pure and true as the author's turnaround jump shot from the corner. They leave no doubt: Bill Reynolds has game.

—Dan Barry
New York Times

EDITOR'S NOTE / ACKNOWLEDGMENTS

LIZ ABBOTT

The initial concept for this book was to compile a "best of" Bill Reynolds' newspaper columns, but it quickly became clear that this idea wouldn't work since the columns that didn't make the preliminary cut were arguably just as good as the ones that did. It also became obvious early on, at least to me, that Bill's very popular "For What's It's Worth" columns were a species unto themselves and, while funny and observant, their subject matter seemed too timely and topical to include in this anthology. Another book for another time, perhaps. I then focused on choosing columns with recognizable names and subject matter in an effort to appeal to readers who might not hail from Rhode Island, but that left out some truly memorable pieces, so again the selection criteria changed. In the end, *Story Days* became a collection that I hope showcases the imagination and talent Bill brought to a wide array of subjects over a long, dedicated newspaper career. Inevitably, it isn't a perfect representation of his work, but it's a start.

This book would not have been possible without the support of many of Bill's former colleagues at The Providence Journal. Special thanks to Alan Rosenberg, Mike Delaney, Bill Coury, and Peter Donahue, who helped me to navigate some legal and technical hurdles. In addition, thanks to freelance photographer Ryan Conaty for his wonderful cover photo, Dan Barry of the New York Times for writing a heart-felt foreword and David Fletcher of Barrington for coming up with the title. If I have overlooked anyone else who deserves a nod, I apologize in advance; any omissions were not intentional. In exchange for copyright permission to republish Bill's columns, a portion of proceeds from the sale of *Story Days* will be donated to a Providence Journal charity.

Happy reading!

STORY DAYS

PART ONE

1980–1989

RICK PITINO

11/10/1986

"It could go in a season."

—Rick Pitino

PROVIDENCE — Last year he came in here like Brother Ricky, a basketball version of a tent evangelist, someone who was going to wake up the echoes and make the past dance in the street again. Brother Ricky's Basketball Salvation Show. Pack up the babies and grab the old ladies and everyone goes.

And then, just when it seemed like he was just one more snake-oil salesman at the door pushing dreams on the lay-away plan, all the promises were delivered. (Providence finished 5th in the Big East, won 17 games and made it to the NIT quarterfinals). Someone might have done a better coaching job last year than Rick Pitino, but I don't know who it was.

You know the story.

But what does Rick Pitino now do for an encore? What trick do you do after you've already pulled the rabbit out of the hat?

For now Pitino no longer is the first-year coach in here to wake up the dead, no longer the new guy in town with a pocketful of mumbles that are promises. Now his reputation extends far beyond the insular world of Five-Star camp and basketball afficionados. A recent Sport magazine had him tops on the list of college coaches who can do the most with the least. Now Rick Pitino is one of the hottest coaches in the country, what Gary Williams was two years ago at Boston College, this year's starlet. Now he's the latest young coach, who — if he can't walk on water — at least knows where the stumps are. Or so the thinking goes.

You could see that last night. Introduced before last night's game against the Russian National Team, Pitino got a bigger ovation than any of the PC players. All this because last year Pitino took a team picked to be the Big East doormat and finished with the best Friars' record in eight years. All this because last year Pitino pumped life back into a Civic Center that had seemed in seasons past to lie there like some big balloon that had had the air sucked out of it. Because last year Pitino did all the things he had promised he would do.

You know the story.

So now what? Will winning 17 games be enough this year? Will going to the NIT be enough? Will winning seven Big East games be enough? Or did the Friars' success last year raise expectations so that a similar season will be seen as a disappointment?

"Everywhere I go I hear we're going to be good," says Pitino. "But what's it based on?"

Certainly it's not based on the Big East coaches' preseason predictions. The Friars are picked for sixth. Nor is it based on returning players. Only Billy Donovan is on the first two teams. Nor is it based on the freshmen. No Friar was chosen on the Big East all-rookie team.

So what then?

It seems Pitino already has become a victim of his own success. That because the Friars were the surprise team of the Big East last year, this year they are supposed to be better. If last year they went to the NIT, this year should be the NCAA Tournament. Why? That's never really addressed.

This is Pitino's mystique, the feeling he's one of the very best there is at doing the most with the least. That he can keep reaching into the hat and coming out with the rabbit. This is the price tag for delivering on all the promises last year. No matter that last year, even by Pitino's admission, was two years ahead of schedule, a magical mystery tour that seemed to take on a life of its own.

"I look at the films from last year and don't know how we won," says Pitino.

But no one wants to hear that. Didn't he deliver last year? Didn't he say last year the Friars were going to be the hardest working teams in America? That they were going to run into scorers' tables and dive on the floor? That playing them was going to like trying to get a shake a mean little dog away from your pants' leg? Isn't that just what happened?

And now the Friars have beaten the Russians. The big bad Russians. A few days before Pitino called them one of the best teams in the world. But there were the Friars last night looking as if someone had put a videotape of last year into the machine and hit the "play" button. There were the Friars knocking down three-pointers as if they were clay ducks in some carnival tent. There was the old never-say-die spirit that Pitino seems to pour over his team from some private bottle. As if there has been no summer vacation, no break from the Friars last game in the NIT last March.

The Friars beat the Russians? Bring on the Big East.

But don't be fooled by last night.

This is still a team that is thin, especially up front, still a team that's going to have to play defense as if it were running up San Juan Hill with Teddy Roosevelt. Still a team that wouldn't get a lot of respect on a playground. This is still a team that has to play every night as if its game plan was a slogan on a locker-room wall. There are four newcomers, soon to be five. All will play, ready or not, because Pitino knows he's going to need them later on those cold night along the Big East trail. Once again this is going to have to be a team whose whole is better than the sum of its parts.

So Pitino will spend this year walking a personal tightrope. He knows everyone expects more this year, that he can be a victim of his own success. He knows there's still a talent-gap between the Friars and the top Big East teams, and that the higher you get to the top the scarcer the rabbits get.

And his reputation as one of the hottest young coaches in the country?

"It could go in a season," says Rick Pitino with a shrug.

But don't bet on it.

POSTSCRIPT: *In his second season, Pitino took PC to the Final Four. He left P.C. after that to coach the New York Knicks. Then it was on to the University of Kentucky, where he led Kentucky to a NCAA championship in 1996. Pitino is the only coach in history to take three schools to the Final Four. He was elected into the Naismith Memorial Basketball Hall of Fame in 2013.*

ANGELO IZZI

9/19/1986

"It never said how many people he made happy. How Angelo gave us thrills we'll remember forever."
—Teddy

PROVIDENCE — Teddy couldn't believe it when he saw the obituary July 17th.

It said Angelo S. Izzi, 53, of Carroll Towers, Smith Street, died at Veterans Medical Center. It said he had been born in Providence, served in the Army in the Korean War, and recently had been employed as a security guard at Wells Fargo for nine months. It said he had four survivors. Fifty-three years condensed into four paragraphs. What it didn't say was that once upon a time Angelo Izzi was a prize fighter.

"I was hurt when I saw that," says Teddy. "Not even a mention. As if it never happened. It never said how many people he made happy. How Angelo gave us thrills we'll remember forever."

That was back in the early '50s, back when Angelo Izzi was known in the ring as Izzy Angelo, a 147-pound fighter from Providence; a kid from Eagle Park who saw boxing as an escape from a second-shift world where too many dreams never got out of a lunchbox and the future often stopped at next week. Izzy Angelo had seen Kirk Douglas in "The Champion" and he wanted to be the champ, the oldest sports dream of all.

By 16 he was fighting professionally, often against older, more experienced fighters. Teddy grew up in the same neighborhood, hung on the same corner, went with Angelo to his fights, even worked his corner a couple of times. And on a day when Vinny Pazienza was to fight in the Providence Civic Center, Teddy was reliving a lot of the same memories.

"The scenario's the same," he says. "A good-looking kid. Italian. All the followers. The excitement. Treated like a kingpin. Vinny saw 'Rocky' and wanted to be the champ. Angelo saw "The Champion." Vinny certainly has more talent, but, on a smaller scale, it's the same scene."

It was a different fight game in Rhode Island then. If now local boxing is Vinny Paz and a lot of memories, boxing then was as much a part of the state as the Democratic Party and shore dinners at Rocky Point. Various boxing clubs were churning out kids, all trying to hitch a ride on the Boxing Express, almost as if each neighborhood's hopes rode on the right hand of some young fighter. The old R.I. Auditorium and the Arcadia Ballroom in downtown Providence had weekly boxing fights. There were promoters who seemed to have stepped out of the pages of a Damon Runyon story, complete with cigar smoke hovering over every syllable.

Not that Izzy Angelo ever was a great fighter. The scouting report was good left hand, no right hand. Mostly he was an undercard fighter, living in the sport's underbelly, trading leather for a few dollars, dreaming his dreams, waiting for his chance.

"But he could take a punch and he had heart," Teddy says. "A ton of heart. A heart like Rocky Marciano. They used to hit him with everything but the stool. All his fights were Pier Six brawls."

The big chance came one night in the early '50s at the Arcadia in his first main bout. He had fought around New England on undercards. This time he was the headliner. Even now, so many years later and seen through the tunnel of memory, Teddy remembers there were 40 guys at the weigh-in the morning of the fight. How there was a stream of guys from the corner, all backslapping Angelo, telling him he was the greatest. Remembers how a victory party was planned for the Biltmore.

He was fighting another local kid, older, a kid supposedly on the way down, and this was a crossroads fight for Izzy Angelo. Win and the dream stayed alive. Lose, and put it away with the rest of the childhood fantasies.

He lost.

Teddy says Izzi just sort of disappeared after that. He went out West for a while and when he came back it was as if something was missing, as if the death of the dream had taken some of the spark with it.

"In a way it was like the end of his life, it really was," says Teddy. "It was like something inside him had died."

And all the hangers-on? All the people who always had wanted to be trailing after him?

"When he lost, they all went away," he says. "Went away in droves. Like they didn't want to be around him anymore."

Teddy would run into Angelo occasionally through the years and he would try and talk about the old days, when they both had been young together and Angelo had had his dream. But Angelo never wanted to talk about the fights; as if it all belonged in the past tense, a life that ended that night so long ago when he was 20 years old and realized the dream never was going to come true.

After a while they fell out of touch, their lives going down different roads. When he did hear about him it always was information that was filtered: He was working with a horse trainer or he was into organic gardening. Second-hand information. Teddy last saw Angelo about a decade ago. Ironically, he ran into Angelo's brother earlier in the summer, asked about Angelo, trying to catch up on a childhood friend.

Then a couple of weeks later he saw the obituary. With no mention of the what Angelo had been. No mention of thrills that he gave the dream he once had.

So now Teddy looks at Vinnie Paz and sees Angelo Izzi. Looks at Vinnie Paz and sees the same dream in a different package. Looks at the glitter and the excitement and can't seem to shake the image of Angelo Izzi's last fight.

"After the fight that night," says Teddy, "no one was there. All the back-slappers had disappeared. All the hangers on were gone. And Angelo and me ended up at the New York System on Smith Street in Providence. There was no Biltmore. No party. It was just me and Angelo sitting in the New York System eating hot dogs alone."

DENNIS 'OIL CAN' BOYD

10/22/1986

*"It is the biggest thrill in my life.
I could never have a bigger thrill."*
—WILLIE BOYD

BOSTON — The sign said, "I came all the way from Meridian, Mississippi, to see #23, Dennis 'Oil Can' Boyd, pitch."

It was held by an elderly black man in a tan jacket and a white cap with "Red Sox" on the front. The woman next to him held a similar sign. They were sitting in the grandstand near first base. It was minutes before the game, the Red Sox were being introduced, the Fenway crowd was pumped up, the electricity started to build in this old ballpark that has seen so many magic nights. The players were introduced, each one coming out to stand along the first-base line, the cheers pouring down on the field like a summer shower.

"And warming up in the Red Sox bullpen," said the P.A. voice, "the man who won the sixth game of the Championship Series, Dennis 'Oil Can' Boyd."

The woman waved her sign back and forth. The man cheered.

"Words can't express my feelings," said Willie Boyd. "It is the biggest thrill in my life. I could never have a bigger thrill."

The Can began walking in from the bullpen, heading across the emerald field for his World Series date, while his father watched him…his father, who had never been to Boston before…his father, who never had seen his son pitch in the major leagues before.

His father, who used to barnstorm through Southern towns in

an old bus that still sits alongside his house in Meridian, just a short foul ball away from the rickety old ballyard where the Can and his brothers learned the game, just as his father and his uncles had before him, and his grandfather before them…his father, who once was a show-boating pitcher who always pitched with a certain style.

"This is the greatest thrill of my life," he said. "The greatest feeling in my life."

And maybe you have to know that Willie Boyd grew up in a Deep South town where racism was as omnipresent as the summer heat. Have to know that his, and his brothers', baseball careers were sacrificed on an altar of prejudice, just as several of his sons' careers were. Maybe you have to know that each time the Can pitches, he pitches for the careers his family never had, for the tradition he comes out of, a tradition whose high priest is Satchel Paige, one of the all-time great pitchers who didn't get out of the barnstorming past until late in his career.

The Can talked about that in Monday's press conference. Said how he'd be "Satchel Paige out there." How he'd have an "old-timey" feeling that was Paige back in the 30's and 40's. How he once met Paige when ole' Satch had come to Jackson State and a young Can had asked him for advice.

"Keep throwing the 'yellow hammer,'" Paige had told him.

The yellow hammer?

"The overhand curve that breaks down," Paige supposedly had said.

"Does Dennis remind you of Paige?" Willie Boyd was asked.

"My brother K.T. Boyd played with Satchel in Kansas City in 1954," said Willie. "Dennis reminds me more of my brother J. C. Boyd, who's still pitching semi-pro in Detroit."

And maybe you have to know that Willie and Dennis never had a relationship out of the "Cosby Show." Willie and Dennis' mother, Sweetie, were divorced when Dennis was a child, and though Willie only moved a couple of miles away, their relationship always was strained. But Dennis had invited him to Boston, and Willie and his second wife had flown in yesterday afternoon with Sweetie and Dennis' older brother, Skeeter. A family whose history sometimes seems as if it came out of a Faulkner novel was in a sense reunited on this night in Boston. A mother and a father, who no longer live together, in Fenway Park to see their youngest son pitch in the World Series.

It would be nice to be able to say the Can went out and threw a masterpiece, went out onto this World Series stage and pitched as if he were pitching back in that rickety ballpark in Meridian with his brothers behind him. Pitched as if Satchel Paige were right out there on the mound with him. Pitched as if the "old timey" feeling were enough for a storybook ending.

But he came out higher than the centerfield flag pole and gave up a home run on his third pitch. By the time the smoke had cleared the score was 4-0, manager John McNamara had been out to the mound and there was activity in the bullpen. He settled down after that. At one point he retired 11 in a row, then 17 out of 18. Then in the seventh, with the bases loaded and two out, he gave up a single to Gary Carter, a hit that essentially sewed it up for the Mets and ended the Can's night.

Later, in the clubhouse, the Can would say that having his family there was the greatest feeling in the world.

"I can look at the night and make it feel okay," he said.

"You win some, you lose some," said his father Willie up in the grandstand. "That's life. That's baseball."

Willie Boyd did not seem too disturbed. Maybe he could take the defeat because he has been around baseball his entire life and knows there are no formulas, no easy scripts and there's always another game. Or maybe because last night Willie Boyd had a reunion with his son, which was more important to him than a win or a loss. Maybe because he knows that not too many fathers ever see their sons pitch in the World Series, win or lose.

And maybe because Willie Boyd knows it's a long trip from Meridian to the World Series. Win or lose.

POSTSCRIPT: The "Can" played in Boston for seven years after making his Red Sox debut in 1982. He went on to play for the Montreal Expos and Texas Rangers, spending a decade in the Major League in total. He came out of retirement at age 45 to pitch for the Brockton Rox of the Can-Am League, then embarked on a barn tour, in the style of the Negro League, called "Oil Can Boyd's Traveling All-Stars."

VINNY PAZ

5/17/1986

"I'm lucky to have been born here and I'm proud of my heritage. That's what Pazmania is all about."

—Vinny Paz

PROVIDENCE — He is a phenomenon. Pure and simple.

Forget that he is not ranked. Forget that he may never be a world champion. Forget that he's not even in tomorrow's feature fight. Forget that there's no guarantee he will beat Harry Arroyo tomorrow afternoon in the Civic Center. Vinny Pazienza drew 13,000 people to the Civic Center in February for his bout with Joe Frazier Jr. and nobody, but nobody, should have been able to do that.

Need proof?

Three years ago, Marvelous Marvin Hagler drew 10,000 people here for a title fight.

"There are no more than five fighters in the United States of America who can even draw 7,000," said Ray Nicosia of Main Events, the New Jersey-based group that manages Pazienza. "Ten thousand would have been a dream. But there were a lot of 60-year-olds in there for the Frazier fight. A carryover from the glory days."

Ah, the glory days. Back when Providence was once a great fight town. That was in the late 40's and early 50's when Providence was the best fight town in New England, where Rocky Marciano got his start, where the Old Rhode Island Auditorium used to sell out a boxing card once a week, and where the unwritten rule was never fight a Rhode Island fighter in Rhode Island. Back before television and the changing times sent the local fight scene to the Ancient History shelf.

But Paz has inherited the legacy. At 23, he is too young to remember the smell of cigar smoke that used to hang over the old Auditorium like haze over Los Angeles, too young to remember Manny Almeida's old gym in Fox Point that was home for a generation that chased the boxing dream. But Paz knows the tradition. Knows that he, alone, carries the legacy. That Providence's reputation as a fight town has all come down to this 139-pounder from Cranston.

Earlier this week, Nicosia sat in Paz' gym on the second floor of a brick building in the Silver Lake section of Providence. A Newsday reporter sat with him. The New York Times was coming later. Understand, this is unheard of for an unranked fighter. They are here for one reason: two months ago Vinny Pazienza put 13,000 people in the Providence Civic Center.

"How big here is the fact that he's Italian?" continued Nicosia. "Very big. Because nobody else could have done what he did in February. It was unbelievable."

A phenomenon.

Pazienza would be a nice story even if he weren't the state's newest heart-throb since P.C.'s Ernie D., the perfect fighter for his time and place. This is a kid who grew up in Cranston, played football and baseball at Cranston East, went to CCRI in Warwick, just another local kid who went to see "Rocky" and swallowed it all. Pazienza walked out of the Park Cinema in Cranston after watching Sylvester Stallone convinced that he was going to be another Italian kid who battles his way to become the champ. As

As the story goes, he came down the stairs the next morning all set to do a little roadwork, all 120 pounds of him. Which is probably what a lot of kids did after they saw the movie: left the theatre dreaming big dreams of being the champ of the whole wide world, dreams that got laid to rest the first time they found themselves on the business end of a left jab.

"I used to tell him, 'Vinny, stay in bed, you don't need this,'" says his father Angelo. "But he did it every day. You couldn't get him to stop."

The rest is already part of the Paz legend. How he became one of the top amateur fighters in the world, compiling a 100-12 record. How he was the national lightweight champ in 1981. How he was a gold medal winner at the National Sports Festival. How he toured Russia and Europe with the U.S. team. How he seemed to be a sure shot to make the 1984 Olympic team before he got tired of the politics of international amateur boxing and turned pro in May of 1983. How he is now 18-0 as a pro, 14 of the wins coming by knockouts.

Until February, "Pazmania" happened out of town. Paz at the Totowa Ice World. Paz in Atlantic City. Paz in Vegas. Paz in Italy. Small stories on his fights appeared in the newspapers. Occasionally he appeared on cable television. But all the while he was chasing his dream out there in obscurity.

Then he fought Joe Frazier Jr. in the Civic Center and brought Pazmania into the Civic Center. It wasn't just that he hit Frazier with everything but the proverbial kitchen sink, or that he threw more combinations in seven rounds than many fighters throw in their careers. Or that he came out in an outfit that would force Liberace to don sunglasses.

It was that he was an Event.

A phenomenon.

Pazienza walks into the gym his father built for him four years ago. Two fighters were warming up in the ring, their every move covered with sweat. He walks into the small office which is a shrine to his career: pictures, trophies, memorabilia. On one wall is the inspiration itself: a picture of Sylvester Stallone, posing as Rocky.

"What is the difference between now and before the Frazier fight?" he is asked.

"When I first started, I used to go around in my USA jacket and no one knew who I was," he said.

"How recognized are you now around here?"

"Let's just say I don't need American Express."

But the real difference?

"Now people know I'm for real," said Pazienza. "Now they know there's the possibility that being a champion from Rhode Island is not a fantasy. Everyone used to doubt me. Everybody knows now I can fight."

Pazienza sat there and tried to describe what it's like to close in on a dream. How it's already been nine years of workouts and sacrifice, nine years of getting hit every day, nine years of sweat. And how now that it is all starting to happen exactly as he once envisioned, it's getting a little scary.

He's cocky, yet almost in a playful way, street-corner bravado mixed with the confidence that comes with winning. He knows that reputations are enhanced on glitter and one-liners. Like the time he first met Randy Gordon of Ring Magazine. This was early in Paz's career, they were watching a lightweight title fight and Paz told Gordon that he could beat both of them right now.

"You got a big mouth," Gordon told him, "and if you can back it up you'll be all right."

So after saying Paz said he'd been watching Arroyo on tape, someone asked him what he saw.

"I saw him stretched out before 13,000 people," he said.

"But what if you don't knock him out?"

"Then he'll wake up the next day and need a huge Tylenol."

Paz also knows his audience. Do you think it's an accident that he has orange and green stripes on his warmups, orange and green stripes on his sneakers? Italy's colors. Pazienza knows that if he didn't exist, Rhode Island might have to invent him. The kid from the neighborhood chasing the biggest sports dream of all.

"I'm lucky to have been born here," he said, "and I'm proud of my heritage. That's what Pazmania is all about."

At ringside, his father is watching two guys beginning to spar.

His father, who kept telling Lou Duva from the beginning that Vinny would sell out the Civic Center. His father, who remembered the old days. His father, who knew that a flashy kid with an Italian name can sell a lot of tickets in this town.

"How big a deal is it that Vinny is Italian in this state?"

"There probably were 4,000 people at the last fight who hadn't been to a fight in 20 years," said Angelo Pazienza. "I know people who had never been to the Civic Center before. It's so big you can't even describe it."

Vinny is asked how he feels about so many people going to the last fight.

"Thirteen thousand people," he said, letting out a soft whistle. "Frank Sinatra doesn't even do that."

Pazmania has been reigning all week.

"Sports Locker" on Channel 6 Sunday night. Going back to Cranston East High School to speak. Monday night live on the "Dick and Dave" radio talk show.

"How would you compare yourself to 'Boom Boom' Mancini?" one caller asked.

"We're both Italian."

Much of the conversation is concerned with a possible future fight with champion Livingstone Bramble. Pazienza's manager, Lou Duva, has offered Bramble $350,000 to come to Providence to fight Paz.

"Why does Livingstone Bramble want to fight you in Providence, Rhode Island?" talk show host Dick Higgins asked.

"Because you don't draw 13,000 anywhere else," Pazienza said. "Why not here?"

Another caller wants to know if Pazienza is the forerunner of a boxing renaissance, or is merely an aberration.

"I could never have been where I am today if I hadn't hooked up with Lou Duva," Pazienza said. "I was moved the right way. I was on TV. It's a long process you go through. If it was easy everyone would be doing it."

On Wednesday, at a morning press conference at the Civic Center, Pazienza traded a little pre-fight banter with Arroyo. "I know you got good people behind you, Harry, but you're going to have to worry about what's in front of you."On Thursday, a noontime public workout in Kennedy Plaza. Paz on the Plaza. He showed up with a picture of the Pazmanian Devil on his back, going three rounds in a makeshift ring in the shadow of City Hall before a few hundred of the curious.

"Oh, he's cute," squealed a female voice, as Paz climbed out of the ring.

"The next champ," yelled another.

"Yo, Vinny," yelled another.

Pazmania, Part II. Complete with TV cameras. Photographers. Close your eyes and it could have been Rocky himself. Life imitating art. But maybe the best evidence of the Paz phenomenon appeared Monday, when he came down the stairs of his father's gym on Laurel Hill Avenue and walked out onto the sidewalk. In front of him two small girls, about 10, were waiting on their bicycles. One of them handed a notepad to Pazienza to be autographed.

"Do you know who he is?" the girl was asked.

"Sure," she said. "Vinny Paz."

"How do you know who he is?"

The girl shrugged. "Everyone knows Vinny Paz."

LEN BIAS

6/22/1986

"He was my idol. When I first heard he was dead
I went into my room and cried."
—CLINTON HAYNES

COLLEGE PARK, MD — The first thing you see is the picture.

On the office door of the sports information office at the University of Maryland is a full-length picture of Len Bias. He is wearing a yellow uniform with red trim. He is holding a basketball. He is smiling. It all seems larger than life.

And until Thursday morning Bias was, indeed, larger than life. Tuesday he had been the second choice in the NBA college draft, chosen by the Boston Celtics. Wednesday he had signed a sneaker contract reportedly in excess of $1 million. He was the culmination of every playground dream, a childhood basketball fantasy come true.

And what made it even better was that this wasn't happening to some kid who had come to Maryland after intensive national recruiting. Not someone for whom athletic greatness had been almost a birthright. This was a local kid who went to high school just a jump shot away from the Maryland campus. Someone who used to sneak into games at Cole Field House with an uncle who sold ice cream, and ended his collegiate career as the all-time leading scorer in the school's history.

This was someone who was all but worshipped by his teammates, loved by his coaches, and called one of the greatest players in Atlantic Coast Conference history. A kid who had spent hours lifting weights to build his body, and more hours refining his jump shot. A born-again Christian who wrote poetry, liked to draw, wanted to design clothes and said he wanted to play pro ball so he could help out his parents and younger brothers and sister.

Someone who seemed, at the age of 22, larger than life.

"He was revered here," said John McAdam, who writes for the student newspaper.

So when Bias was found dead Thursday morning of cardiac failure, after a night celebrating his selection by the Celtics, it was not merely the death of a great athlete, a personal dream reduced to ashes. Nor even was it, in the words of Larry Bird, the "cruelest thing I ever heard of." It was a death in the family. Here in Prince Georges County, where there have been unemployment and busing problems — here in this county in southern Maryland that is a forgotten stepchild of the Washington suburbs — Lenny Bias was a certified hero.

"He was my idol," said Clinton Haynes, 17, in a red warmup jacket. "When I first heard he was dead I went into my room and cried. I was crushed."

Haynes was one of about a dozen black kids, from 8 to 18, shooting baskets on an outdoor court Friday in Landover, just down the street from where Bias grew up.

"Everyone watched the draft, and when they said Lenny Bias, everyone cheered," he continued. "He was somebody from the area who had made the big time. I used to see him down the rec center all the time. He would come over and do a couple of dunks, put on a show for us."

Haynes and the others were down at one end of the court. Two wore Reebok sneakers, the company Bias had signed a contract with Wednesday.

"Do they know why he died yet?" one of the younger kids asked.

"They said on the news there was traces of cocaine in his urine," said one of the older ones. "He was out celebrating."

No one said anything, the silence hanging heavy in the humid air. Suddenly, a kid threw up a shot that missed, and a few others fought for the rebound. A scene as timeless as an American schoolyard.

"We play out here every day," said Haynes. "We're always playing. But you know, the day he died, no one played. Everyone just stayed inside and watched the news. It was like everything just stopped."

Bias grew up the oldest of four children in a primarily black middle-class neighborhood in Landover called Columbia Park. His father, James, is a repairman for a company that supplies medical and research gasses to hospitals and government agencies. His mother, Lonise, is a supervisor in the customer-service department of a Washington bank. Columbia Park is just 7 miles from the urban blight of the Washington ghettos, but it is far removed in lifestyle. It is a quiet place of small one-story houses and tree-lined streets, about 8 miles south of College Park, home of the University of Maryland.

Sugar Ray Leonard grew up in nearby Palmer Park, and Brian Waller, the former Providence College basketball player, grew up only three blocks away. Bias and Waller became best friends, inseparable as kids. Even now at the Columbia Park Recreation Center, the walls have pictures of Bias and Waller together, Polaroid memories of gone-forever times.

"I first met him at the rec center about 12 years ago," said Waller, who knew Bias as Frosty, a childhood nickname. "Both of us weren't into basketball then. He was playing Boys Club football."

Bias was cut from the junior-high basketball team as an eighth-grader and played the following year, a gangly 6-foot-4 kid who had trouble catching the ball. Which is when Bob Wagner, the coach at Northwestern High School, first met him.

"His team had just lost a game and he was crying in the locker room," Wagner recalled.

The following year, as part of the school busing program in Prince Georges County, Bias was assigned to Northwestern. The racially mixed school in Hyattsville is less than a mile from the University of Maryland. Waller also went there, a year ahead of Bias.

"Lenny Bias was not a ghetto kid," said Wagner. "He had a very strong family situation. But he was very impressionable as a 10th-grader, with an infectious grin. Everyone liked him. He was a good person."

As a player then Bias was as green as a Celtic warmup suit, and Wagner began slowly transforming him from a raw talent into a player. They also started lifting weights together.

"That body wasn't an accident," said Wagner. "He worked at it. I started him with weights when he came here as a sophomore, and then he asked his father for some for Christmas so he also could lift at home. He wanted very much to be a good basketball player. It was very important to him."

Wagner, 39, who is white, attended Northwestern and then returned to teach math, and he has been coaching the basketball team there for 10 years. In his small, cluttered office off the gymnasium lobby there are many slogans about working hard and paying the price, about discipline. About how special it is to be a Northwestern Wildcat.

"We always say, 'Once a Wildcat, always a Wildcat,'" said Wagner. "I try to do more with these kids than just teach them basketball. I keep hearing about how much natural talent Leonard had, but I had some kids who had more natural talent than he did. But never anyone who wanted it more. There are some kids who hear what coaches say and go out and do something else. Leonard was the type of kid who heard what coaches say and went out and did it."

By his senior year Bias had become one of the most dominating players in greater Washington, recruited by North Carolina State and Georgia. But even then his overall game was suspect.

"All he did in high school was dunk," said McAdam, whose team beat Northwestern by one point in the state finals at Cole Field House on the Maryland campus. "He couldn't shoot at all."

By this time the word was that he had an "attitude" on the court, supposedly one of the reasons he wasn't more highly recruited. Wagner once said that Bias could be, at times, his own worst enemy.

But Phil Ness, the assistant coach at Brown University, recalled the time he visited Bias's home while recruiting for Northeastern University.

"He was a great kid, a super kid," Ness said. "One of our players had been his counselor at a summer camp and thought he was the nicest kid there."

If Bias could sometimes be intense to a fault on the court, there was another side, a softer side. He liked to draw. He liked gospel music. Once Wagner brought the team to a Baptist Church tournament, and then almost cringed when, between games, the players were asked if they wanted to go to another room and discuss the Lord. Bias was the only player who wanted to.

During Bias's senior year, Wagner also worked on the youth's speech.

He would stick a fake microphone in his face and make Bias practice responding to interviews. He made sure Bias visited some schools around the country so he would know what being away from home really meant.

"His mother was the biggest factor in him going to Maryland," said Wagner. "She is the guiding force in that family — wanted him to stay close to home. I think she thought he wasn't ready yet to handle being away."

So in the fall of 1982, Lenny Bias went up the street to the University of Maryland, the neighborhood school, where he had known Coach Lefty Driesell since the time he was a kid and had gone to his basketball camp. Where he had been walking through the campus all three years of high school. Where he had used to sneak into Cole Field House. Where he had played his last high school game.

The local kid.

The red banners honoring great teams of the past hang from

one side of Cole Field House, the amphitheater in the middle of the Maryland campus that seats about 12,000. Next to them hang white banners with names like McMillen, Elmore, Lucas, Williams, King. All great players at Maryland, all of whom later went to the pros.

The basketball tradition leans down heavy at Maryland, this large university whose red brick sprawls across Route 1 and whose national reputation centers on its basketball team.

Bias didn't play much as a freshman, only averaged seven points a game. Waller says Bias had found out that just trying to dunk the ball all the time was no longer enough at this level. So that summer Bias began developing an outside shot. He worked at an elementary school in Landover, and spent the summer shooting endless jumpers. Unlike many players who get a college scholarship and figure all the work is over, Bias continued working on his game, fueled by his dream to one day become a pro.

When he returned for his sophomore year he was a different player.

The rest is all there in the resume: twice player of the year in the ACC, an All-American. A fantasy career, Horatio Alger with an incredible vertical leap and a body sculpted by the Hoop God.

Bias often complained he got too much media attention at the expense of his teammates, just as Larry Bird once did at Indiana State. At this year's media day, when everyone rushed to interview Bias while leaving his teammates sitting by themselves, he got angry. Bias could be surly to people he didn't know. His on-court appearance could be, at times, menacing, the intensity stamped all over his face. Reporters who covered the team often found him uncooperative. His locker was next to the bathroom, and sometimes after games he would go in there and hide, waiting for the reporters to leave.

It was almost as if there were two sides of Lenny Bias, the public and the private.

He also had become the most recognizable figure on campus

— always dressed impeccably. He wore fur coats, Italian loafers and designer jeans. He had a leather trench coat with an ermine collar. He majored in interior design, and said he one day wanted to design clothes.

"I've got to look good, you know," he told the campus newspaper. "I don't want anyone to see me looking like a rag."

If he had been easily impressionable as a 10th-grader, now he was impressed with the Good Life, the life offered to top NBA draft choices. His dorm room had pictures of a Lamborghini and a Porsche. He talked of getting a Mercedes when he finally signed a pro contract. But for all his attention to high style, Bias didn't have a reputation as a partier. The word was he was down on drugs, wasn't a drinker.

"I like to play basketball, draw and design clothes, in that order," he once said.

And all the time he was making his fame at the university, he often went back to Northwestern to visit. Once a Wildcat, always a Wildcat.

"We rarely talked about basketball," Coach Wagner said. "I think he came back here because he could be just plain Lenny Bias here. To come and be around me was to get away from everything else."

"He is a very private person," his mother said a few months ago. "It's as if he lives in two separate worlds."

On Friday, Wagner stood in the lobby of Northwestern High School. A dusty trophy case was off to one side. The school crests of opponents were on a gym wall. It all seemed a long way from Cole Field House, just up the street — a long way from a multimillion-dollar contract. Wagner has been witness to much lost potential in his 16 years as a teacher, a lot of crushed hopes and broken dreams. The best player he ever coached died of a heroin overdose in Washington. Every day Wagner deals in a reality where drugs are as omnipresent as slam dunks.

"He was even bigger than Sugar Ray Leonard around here,

because basketball is bigger than boxing," said Wagner. "The average kid has a need to know that if he works hard he can make it. And Lenny was such a great role model. His image was so pure."

He shook his head at the incongruity of it all, the senselessness of Bias's death. Then he talked about a society that takes a 22-year-old kid and makes him larger than life.

"I tell all my kids that life is not like a basketball game," he said. "There are no time-outs. Maybe Wednesday night he just wanted a time-out from the rest of his life for a while."

He said he would remember Bias for all the good things he did, not for maybe the one mistake he made.

"Lenny Bias is a tragic hero," he said.

Thursday night, 12 hours after Bias had died, the Wildcats played a summer-league game in nearby Silver Spring. There were about 100 people in the gym on the humid night, almost all of them black — just another summer-league game in a hot gym. Except playing for Northwestern was Jay Bias, Lenny's little brother, who will be a junior in the fall. Jay had said that he wanted to play because Lenny would have wanted him to — that his brother had told him if anything ever happened to him, Jay was just going to have to work twice as hard.

So Jay Bias had already decided that one day he was going to play basketball at Maryland. He plans to pick up where his brother left off and "let the good memories carry me through."

Jay Bias is about 6 foot 5 and gangly, and he seems to have a little trouble catching the ball. Take away six years and it could be Lenny Bias — a young kid with basketball all ahead of him. Wednesday night it almost seemed eerie. Jay Bias is not yet a finished basketball player, but already he can jump out of the gym. Wagner says that, for what it's worth, Jay is better than Lenny was at the same age.

The mood in the gym was subdued, almost like a basketball wake. The talk in the stands, almost in whispers, was about Lenny Bias and the tragedy that had happened that morning. Then, with

2:55 remaining, Jay Bias got the ball on a break, went up in the air, double-pumped, and slam-dunked.

The small gym exploded in cheers — almost as catharsis after a long, sad day. "BIAS…BIAS," came the shouts. "BIAS, he's the Man."

The legacy continues.

POSTSCRIPT: *Maryland's Chief Medical Examiner concluded Bias died of "cocaine intoxication" after ingesting an unusually pure dose of cocaine. His younger brother, Jay, died four years later at the age of 20 after being shot twice during an argument at a Maryland jewelry store.*

REGGIE JACKSON

*"I am a professional and I consider that
question an embarrassment."*
—Reggie Jackson

BOSTON — Reggie Jackson came out of the trainer's room and started walking through the Angels' clubhouse. The same Reggie Jackson who, at 40, is hitting .286, just when it appeared his baseball career was over. Another Lazarus risen from the dead.

"Do you have a minute?" I asked.

Reggie stopped and stared, silent.

"Did you do anything different to get ready for this season?" I asked.

Reggie just stared for a second, then turned his back and walked away.

"Do you believe this guy asked me that question?" he said to a teammate. "I must have answered that question a thousand times."

He went into a small, equipment room and started searching through a bag of bats.

"Hey, I'm sorry if you've answered the question a thousand times," I said, as Jackson continued looking through the bag. "But for what it's worth I read your book last night and thought it was good. For what it's worth."

Reggie looked up.

"It's worth something," he said. "Maybe not an interview, but it's worth something."

"Is it worth two minutes?"

He stared for another beat. "Okay," he said. "I'll talk to you."

Welcome to Reggie World.

The seasons come, the seasons go, the years fall off the calendar, and still there is Reggie. Somehow, it makes no difference whether he's with Oakland, or the Yankees or, now, the Angels. The years start to blend and still there is that buzz of excitement when he comes to the plate. Still Reggie, after all these years. Has there been a more dramatic figure in baseball in the past 20 years? Anyone with more charisma?

And it's more than just that he's already assured of a measure of immortality, assured his memory will live forever in Cooperstown long after he has taken his black bat and big swing and gone wherever Reggie Jacksons go when they retire. It's more than that he entered this season as the eighth all-time home run leader, 18th on the all-time runs batted in list. Or that he's tied with Mickey Mantle for the most postseason home runs. Or that he's one of only four players in the history of the game to have more than 400 home runs and 228 stolen bases in his career.

It's more than all the stats.

More than the fact that he's been one of the premier power hitters in the game for nearly two decades now. That he's "Mr. October," the straw that stirs the drink, the inspiration for the late Reggie Bar. More than all that. It's that long ago he moved from the realm of superstar athlete to national celebrity. A recent ad agency survey found him the most recognized athlete in the country.

Reggie.

No last name needed, just Reggie. Larger than life.

You could see that Thursday night. He came out of the Angels' dugout a few minutes after six. The Red Sox were finishing batting practice, many of the Angels beginning to stretch on the sidelines, as Reggie began talking to Sox coach Rene Lachemann behind the batting cage.

"REGGIE…REGGIE," came the voices. "OVER HERE, REGGIE. PLEASE, REGGIE. REGGIE."

Several rows of people were lined up in the box seats, all yelling for Jackson. He continued talking to Lachemann, seemingly oblivious.

"REGGIE...REGGIE...HEY, REG."

"REGGIE, COME OVER HERE AND SIGN SOME AUTOGRAPHS."

It was as if there weren't another player on the field. No Red Sox players. No California players. The fans didn't yell for anyone else. Just Reggie. A year ago I had witnessed the same scene, everyone yelling for Jackson, while he was standing near the batting cage and by chance I was next to him. I asked him if it was like this everywhere he goes.

"All the time," he had said. "It started with the Yankees. I've gotten used to it. I take it as a compliment."

After he had taken some batting practice, the crowd still yelling for him, he had walked back to me.

"Watch this," he had said. "Watch them go crazy."

And with that, he had walked over to the stands and signed a few autographs, the crowd all but squealing in delight. A few minutes later he came back to the batting cage, walked by me and shrugged.

So here it was Thursday night a year later and nothing had changed.

"REGGIE...REGGIE."

"YOU'RE MAKING A MILLION A YEAR, AT LEAST YOU CAN GIVE US AN AUTOGRAPH."

"REGGIE, WHAT HAPPENED TO THE YANKEES?"

"REGGIE...REGGIE..."

"REGGIE, YOU...."

Reggie World.

Last winter it seemed Reggie World was nearing the end of its run. He was going to be 40 years old this season, his baseball future behind him. Even if he had led the Angels in home runs three out of the last four years, there had been rumblings of discontent. His last three years he had hit .194, .223, and .252. Not real big numbers for a man about to be 40 who makes more than the gross national product of some Third World countries.

And then there was his book, written last year with sportswriter Mike Lupica. "Reggie." No last name needed. Three hundred and nine pages of Reggie, up close and personal. The golden years with the A's, back when he was coming of age as a baseball celebrity. The tumultuous years with George Steinbrenner and Billy Martin, when he was on center stage in the dance macabre that was the Yankees. Through the years with Reggie.

In a sense the book was a way of wrapping up his career and putting a big bow on it. And if some of it is self-serving in the way all autobiographies are, it is also insightful, a peek behind the public persona of Jackson being a star in his own movie, a man always in the fast lane. The book tells of growing up in a white area outside Philadelphia. How his parents divorced when he was six. How he went to live with his father, separated from his mother and siblings. How his father went to jail for six months for having bootleg liquor in the car while Reggie was a senior in high school, essentially leaving him without a mother or father at a vulnerable time in his life. And how when he went to Arizona State in 1964, "I didn't look back for a long, long time."

It also tells of encountering the hurt of racism in the South while in the minors. How being traded from the A's was so traumatic because they had become the family he had never had. How his inability to express his feelings, to be trusting, torpedoed his first marriage. It is a portrait of a bright, sensitive, complex man; an essentially private man who has had to come of age in the public arena. A look at Reggie through a different lens.

And there he was last winter, on a team that had said publicly it didn't want Rod Carew anymore, no longer wanted over-the-hill superstars with megabuck salaries.

"They didn't want me," said Jackson.

So why did he play again this year? Why put himself through the possible public embarrassment of being released, like Steve Carlton was? Why does a 40-year-old man who has all the money and fame he'll ever need, risk his reputation?

"I like to play," he said. "It's a privilege to play. And it's exciting to be able to still play well in young man's game."

But he also knew that he would have to pay a higher price than he had before.

"I worked out like a fool," he said. "I worked out 29 days a month, a much more concerted effort. And I didn't have a beer for five months."

"Do you still enjoy the game?" I asked.

"That question is an embarrassment," he said, starting to turn away again.

"I am a professional and I consider that question an embarrassment."

Jackson took a bat out of the bag and gripped it. He was wearing a red T-shirt, his arms still thick and powerful. His hair has a trace of gray, but the body hints of younger days, not of a man turned 40.

Jackson can go through three or four mood shifts in a 10-minute conversation. He can look at you one minute as if you're involved in an intimate conversation he will remember forever, the next minute turn away in disgust, then go back to being your buddy again. Welcome again to Reggie World. But, hey, no one has ever said he was easy to understand.

He talked for a minute about his collection of antique cars, his various homes, his 15 or 20 pieces of commercial real estate, his businesses, his endorsements, and…you get the point. Still Reggie, after all these years.

"Do you ever sit back and wonder about just how far you've come," I asked, thinking about the background, the Pennsylvania town he once left without looking back.

"Maybe when I retire I'll reminisce," he said, "but right now I'm caught up in my personal situation. Because my life is something that is no big deal to me. I mean, I get out of bed in the morning and I'm sore, but that's just the way it is. That's just my life. It's not anything I think about it."

But even if he's sore when he gets up, even if he no longer is the straw that stirs the drink, even if he no longer feels he's a million-dollar-a-year player anymore, Reggie Jackson still would like to play another year.

Why?

"Because I can still swing the bat," he said.

"Then what will you do?" I asked.

"Whatever I want to," said Reggie.

LOU CARNESECCA

3/6/1986

"I know you guys have to fill up space so just make something up and tomorrow we all come back and do it all over again."
—LOU CARNESECCA

NEW YORK — Lou Carnesecca was at a posh midtown restaurant for a picture session and two blue-haired old ladies, who wouldn't know the Big East from a beach ball, were in the lobby.

"That's 'Looie' Carnesecca," said one to the other.

"How do you know who he is?" Katha Quinn, St. John's sports information director, asked.

"Oh," said the woman. "Everyone knows Looie."

No doubt. This rumpled little man, known as 'Looie' to friends and fans, has become as much a part of New York as egg creams, hot chestnuts and carriage rides around Central Park. He is 61 years old now and Looie Carnesecca has become college basketball in New York. "We are St. John's," the cheerleaders shout. They are wrong. Looie Carnesecca is St. John's.

And this has become Looie's tournament. The number one seed. The hometown team. St. John's in Madison Square Garden. Looie in New York. All that's missing is Sinatra on the soundtrack.

And it's hard to say just when Carnesecca passed over into myth, but certainly it was a while ago. In the beginning it was the God-father voice, the Columbo clothes, the hangdog face, and the fandango he always did along the sidelines. Cowards die a thousand deaths? So do coaches during a game. And no one ever died more than little Looie.

Now it's more than that.

The players have changed from McIntyre to Jackson, from Mullin to Jones, an entire assembly line of city kids worshipping the City Game, and still there is Looie. A tough city kid coaching tough city kids. The game has changed from campus gyms and Sisters of the Poor schedules to the big arenas and big bucks of the Big East, and still there is Looie. The seasons come, the seasons go, and still there is Looie. Still the same after all these years.

And did he really go into the wrong dressing room after the St. John's-Louisville game early in the year, then say to Katha Quinn, "How can I be in the wrong place? The uniforms are red." Did he really once sit on the Providence College bench in the Civic Center after he had roamed too far down the sidelines and didn't want a ref to see him? Did he really once sit down on a woman's lap, thinking it was his bench?

Who knows.

But it's all part of the legend. Right there with his resume that's as New York as the Bowery. How he grew up on the East Side, where his father owned an Italian deli. How he went to Our Lady Of Perpetual Help grammar school. How he played baseball at St. John's and then came back to the school as an assistant to Joe Lapchick in 1957.

Right there with how he always loses his keys to his office, so that now campus security virtually always follows him back to his office after practice. Or recently, when he was posing for pictures with some Girl Scouts and he turned around to Quinn and said, "I forgot I remembered."

Forgot I remembered?

A Looie-ism. Right there with his recent statement that sometimes he has a dream that a game is close and suddenly the ceiling parts and Chris Mullin comes floating down in a parachute. Or the time three years ago when, after winning the Big East Tournament, he said his team walked with kings. A million Looie-isms.

And there he was yesterday in a conference room in the Grand Hyatt, a monument to corporate America on Park Avenue, being introduced as the Big East's coach of the year. Somehow he looked out of place. Lou Carnesecca in a blue blazer looking as if he's about to teach an accounting course? Somehow he looks better on the sidelines with his shirt hanging out.

Not that Carnesecca was an obvious choice for Big East coach of the year. Certainly you can make a But certainly Carnesecca did a better coaching job than he did last year when St. John's looked ragged and confused in the national semifinals against Georgetown. The knock on Looie's coaching always has been that his reins on his players were too tight, that he took city players and tried to get them to play some CYO game. This year he turned them loose.

"You could get a hernia," said Looie in his raspy voice, picking up the trophy. "It's nice to be honored by your own."

It's also nicer when it's not supposed to happen. After all, last year was Looie's year, wasn't it? Last year was Mullin and Bill Wennington and the 31-4 record. Last year was the first trip to the Final Four for Carnesecca, the culmination of a coaching career that started 36 years ago at St. Anne's Academy in New York. Last year was the roses.

This year?

This year was not supposed to end 27-4, fifth in both national polls, and the first seed in the Big East Tournament. This year was not supposed to end with Carnesecca being the coach of the year in the Big East. But Walter Berry turned into Superman, Mark Jackson started playing like a future NBA guard, and yesterday reporters asked Looie if this year's team is as good as last year's.

"WHO KNOWS about the NCAAs?" he said a while later, down at a small table in one corner of the room, microphones in his face. "The NCAAs is Monte Carlo. You just play the games one at a time."

"Aw Looie, you coaches always say that," a reporter said.

"Come back in 50 years and there will be some guy sitting here in a beard and he'll tell you the same thing," Carnesecca said.

His voice is now hoarse, the result of years of yelling at players in noisy gyms, and now he wears glasses to see all those calls referees miss. Other than that, nothing has changed. He says he still coaches the same way he did 25 years ago. He says he still enjoys being in the gym every afternoon with the kids, still teaching the game. Says he still has the same passion he has always had, even after all these years.

"If I didn't I would put the ball away forever," he said.

The questions kept coming and Looie kept working the room as skillfully as the string band in the Hyatt lobby.

"How can I tell Walter Berry not to turn pro if he really wants to? That's like telling him to play in the local hall instead of Carnegie Hall," he said to one guy.

"Sure Ron Rowan's had a hell of a year. And it's not like he had many rehearsals last year," he said to another.

"I know you guys have to fill up space," he said, "so just make something up and tomorrow we all come back and do it all over again."

Then he winked.

BILLY DONOVAN

11/4/1988

*"Sure, it's tough to let a dream go, but I know in my
heart I did everything I possibly could."*
—Billy Donovan

He got up Wednesday morning in his parents' home in Rockville
Centre, N.Y., and all of a sudden Billy Donovan knew something
was different. Knew in some definite way that not only had his life
changed, but it probably never was going to be the same again.

"For the first time in maybe 10 years I didn't have to be guilty
about not lifting weights or going to shoot 500 jumpers," he says.

The day before he had been one of the last cuts of the Utah Jazz.
Last year he also had been released by the Jazz shortly before the
season started, then was reunited with his former Providence College
coach, Rick Pitino, in December, spending about 40 games with the
New York Knicks before being released in March. Last spring he had
started getting ready again to chase his dream of playing in the best
basketball league in all the world. Tuesday the dream died.

Just like that.

So when he woke up Wednesday morning and realized he would
feel no guilt if he failed to shoot 500 jumpers, he also knew a part of
his life was probably over.

For the thing to understand is, no one ever worked any harder
than Billy Donovan. He never had great physical gifts, never was
someone for whom the game came easy. In a sense he's always been
the kid next door, the one you always see shooting baskets in the
driveway, out there by himself playing imaginary games, fueled by

fantasies. The kind of kid who always had to struggle, every step of the way.

His first two years at Providence College he always looked as if he had stumbled out of a CYO game, a little too small, a little too slow. In a league as competitive as the Big East, he always looked a little like the kid who hoped to get chosen into the game. We all know the rest of the story. How Pitino came in and told Donovan to lose 20 pounds. How Donovan became the most visible symbol of the Pitino era at PC. How Donovan became one of the top guards in the Big East, the one who dribbled the Friars all the way to the Final Four, one of the best stories in all of college basketball.

What we didn't know then was how hard Donovan worked at it. How every summer he went back to his own little torture chamber where he shot his 50 jumpers a day, off in a gym by himself, far away from the cheers.

When he was released by the Knicks last spring, he hired the Knicks strength coach to live with him for two weeks and get him on a serious conditioning program. A month later he could see the difference. He was able to shoot the pro three-pointer effortlessly, a failing he thought had hurt him with the Knicks the year before. He played in a summer league in Harlem. He spent two weeks at rookie camp with the Washington Bullets. He went out to Utah for another two weeks. His goal had been to play against as much good competition as he could find, and when he went back to training camp with the Jazz in early October he felt he had done that, felt he had taken his game to another level.

Four games into the exhibition season, the Jazz cut Ricky Grace and Eddie Hughes, two guards who were competing with Donovan for the backup-guard spot behind John Stockton. He was playing about 10 minutes a game, feeling more comfortable than he had the year before. But no one ever told him anything. Not how he was doing. Not if he were going to make the team.

Nothing.

Every day he would practice, then go back to his room in the Salt Lake City Marriott, then go back to practice, all the time not knowing what his fate was going to be. With two exhibition games to go, the Jazz brought in Jim Les, a backup guard who had been cut by Milwaukee. And it started to play with his head. The uncertainty. The doubt. The never-knowing what the coaches are thinking. The never-ending emotional roller-coaster. He had spent nearly two years chasing a dream to get into the NBA and now, when it was so close he could reach out and touch it, the chase seemed much more complicated than it was supposed to be.

"I think for the first time in my life I didn't enjoy playing basketball," he says.

Then Tuesday he was told he was released. Coach Frank Leyden told him that he didn't know if Les was any better than Donovan, but he was keeping Les anyway.

What do you say?

So now Donovan has to deal with the fact the dream is probably over. For even if he thinks he's good enough to be a backup guard in the NBA, he doesn't want to go to the CBA, doesn't want to be one of those guys who's always chasing the game, always looking for another tryout, clinging to the dream that year by year fades a little more. He also knows that to try again means waiting until next fall for another training camp, another year of lifting weights and shooting 500 jumpers a day.

"I don't want to be someone who ends up bitter with basketball," he says. "I am a little upset with the way things were handled in Utah, but basketball has been great to me. My dream always was to play in the NBA, so my time last year with the Knicks was the best thing that ever happened to me. And I know that if I could go back and live the last 10 years of my life over again, I would do everything the same."

The plan now is to get on with his life. Maybe work on Wall Street. Maybe get into coaching.

Anyway, he thinks maybe now it's time to let the dream go and write his basketball obituary.

He says that what kept him motivated in the past, what kept him in going through all those lonely hours in all those lonely gyms, was that making the NBA was a realistic goal. Now it's as if he sees a chilling future of always being in limbo in some training camp, trying to hang on, living with the uncertainty.

"Sure, it's tough to let a dream go," says Billy Donovan, "but I know in my heart I did everything I possibly could."

He got up Wednesday morning in his parents' home in Rockville Centre, N.Y., and all of a sudden Billy Donovan knew something was different. Knew in some definite way that not only had his life changed, but it probably never was going to be the same again.

POSTSCRIPT: *Billy Donovan worked briefly on Wall Street after being cut by the Utah Jazz. Then he turned to coaching. Highlights from his coaching career include leading the University of Florida Gators to back-to-back NCAA championships in 2006 and 2007 and, in the NBA, being named Coach of the Year after his 2019-2020 season as head coach of the Oklahoma City Thunder. He has been head coach of the Chicago Bulls since 2020.*

BOBBY RIGGS

9/13/1988

"It was the first battle of the sexes and considering all the ones they had after that I should have gotten royalties for it."
—BOBBY RIGGS

EAST PROVIDENCE — He has just won a first- round match in the 70-75 age division in the National Super Senior Grass Court championships at Agawam Hunt and now Bobby Riggs is walking off the court. He is wearing a green hat, white shirt, and gray shorts. All the rest of the players are wearing white shirts and matching shorts.

"Er, Bobby," says a man in a blue blazer. "They want you to wear whites tomorrow."

"Whites?" asks Riggs incredulously, glancing down at his gray shorts. "This is good enough for Wimbledon."

The man looks apologetic. "They asked me to ask you because they know I know you."

"Whites," says Riggs, a sly smile sticking out from underneath the green cap. "Are they going to buy me some?"

Bobby Riggs, always looking for the edge.

He is 70 years old now, and it's been 15 years since Bobby Riggs played Billie Jean King on national television in the Astrodome, the event that took tennis from the country clubs to America's living rooms. The event that also made Riggs a genuine celebrity, America's favorite Male Chauvinist Pig.

No matter that he had been a name in the tennis world ever since he won the national juniors in 1935, then came back and won the national amateur the following year when he was 18. No matter that he always had the red-carpet treatment, his tennis ability the passport to the good life. No matter that he won Wimbledon, the U.S. Open, and now has won more than 70 national titles. It wasn't until he first beat Margaret Court, and then lost to King in the Battle of the Sexes, that Bobby Riggs became a part of the culture.

TV commercials. Endorsements. The whole enchilada.

And he made the most of it.

If he always had been a hustler, ever since he came of age in Los Angeles in the '20s where he first learned to play tennis by "loser pays for the balls," now he took his act on the road.

He's played with one foot in a water bucket. He's played holding an umbrella. He's played with frogman flippers on his feet. He's played in a scuba diving suit. Once he played the Chicago Bears. Once he played an Australian football team.

"That was easy," he said. "They kept bumping into each other. But you name it, I invented it," he says.

"One time I played Minnie Pearl, the singer from the Grand Ole Opry. I had 45 chairs on my side of the court. She didn't even play tennis, but I told her that all she had to do was hold out her racquet and I would hit my serve into it. I reassured her she would win and she did. So this guy who was the chairman of the board of Holiday Inn sees this and sends me a note telling me that he'll play me the same way for $1,000. He doesn't know I faked it with Minnie Pearl. So I keep serving aces, he never gets the ball back, and I pick up the grand. That was one of my greatest hustles of all time."

For the last few years, he has added a new hustle: golf. Complete with his own motto: "A throw a hole and I'm as good as a pro."

"I don't want strokes," he says, "because with strokes you still have to make the shots. I want one throw a hole. Give me that and I can play with anyone in the world. Give me one throw a hole and

I can play scratch golf. I get near the green in two shots, I use my throw, and I'm putting for a birdie.

He has done this all over the country, played against pros, against anyone who wants to play a $100 Nassau. All he wants is his throw a hole. His edge.

The hustling started early. He had four older brothers, so he learned how to compete early. Sports. Pitching pennies, marbles. Anything. Beat the kid next door in a race, and you can go to the movies. Lose, and get a kick in the butt. Competition as a way of life. And from an early age he learned how to evaluate talent, to know who he could beat and who he couldn't.

"I always wanted to play for a prize," he says. "To play for something. A trophy. A cup. A championship. Glory. Money. Something."

He is sitting on the green lawn in back of the yellow Agawam clubhouse, a different world from the one he grew up in. For he learned his tennis in the public parks, not the country clubs; and even now, after all these years, there is still the side of him that thinks he is in here on a pass, always a little bit of the outsider. Still the hustler, after all these years.

"But I never hustled anyone who needed the money," he says. "Only rich guys. Country club guys. And a lot of times I didn't hustle them at all, I just beat them because I was a better competitor. I didn't miss the putt. I didn't choke. I won because I was used to competing and they weren't."

But his all-time greatest hustle, of course, was to issue a challenge to the women pros. It was 1973. He was 55. It also was a time when feminism was in flower, a time when sisterhood was powerful.

"It was the first battle of the sexes and considering all the ones they had after that I should have gotten royalties for it," he says with that sly smile, "but I guess I couldn't get a copyright."

Now Riggs runs a bowling alley outside of Fort Lauderdale, in between trying to round up a golf game where he can get a "throw a hole." In January he had an operation for prostate cancer. Then he underwent eight weeks of radiation. This summer he started playing tennis again, already has won two national doubles titles in the 70-and-over division, even though he says he's still "only 40 percent."

But he is here all week gunning for another national title, this time in the 70–75 age group. And it's not only because he's already won all the age groups. And it's certainly not that he needs another national title. No, he is here this week because it long ago became a way of life for Bobby Riggs.

"I always wanted to play for a prize."

"If I were healthy I'd win it easy," he says, "but who knows now."

He starts talking about how he now gets winded, and how he recently caught a summer cold and how his throat hurts, and how his knee aches, and how he might need a shot of penicillin to get through the week. And just when you start to think there's no way he'll be able to play at all, he gives you that sly little smile and you start to wonder. Because in the next sentence he starts to talk about some of his hustles. And when Bobby Riggs talks about his hustles, the smile of memory on his face, it's a little like an old man talking about his past lovers.

JIM RICE

8/21/1988

"I do my job. I've always done my job."
—JIM RICE

ANDERSON, SOUTH CAROLINA — It is a one-story red-brick building a few streets away from downtown Anderson, S.C.: an old elementary school that's been turned into a youth center. The sign outside says, "Jim Ed Rice Center," and in the lobby inside is a large picture of a young Jim Rice in a Red Sox uniform, the center-field bleachers in Fenway Park behind him. There is a smile on his face. A large Afro sticks out from under a red hat.

And on this summer afternoon, with the heat shimmering off the pavement outside, a dozen or so kids are in the rec room, just down the hall from that picture. So is Barbara Mack, a woman who grew up in Anderson and now runs the center. On the desk is a letter she's writing to Rice. She wants him to stop into the center sometime, this place that honors him here in his hometown. She says the kids here don't know him. That they see him once in a while on television; they see his picture in the lobby every day. But they don't know who he is.

Exactly.

For though he is now in his 13th season in Boston, in a sense we know as little about Jim Rice as we did when he first came to Boston, in 1975. He has long been the great enigma, the Greta Garbo of Boston sports. Certainly, he's the least-known superstar ever to play in Boston. He seldom gives interviews. When he does, they tend to be perfunctory at best, given about baseball and baseball only. There have been virtually no peeks at Rice the man: what he thinks, what he feels, who he is.

In his new book, "A Player for a Moment," John Hough Jr. spent a season following the Red Sox. He describes Rice this way: "He won't look at me, won't say hello, carries an indifference to me and my business that is so colossal, so absolute, that the sheer weight of it seems aggressive."

Hough is not alone. Almost every sports writer who covers the Red Sox has endless stories of Rice's being difficult, moody. The impassive mask he puts on his face has become part of Boston sports lore. He has turned being unapproachable into an art form.

But these are not the best of times for Rice.

Last year, he had the worst season in his career, hitting .277, with only 13 home runs. Then he began this year in a horrible slump. The picture seems to be of a fading superstar in the twilight of his career, trying to survive on memories and rust.

For he's now 35, and if he is one of the highest-paid players in the game, all the birthday candles show. He no longer plays in the field, but is relegated to being a designated hitter, a one-dimensional player. He has trouble pulling the ball. He shows little power. Where once he was one of the most feared hitters in the game, now he seems a parody of himself at the plate, swinging late, hitting most balls to right field. At the All-Star break in mid-July, the symbolic halfway point of the season, he had only four home runs. So different from his prime, when opponents tried to pitch around his power.

A month ago, he was suspended for three games after he threw a temper tantrum. New manager Joe Morgan had replaced him for a pinch hitter against the Minnesota Twins and Rice felt he was being publicly embarrassed.

Now Rice is being booed in Fenway, as if all the years when he has produced no longer count, as if there is no memory of the past. Not that this comes as a great surprise. Rice has never been a favorite in New England, not really. There have always been the subtle knocks on him, even in all the good years, the negatives that have followed his career like shadows trailing a summer sun: he doesn't hit in the clutch; he's a poor fielder; he hits into too many double plays. He has been admired, but never revered.

And even now, when he is seemingly close to the end of his career with the Red Sox, an air of mystery still surrounds Rice, as opaque as it was 13 years ago.

There are several theories as to why Rice's career in Boston has evolved this way, why he long ago decided to erect a wall around himself. The most prevalent is that he has never forgotten that Fred Lynn got most of the attention back in 1975, the year the Red Sox won the pennant. Lynn and Rice had both come up from Pawtucket that year, two rookie outfielders having a great year in the middle of a pennant race. They were nicknamed the Gold-Dust Twins. But Lynn was everything Rice wasn't. He was graceful in the field, smooth, articulate, the college kid from USC. He was also white.

So maybe it was inevitable that Lynn became the media darling. Then, shortly before the play-offs, Rice broke his wrist. He spent the World Series sitting in the dugout in relative obscurity, while Lynn spent it in the middle of the media microscope. And then Lynn was named the American League's Most Valuable Player.

"I was hurt by all the attention he got at the time," Rice said three years ago. "Anyone who looked at the stats had to think I deserved the MVP as much as he did."

Another theory is that Rice resents the fact that he's never gotten the appreciation he felt he deserved in Boston, that he's always been overshadowed. It only started with Lynn. Then it was Carlton Fisk. Then it was Carl Yastrzemski, who by the end of his career had become a New England folk hero.

But on Yaz's last day at Fenway, a day emblazoned in New England sports lore, Rice came to the plate late in the game and received a standing ovation. It was seen as a passing of the torch. It was 1983. Rice was the only one left, the last link to the past. It was going to be Jim Rice's team.

Finally.

Two years later, new manager John McNamara named him the team captain, only the third captain of the Red Sox in the modern era.

But it never really turned out to be Jim Rice's team, after all. Shortly thereafter, Wade Boggs became the new Fenway darling. Then it was Roger Clemens. Once again, the Red Sox seemed to belong to someone else, not Jim Rice. Even in the pennant year of 1986, Rice was overshadowed by the overwhelming clubhouse presence of Don Baylor, a veteran obtained from the Yankees. Rice may have been the captain, but everyone knew Baylor was the leader. Once again, Rice seemed to be sitting in one corner of the clubhouse while all the attention went somewhere else.

How much has this affected him? How much has it played with his psyche?

Who knows.

Rice's current explanation is that he's never cared for the limelight, that he just wants to come to the park, do his job, and go home. That if he had to do it all over again, he would do things the same way. That he's never cared for crowds, nor sought any attention.

Then there is the delicate subject of race. Rice is a black man who grew up in the segregated South and then came to Boston to play several games in 1974 — the year the city was starting forced busing, a traumatic time when racial tensions were like tinder waiting for a match.

He also came to an organization with all the sympathies of the Old South. The Red Sox, the last team in the major leagues to integrate, have long had the reputation of being insensitive to blacks and other minorities, a holdover from the days when the tone was set by owner Tom Yawkey, a paternalistic South Carolina farmer. Even in the past decade, when blacks and Latins are all over the rosters of most major-league teams, the Red Sox have had few of either. There are few blacks that work in the Red Sox organization. There are few black fans in Fenway Park.

In fact, Boston is a city that's never embraced black stars. Bill Russell, one of the greatest basketball players in history and the foundation of the hallowed Celtic teams that dominated the sport in the '60s, called Boston "racist."

"I think race has been a factor in the way I've been used," Rice said in 1978, "because the front office let it be a factor. Lynn can hit .240 in the minors and I can hit .340, and he gets a starting job before I do."

That same year, Carlton Fisk was named the team's most valuable player, even though Rice was the league's MVP. Rice blasted the Boston media, the implication being that it had been a racist decision; that once again Rice had been cheated out of something he deserved.

Whatever the reason, Rice long ago built a wall around himself. After games, he often sits in the Sox clubhouse in silence, glaring at people he doesn't know. Once he threw Tom Boswell, a baseball writer for the Washington Post, into a clubhouse trash can for something Boswell had written. An article last year in Sport magazine essentially asked what is wrong with Jim Rice? Why all the belligerence? The article went on to point out that Rice was surly and hostile, giving short, one-word answers, and never looking at the questioner.

How much of this is Rice's personality?

How much of this is the result of being a black man who came of age with the Boston Red Sox and still carries the scar?

You come to Anderson looking for some clues to who Jim Rice really is. It is a town of about 40,000 in the southwest part of South Carolina, about 20 miles from Clemson University. This is the Deep South: farm country of red clay and fields, where every September they have the Anderson County Fair, just a few blocks from downtown.

The town is a mixture of the Old and the New South. Downtown is the Old South, with its wide one-way streets and main street full of small stores whose glory days seem in the past tense. Cars park diagonally, and it all seems to belong to another time, back before the interstate just a few miles away became the main thoroughfare between Richmond and Atlanta. It is sleepy in the summer heat, with white frame houses nestled under leafy trees. It could be a scene out of To Kill a Mockingbird.

The New South is the street that leads out of downtown to Interstate 85, full of new malls and franchise restaurants. Anywhere, U.S.A.

This is the town where James Edward Rice grew up, the fourth of Roger and Willie Mae Rice's nine children. His father was a factory supervisor. It was a disciplined home, where the children said, "Yes, sir" and "No, ma'am," and didn't talk back. Rice has said that he is raising his two children in the same way. It was still the segregated South, where whites and blacks often lived on neighboring streets yet in different worlds.

"That was just the way it was then," remembers William Roberts, who first met Rice when Rice was 12 and coached him in football and basketball at all-black Westside High School. "He was a nice kid. He never was a problem. I wouldn't classify him as moody. He was treated just like all the rest of the kids."

Right from the beginning, Rice's athletic ability set him apart. He was a starter for Westside while only in the seventh grade. As a sophomore he supposedly hit a ball 500 feet, an achievement that became part of Anderson's oral tradition. He was 15 years old. He was also Ed Rice then. Or else Jim Ed Rice. Never Jim Rice.

It was about then that he met Olin Saylors. Saylors, 49, owns Saylors' One Stop, a gas station — variety store a few blocks from downtown. When Rice was growing up, Saylors coached an American Legion team. One night Rice and a couple of his friends came over to McCant's Field for a tryout; it was the first time blacks had shown up. Rice immediately began knocking the ball out of the park, the ball all but jumping off his bat.

But the next day Rice didn't come to practice. So Saylors went looking for him. He found him hanging out in front of a variety store near his house, on Reed Street, drinking Pepsi and eating potato chips. Saylors asked Rice why he wasn't at practice. Rice replied that he didn't want to waste his time playing baseball, that he was going to get a job so he could have money to buy clothes.

"I'll never forget what I said to him, right there on the front steps of that store," Saylors says. "'Listen,' I told him. 'I don't know anything about clothes, but I know something about baseball. You stick with baseball, and someday you'll be wearing silk underwear.'"

Saylors remembers Rice as being no different than any other 15-year-old kid. He was loyal. He always was on time. He never missed a practice.

"I liked him. I still do," says Saylors. "I had many long talks with him in those days, out in front of his house late at night. One of the things I tried to get across to him is that when someone hits a home run, it doesn't matter if he's black or white. His best friend on the team became John Campbell, a white kid."

It was just before Rice's senior year that, in retrospect, was a turning point for Rice. Integration was coming to Anderson. It was 1970 — 16 years after Brown vs. Board of Education, the landmark Supreme Court case that brought civil rights to the South; almost a decade after the civil — rights marches; two years after Martin Luther King Jr. had been assassinated in Memphis — and Anderson was coming into the 20th century.

Although he lived close to his school, Westside, Rice was designated to go to all-white Hanna High School, miles away. So he had to leave his neighborhood and friends and become a pioneer in Anderson's integration. School officials denied gerrymandering, but to this day there is strong suspicion that Hanna wanted Rice because of his talent, both in baseball and in football. The evidence: Rice's sister, who lived in the same house, went to Westside.

"They used him," says Beatrice Thompson, a guidance counselor at Westside and a distant relative, who remembers Rice as being well liked, though not outgoing. "He knew they only wanted him there to play ball for them."

Yet the opportunity to go to Hanna undoubtedly helped Rice's career get started. Even as recently as the late '60s, black high schools in the Deep South often played in obscurity, ignored by many baseball scouts. But at formerly all-white Hanna, Rice — hitting nearly .500 in one year — became the Red Sox's first pick in the June '71 draft. He also turned down football offers from North Carolina, Nebraska, and nearby Clemson, and signed for $46,000.

Three years later, he was in Fenway Park.

Rice was brought to Boston for the last month of the 1974 season, his arrival coinciding with the court-ordered busing. For a young black man from small-town South Carolina, it must have seemed like a different planet. Even a decade later, his father said, "He don't like Northern states, but his job calls for it."

By the time Rice got to Boston, he had made all the predictable stops through the Red Sox organization, coming up quickly: One year at Williamsport, Pa., in the rookie league ("I lived in a big house with five other guys, three blacks and two whites. It was my first year away from home, but we were all going through it together. It was like one big family"); one at Winter Haven, in Class A; one at Bristol, Conn., in Double A; and then a year at Pawtucket.

At Pawtucket, Lynn was brought up by the Sox before Rice, even though Rice had appreciably better numbers.

"I remember (Rice's) mother calling me up the next morning at 6 a.m. and telling me I had to talk to Jim right away," remembers Willie Binette, a sports writer at the Myrtle Beach (S.C.) Sun News. "He was upset. I told him not to worry about it. That there wasn't any way they were going to be able to keep him out of Boston much longer, and once he got there, he would stay there."

Binette used to be a sports writer on the Anderson Independent.

More important, he was Rice's friend. It was a relationship that had started when Binette covered Rice's games at Westside High School; Binette was one of the few white people who went to the games there. It was also a relationship fueled by a shared love of golf. Binette often got Rice, as his guest, onto golf courses in the Anderson area, courses that would not normally have let blacks play.

"I was the only white person present when he signed a pro contract," says Binette.

Even now, Rice keeps in contact with Binette, one of the few who are allowed inside the wall, someone who was there in the beginning. Rice often comes down to Binette's benefit golf tournament in Myrtle Beach, has gone out of his way through the years to help Binette.

Tony Pennacchia, now a Cranston sports agent, first met Rice that year he was at Pawtucket, in the summer of 1974; they were introduced by a mutual friend. A year later, after his rookie season, Rice asked Pennacchia to represent him. Rice became Pennacchia's first athlete client.

"He was shy," remembers Pennacchia. "And he was moody. When he smiled, he'd melt your insides, and when he frowned, you quaked. His whole personality is so incongruous. It can change from second to second. But it definitely affected him in 1975 when Lynn got all the attention. There's no doubt about that."

Pennacchia and Rice became fast friends. Pennacchia also loved golf, and often the two flew around the country in the off-season to play golf.

"He started out like my son and became like my brother," says Pennacchia. "He was my man. He made my life. In 1979 we negotiated the biggest contract in sports. He was getting $1.2 million a year, plus endorsements, and that was incredible money in 1979. I still have a house in North Conway I call the Rice House."

A few years ago, Rice dropped Pennacchia as his agent, although the two remain very friendly.

"We used to go everywhere together, and Jimmy always was impeccably dressed," says Pennacchia. "And with the public, no one's better than Jimmy. With just a few people he's very gracious. But he created a lot of the problems he's had with the media. He dumped Boswell in a trash can. He can be surly and caustic. Maybe I shielded him too much. Overall, I could never get through to him about press relations."

"I can understand it he went into a shell," says William Roberts, Rice's childhood coach. "From what I hear, Boston's as segregated a place as it used to be down here. Maybe he dealt with it the best way he could."

Beatrice Thompson believes that Rice's behavior is little more than a defense mechanism, a survival tool for existing in an unfamiliar world.

Once, a few years back, I got some insight into just how unpleasant it is for Rice to operate as a public figure in Boston. There was the usual media circus in the locker room, about a dozen or so reporters waiting by his locker. Rice came out of the shower room and walked over to his locker, seemingly oblivious of the people a few feet away who were obviously waiting for him. By chance, I was at one end of the group, able to see Rice's face as he stared into his locker, the crowd to his back. He put his shirt on and then clenched his face before turning around to deal with the reporters: his face was rigid and impassive, the mask in place, revealing nothing.

It was the only time I ever felt I had gotten a glimpse of the real Rice.

By the middle of his career, the walls were securely in place. At the All-Star Game in 1979, asked to do a small spot on TV to hype the game, Rice announced that he wouldn't endorse anything unless he was paid for it. By this time, Rice may have been the least-quoted figure in sports, Howard Hughes in double-knits, hiding behind his stare and his curt, one-word answers. And his numbers.

Ah, the numbers.

Rice's answer to all his critics. The numbers he kept putting up every season, as if as long as he kept putting up the numbers, he didn't have to do anything else. And for the longest time they were as impressive as any in baseball. For 10 years, Rice was one of the best hitters in the game, someone who hit for batting average while also hitting for power. He has also always played while injured. He's never complained. He has worked hard during the season, taking countless hours of extra batting practice under the center-field bleachers, working on his fielding until he became a decent left fielder for most of his career. In a day and age when many athletes take the big money and go on cruise control, Rice has always played hard. He has also never shirked taking his share of the blame; he has always been more accessible after a bad game than a good one.

Now there are no numbers.

Some say it's bad eyesight and his refusal to wear glasses at the plate. Some think that for all the hard work Rice puts in during the season, he doesn't work out in the off-season, preferring to play golf instead and it has caught up with him. Regardless of the reason, there's little doubt that we are witnessing the winding down of the career.

Jimmy, we hardly knew ye.

There seems be few connections now between Rice and Anderson, his hometown. Unlike certain small towns that almost become shrines to the famous kids they've sent out into the world, there are few remembrances of Rice in Anderson other than the Jim Ed Rice Center. Rice's wife, Corrine, is also from Anderson, and there was a time when they would go back every winter. Now he rarely goes back, and when he does it's in and out, with little fanfare. There used to be a "Rice Watch" in the local paper, but it stopped a few years ago. Now Rice will not deal with any of the sports writers at the Anderson Independent. This is a legacy of the time when Binette got an offer from the paper in Myrtle Beach and Rice was upset that the Independent didn't offer Binette more money.

On a recent afternoon at the Independent, three sports writers sitting around the office displayed little knowledge of Rice. They did not know where in Anderson he had grown up. Did not know whether he still had family there now. Did not know where the Jim Ed Rice Center was.

"He's gotten a lot of adverse publicity here," says Beatrice Thompson, Rice's guidance counselor. "People see him as arrogant. But I think a lot of it was his being uncomfortable…Outside of his family, I don't think there are a lot of close ties here."

But Rice doesn't see it that way. Though he has built an expensive house in North Andover, Mass., Rice still considers Anderson home.

Jim Rice is about to leave the Red Sox clubhouse when I approach him. His locker is in a far corner of the room, the farthest from the manager's office. The room is dark, almost dingy, with a faded-brown rug on the floor. Rice has on a blue blazer, eyeglasses. He starts walking toward the door. It is a Thursday night. The Red Sox have just been rained out.

"Jim, if I make an appointment, can I meet with you on Tuesday?" I ask.

Rice doesn't look at me, but continues walking toward the door.

"What for?" he says.

"A story."

"No way," he grunts, still not looking at me, going through the clubhouse door and out into a small hallway. "Everyone's done stories on me."

"Maybe I'll do it different," I say loudly, as he opens the door that takes him out underneath the first-base grandstand. By this time, he is five yards ahead of me.

"Four o'clock," he yells back, without ever turning around.

Tuesday, four o'clock.

Rice is sitting in front of his locker. The room is nearly deserted. I sit in a chair next to him, and ask him if he knows that he is a mystery.

"I don't care," he says. "I do my job. I've always done my job."

But in almost the next breath he denounces the media.

"They don't write down what you say," he says. "They stand in the back and don't hear everything, or else they get it from somebody else and put it in the paper anyway. And they don't respect that sometimes I want to be alone. If they don't respect me, why should I respect them? Or they want me to talk about my teammates, or what's wrong with the team. Well, I'm not going to do that. And if I have to tell a lie to please them, then I'm not going to do it. I wasn't raised that way. And what did they ever do for me, anyway?"

Rice has always been better with reporters one-on-one. Has always been more surly, more uncommunicative, the larger the group around him.

"I don't like crowds," he says. "I never have. Even now, if I go to the movies and it is crowded, I will always wait and go in late."

If a few days before he was reluctant to do the interview, now he is downright effusive, as if he couldn't wait to unload his pent-up feelings. He says the booing in Fenway doesn't bother him ("They booed Williams and Yaz, didn't they?"); says if he were released tomorrow he would feel no bitterness, that he understands "it's all business"; says he deals with the uncertainty of his future by learning to block everything else out: just come to the park, play hard, and forget everything else.

And he also talks about his past.

He says he has no bad memories of growing up in segregated Anderson, and that "we had no trouble with integration down there. You had all the problems up here."

"Did you have any problems when you first came to Boston?" he is asked.

"No," he says. "The biggest problem I had was adapting to the different ethnic groups. Back home, everyone is more of the same.

"When I first came here," he says, "I used to sit and watch Yaz every day. How he used to come into the clubhouse and let nothing bother him. How he just went about his job every day. I learned from him."

Rice goes on.

"I'm the same person I always was. When I do go home, I hang out with the same people, in the same places, I always did. When I'm home the word gets out, and there are about a dozen of us who play golf all over the place. I haven't changed. I'm still the same person I always was. If someone respects me, I respect them.

"And I don't bother anyone," he says, looking around the clubhouse. "I sit here every day."

Rice says all this with pride. As if, in his view of the world, he has done it his way. As if he has convinced himself that to have done it any other way would have been to compromise his principles.

And as he sits in front of his locker, off in one of the corners of the clubhouse, it is as if he's become a baseball version of Existential Man: Jim Rice against the world. Proud. Imperial. Mysterious. As if he long ago learned to remove his emotions from his career, long ago learned to exist in some private place where the world can't touch him.

DOUG FLUTIE

10/06/1989

"It's like I live in Flutie World," I said.
"I can't stop thinking about Doug."
—BILL REYNOLDS

PROVIDENCE — "Doc," I said, lying down on the couch. "You got to help me."

"What is it?"

"It's like I live in Flutie World," I said. "I can't stop thinking about Doug."

He gave me a long look. With glasses perched on his forehead and wearing a white coat, he was trying to look as learned as Freud. But he reminded me of Victor Kiam.

"Okay," he said finally. "Let's see how bad this obsession really is. I'm going to say a word, and I want you to say the first thing that comes into your head. Got it?"

"Anything, Doc," I said. "I'm desperate."

"QUARTERBACK," he said.

"Doug."

"FOOTBALL PLAYER."

"Doug."

"NEW ENGLAND PATRIOTS," he said. "What's the first thing that comes to mind when I mention the Patriots? Think of the possibilities. The Sullivans. Raymond Berry. Traffic jams. Chaos. Surely it's something other than Flutie?"

"Sorry, Doc," I said. "I only think of Doug."

"Is there anything remotely connected to football in which you don't think of Flutie?

"No. Doug has become football to me. The two have become synonymous. Doug and football. Football and Doug. Like you can't have one without the other."

"Okay," he said. "It's obvious you have a real fixation."

He started making notations on the legal pad in front of him, sneaking looks at me out of the corner of his eye. I tried to clear my mind. No football, I told myself. Don't think of anything that might lead to Flutie. No quarterbacks. No New England Patriots. No short people. No temptation. I leaned back on the couch and closed my eyes, zen-like, trying to turn my mind into a blank slate.

"IMPROVISATIONAL," he said, his voice harder now.

"That's easy, I said. "Doug. The way he scampers around."

He gave me a long look.

"Okay, let's take a different tact," he said. "CUTE."

I shrugged.

"Doug again," I said. "It has to be Doug."

"Be serious," he yelled. "Women are applicable here. Movie stars are applicable. Kim Basinger is applicable. Anyone you want. Pick a fantasy. Puppy dogs are applicable. And the first thing you think of is Doug Flutie?"

"I can't help it," I wailed. "Every time I pick up the paper I read about Doug. Every time I turn on the TV there's Doug. It's all anyone talks about on the sports talk shows. Doug this. Doug that. Doug can do it. Doug can't do it. Doug is too small to throw over the line. Doug is a miracle man. Doug, Doug, Doug, Doug, Doug, Doug. I'm telling you it's driving me crazy. I go to sleep thinking of Doug, and I wake up thinking of him. You're not listening, Doc. I'm in the middle of Flutie World, and there's nothing I can do about it."

The doctor leaned back and took a puff on his pipe.

"You have to get your mind off it," he said finally.

"How can I?" I wailed. "How is anyone supposed to get away from it? It's out of control. Flutie World is everywhere. And it's not just football. He sells Pepsi on TV. He sells Wheaties. Soon he's going to be selling Remington shavers. I'm telling you we're all living in the middle of Flutie World and there's no getting away from it. I don't even want to hear the word miracle anymore. Or Hail Mary. I can't even watch Miami Vice. The other night I heard the Miami Sound Machine on the radio and thought of Doug. It's out of control."

"When did this Doug obsession start with you?"

"I thought I had it under control," I said. "But the past two weeks it's done me in. It's ruined football for me. It's ruined the season. It's all Doug, Doug, Doug. It's unbearable. Doug used to be a great story. Now he's a monster that dominates my life. You got to kill the monster for me, Doc. You got to. I can't keep living in Flutie World."

He took out a gold medallion.

"Hypnosis," he said. "It's the only answer. I'm going to put you under and when I bring you out of it you will be cured."

"Anything, Doc," I begged. "I don't want to live in Flutie World anymore."

I remembered nothing. But all of a sudden I felt differently, as if some awful curse had been lifted.

"Okay," said the doctor. "Some more word association."

"Go," I said.

"QUARTERBACK."

"Bubby Brister," I said.

He shrugged. "Whoever turns you on. FOOTBALL PLAYER."

"Brian Bosworth."

He gave me a strange look. NEW ENGLAND PATRIOTS."

"Victor Kiam."

"Okay," said the doctor. "One last word. And it's a key one. SHORT. What's the first thing you think of when I say short?"

"Randy Newman."

"Fair enough," he said. "Your responses show that you probably need treatment in other areas. But the point is the hypnosis
has worked. See, all your responses had nothing to do with Doug
Flutie."

"Free, free, free at last," I said, dropping to the floor at the feet of
the doctor. "Thank you, Doc. I'm out of Flutie World. I can tell."

I got up to leave. I felt weightless, free. Stripped of Doug, the
world somehow seemed a simpler place. Outside, I could hear birds
sing. I looked at the sky for the first time in weeks. Everything
seemed clear and bright. Life seemed worth living again.

"Oh, by the way?" asked the doctor. "Is he going to start this
weekend?"

PART TWO

1990–1999

MARVIN BARNES

8/17/90

"Think of it this way. A normal person who lived
like I have would have been dead a long time ago.
So somebody up there must like me."
—MARVIN BARNES

PROVIDENCE — One of the first things you learn in this business
is there's always a sequel.

Ten months ago, I wrote a story on the incredible saga of Marvin
Barnes, the onetime Providence College basketball great who had
ended up on the seedy streets of East San Diego, a sunny cesspool at
the bottom of the American Dream where even the palm trees look
tired. At the time, Barnes was in the county jail with an admitted
drug problem, awaiting sentencing on a charge of shoplifting.

Shortly after the story appeared, John Marinatto, the Providence
College athletic director, approached me one night at the Civic
Center. He never had met Barnes, arriving at PC as a student in
1975, the year after Barnes left. But he had heard all the stories, knew
full well how Marvin Barnes was a textbook example of squandered
potential, a basketball tragedy. Curious, he had pulled Barnes' college transcript from the school's files.

"I was shocked," Marinatto recalls. "He only needed one course
to graduate."

When Barnes was in prison in the late '70s, three of his former
teachers used to go down there to help him work toward his degree.
He had come very close to graduating then. He just never finished.

So began a rather strange scenario.

One of the unfortunate aspects of Barnes' demise was his belief that Providence College had been quite willing to use his basketball talent, only to forget him when his life got more complicated. It's not surprising he would believe that. He never has been inducted into the school's athletic Hall of Fame. Though the school claimed that graduation was a requirement to be inducted to its Hall of Fame, the perception was Providence College was embarrassed by Barnes, and would like everyone to forget about him.

Now here was Marinatto taking an interest.

"After I read the story in the paper I realized that no matter what he's done, he is one of ours." Marinatto said. "And I guess I always was intrigued by the reputation and mystique of Marvin Barnes. And that everyone who had known him when he was here had liked him. It also seemed from the story in the paper that he was reaching out for help, and that we should help if we could."

Barnes was told that he was only one course short of graduating, and the school might be receptive to him finishing. He called Marinatto, asked what he had to do. Marinatto told him to call Father Robert Morris, who in 1974 had taught the course Barnes now needed to graduate. Barnes called Father Morris, who told him he had to write a paper.

But these were not the easiest of times for Barnes. He was facing sentencing, and the prospect of jail. It seemed like just one more chapter in a life full of chaos. So it wasn't very surprising to me that he didn't write the paper back then. Barnes was having enough trouble getting through the day, not to mention trying to write a paper for a course he'd begun 16 years earlier.

And since this is Marvin Barnes we're talking about, this was all being done with a certain unique style. For all his problems, he had not lost his charm. Like the time he called me back in December.

"Hey Bill," he said. "As one writer to another, what do you do when you've written all you have and it's not long enough?"

"How long's the paper, Marvin?" I asked.

There was a pause.

"Two pages," he finally said.

Vintage, Marvin.

Needless to say, the paper didn't get written.

In January he was sentenced to a state prison outside of San Diego. And a curious thing happened. We would periodically speak on the phone and Marvin began saying all the right things. How he was off drugs. How he knew he was getting too old to still be running in the streets and fooling around. How he knew that if he didn't start to change his life he would soon be dead. How he even had started reading the Bible and begun working his long-overdue paper.

"When I first started to read a book for the paper, I couldn't read more than one page at a time before I got a fierce headache," Barnes said. "My concentration span was limited. It had been 15 years since I had read anything but the sports page. I had to make myself read."

He began accompanying the prison warden to schools in the San Diego area to talk about the dangers of drug abuse. He was Exhibit A.

"He called me up and said that he was applying for a job with the California Youth Authority," Marinatto said, "and that there were two requirements. One was that you had to have a college degree. The other was that you had to have been to Hell and back. He said he'd been to Hell and back, now he only needed the degree. And he said he wasn't looking for anything. That he was willing to do what he had to do."

A couple of months ago Barnes was transferred to a halfway house in San Diego. During the day he works at a restaurant supply business. At night he goes back to the halfway house. All the while he kept working on his paper, reading a few pages at a time, teaching himself to concentrate again. Eventually, he wrote 13 pages and sent it to Father Morris, who accepted it and gave Barnes a passing grade. Father Robert Bond, the dean of the college, and some other members of the P.C. administration decided that Marvin Barnes had finally satisfied all his degree requirements.

"The thing that impressed me," Marinatto said, "was that he did it on his own. We didn't put a gun to his head. No one forced him to do it. He should feel proud."

"I do," Barnes said. "I'm the first one in my family to graduate from college. It took me 16 years but I finally got it, so nobody can say now that I just went to P.C. to play basketball."

Barnes is scheduled to be released from jail in September, and says that this time it's going to be different.

"I have to change my game around," he said. "Instead of doing everything the wrong way, I have to do all the right things. I can't keep doing what was I doing before. I can't keep fooling myself. I'm 38 years old and I'm getting tired."

I want to believe him. The only problem is there have been many times in his past when Barnes has said all the right things. He still has to prove himself, and that will take some time. He always has lived in the present tense, and it will no doubt take some hard adjusting to begin to live another way.

"Think of it this way," he said the last time we talked. "A normal person who lived like I have would have been dead a long time ago. So somebody up there must like me."

So now he's ready for another sequel.

There's a difference now, though. He squandered the money. He squandered the fame. He squandered the talent. He squandered his basketball future. Many would say that so far he's squandered his life. But Marvin Barnes is now a graduate of Providence College, and that is something no one can ever take away from him, no matter what happens in the future.

POSTSCRIPT: *Marvin Barnes died in 2014 at age 62. In his later years, he often spoke to kids about the dangers of drug use, using his life as an example. "If you take drugs, if you run the street, you are destined to fail," he told a group in 2003.*

JOE MULLANEY

3/90

*"When I resigned at P.C. I figured that was it. But then
this opportunity came up and I said why not?"*

—JOE MULLANEY

ALBANY, NEW YORK — It seemed a strange place to find a
coaching legend.

There were nearly 5,000 people rattling around in the Knickerbocker Arena, a splashy new building that's trying to revitalize a
tired downtown. There were many players on the court you never
heard of. One of them had to be reminded near the end of the game
that he couldn't go into the game wearing a gold chain around his
neck and an earring.

The basketball world may have been obsessed with the NCAA
Regionals, but in this little corner of the world last Friday night the

big news was a playoff game in the Continental Basketball Association between the Albany Patroons and the Pensacola Tornadoes. And there on one of the benches was Joe Mullaney.

The same Joe Mullaney who built the Providence College basketball program more than 30 years ago, and once in 1970 came within a game of winning the NBA title.

The same Joe Mullaney who, when he left college coaching in 1969 for the Lakers, had the third best winning percentage among all college coaches, behind icons Adolph Rupp and John Wooden. The same Mullaney who then came back to coach at PC in 1981, before eventually realizing that Thomas Wolfe may have been right after all, that you can't really go home again.

He was wearing a blue blazer and tan slacks, a rolled-up program in his left hand. If you didn't know better it could have been any year from the past. He still looks the same. He still sits on the bench the same, looking at everything with a jeweler's eye. Still coaching, after all these years.

That's because Mullaney is a basketball coach. Unlike many contemporary coaches who have used the game to become rich, Mullaney came of age in a different era. He never set out to make a lot of money. Never set out to become a celebrity. He never saw coaching as a means to some other end. All he ever really wanted to do was coach a team.

Some people look at a basketball court and see players. Mullaney looks at it and sees a giant chessboard, a canvas for his vision of how the game should be played. Back in the late '70s when he came back to Rhode Island to coach at Brown University, he was asked how someone who had once coached Wilt Chamberlain and Jerry West could now coach in the Ivy League.

Mullaney looked perplexed.

"What's the difference?" he said. "They're all players."

His coaching odyssey has lasted nearly 46 years. Norwich University. Providence College. The Lakers. The Kentucky Colonels.

The Utah Jazz. The Memphis Tams. The Spirits of St. Louis. The Baltimore Claws. The Buffalo Braves. A pro team in Italy. A summer-league team in Puerto Rico. Brown. Providence College again. Mullaney's coached them all. Have clipboard, will travel.

The last two years it's been Pensacola of the CBA. Not that he ever planned to end up on the Florida Panhandle.

"When I resigned at P.C. I figured that was it," he said.

"But then this opportunity came up and I said why not?"

He had resigned as the P.C. coach in February of 1985, feeling that, for whatever reason, it was not happening for him anymore in Providence. Not that he resigned from basketball, understand. He still watched games. He still analyzed teams, endlessly toying with the questions he'd asked himself all his life: Why do teams do what they do? What can you do to prevent them from doing it? No, Joe Mullaney never retired from basketball. He just didn't have a team to coach anymore.

He was given a title at P.C. and a third-floor office. But he was not given a lot of responsibilities, as if he belonged to some other era, some living piece of nostalgia. By the second year he was looking for a way to get back into the game. Not as a coach necessarily. He knew the NBA doesn't come courting 63-year-olds. Nor did he want a college job with its endless recruiting, a carousel that goes around and around. Maybe he could scout for an NBA team, he reasoned. Anything to feel connected to the game that had defined his life. Anything but sit in a third-floor office with a title and nothing to do.

Two years ago, he got a call from an old friend, Mike Storen, who had been his boss back in Kentucky. Storen was now general manager at Pensacola, and he was looking for a coach. At first Mullaney wasn't interested. The CBA? Wasn't that some Basketball Beirut, where they played in drafty, old CYO gyms and rode rickety buses to nowhere? Not so, said Storen. Mullaney went down for a look, saw a shiny new facility, and that was it. He and his wife Jane rented a condo on the beach and he began another coaching job.

"I've really enjoyed it," he said. "It's been everything Mike said it was. Pensacola's a great place to live in the winter. The league is a lot better than people think. It's only a seven-month job, and there are no discipline problems because there are no long-term contracts. From a coaching standpoint there's a lot of pluses."

Yet it's still the CBA, a minor league that might only be a jump shot away from the NBA, but light years away in lifestyle. One of his players often misses practice to fly airplanes. Another came up to him one day and said he had found God. Still another said he can neither play nor practice on Sundays because of religious reasons. Onetime last year he was mugged after a game in Huntington, W. Va.

He has seen players come and go, either to make money in Europe or go off to basketball obscurity somewhere. A few have gone on to the NBA. This year he's lost three to the NBA, so now he's in the playoffs with a team that includes former UNLV star Mark Wade, Todd Jadlow of Indiana and Gary Wright of Iowa.

It is, of course, a league fueled by ambition. Mullaney is the anomaly. He doesn't have any ambition. For the last two years he's coached because he wanted to coach, not for where he hopes it can take him. A purist in a complicated world.

Friday night the Tornadoes won the game in double overtime, 128-127, and took a 2-0 lead in the semifinals of the Eastern Conference. When it was over, Mullaney pumped his fist in the air in triumph, as if the game had been played in the Fabulous Forum during the prime of his career. Afterwards, he stood in the bowels of Knickerbocker Arena.

"You won't believe this," he said, rolling his eyes at the incongruity of it all. "I'm at the board during halftime and I look over and the pilot has taken the ace bandage off his knee and wrapped it around his head like it's a turban."

Ah, the CBA.

An hour later Mullaney sat in a restaurant-bar a few blocks from the arena. On the TV was the Michigan State-Georgia Tech game. The room was noisy. On the screen was a closeup of Tech coach Bobby Cremins. He's now recognized as one of the coaches on the fast track, a builder of programs. The same thing Mullaney was 25 years ago.

The next morning Mullaney was flying back to Pensacola, and the resumption of the playoffs. When they end, he will announce he's not coming back next year.

Somewhere along the way this past season he decided that enough was enough. Maybe it was too many bus rides through the mid-west, too many times when it was just him and the players on the road, guys who weren't even born when he was becoming one of the big names in college basketball. Maybe it was too many early wake-up calls. Maybe it was just not enough coaching rewards, not in a league where everyone's first priority is his own career.

"I just asked myself one day what am I still doing this for, and I couldn't come up with enough answers," said Joe Mullaney.

Coaching legends don't die.

They just get tired of road trips.

POSTSCRIPT: *Joe Mullaney became head coach of the Providence College Friars in 1955. With Mullaney, the Friars won the 1961 and 1963 NIT championship. Mullaney also brought the Friars to the NCAA tournament three times. He died in 2000 at the age of 75.*

SIMULCASTING AT THE TRACK

1991

"…the track is the only place in the world where you can walk in a bum and walk out a gentleman."
—An old-timer at the track

LINCOLN, RHODE ISLAND — I am here at Lincoln Greyhound Park and the first thing I am learning is that no one wants to disclose their real names.

"No names," says the "Dog," so named because he made his living for years betting dogs.

"No names," echoes the "Kid," so named because he started horse handicapping when he was still in his teens, two decades ago.

"No names," says "Late-Double Pete," so called because of a propensity for hitting the late double.

Here at the track, giving out your name to a reporter is right up there with a "tough beat," a track euphemism for an animal that just misses.

"I've known guys here for years and I don't know their last names," says the Dog, who is wearing a green boat shirt and shorts and looks like he's on his way to the beach, not to the ticket window.

"You know them by nicknames: 'Elbow Grease,' 'Fast-Talkin' Johnny,' 'Louie the Throat,' 'The Screamer' (because he spends the entire race screaming for his horse), 'Louie Tony.' That's just the way it is around here. No one wants to know nothin'."

"Louie Tony?" I ask, perplexed.

"Yeh," says the Dog. "We didn't know whether his name was Louie or Tony so he became Louie Tony."

It's a Friday afternoon and they are sitting upstairs in the Queen of Clubs. Down on the track, the greyhounds are being paraded around, minutes before the start of a race. But the interest is on the TV monitors in front of them, where the afternoon races from Saratoga are being shown.

Simulcasting has come to Rhode Island. Welcome to a brave new world.

But if it's a new script in Rhode Island racing, a lot of the characters are still the same. Where are you, Damon Runyon? Downstairs in the grandstand, guys sit at small tables in the back, poring over forms that are supposed to be clues to understanding the universe, never mind a two-dollar Exacta. Upstairs, the Dog and his gang toss insults at each other.

"Whadda you know?" says one. "I've lost more than $200,000. How much do you know? I've lost more than you can ever know."

"How's that for logic. But you know what I like about the track?" says the Dog, looking around the room, a king surveying his subjects. "Everybody walks in here even. An old-timer used to say the track is the only place in the world where you can walk in a bum and walk out a gentleman."

Ah, the Sport of Kings.

And others, too.

The Dog says he's retired now, but for seven years he never missed a card here at Lincoln. Day after day, week after week, grinding. He says there was no mystery to it. It was work, pure and simple. Being here every day. Watching the races. Then watching the taped replays of the races the next day. Studying.

"It become an obsession," he says. "You never know when that big score is going to happen."

Like maybe now, right?

It's the second race at Saratoga and the Dog and I have boxed an Exacta, a pick courtesy of the Kid, who bunked school one day when he was 16 years old, won his first double and got hooked.

"Even now I remember the two horses," he says almost reverently, like a man at the end of his life remembering past lovers. "Ron Du Nord and Rushin' Fleet. It paid $40, and I remember thinking: Doesn't my father know this place exists? Why's he going to work every day? I never went back to school."

When the horses left Lincoln and Narragansett in the '70s, everything changed for The Kid. A lot of horse players became dog players, even though it's two different games, two different ways of handicapping. Dogs are more susceptible to being bumped, known here as "trips." But the Kid stayed true to the horses. Driving to off-track betting at Killingly, to Teletrack in New Haven, to Suffolk, to Rockingham; for 22 years. Now comes simulcasting, and he can come home again.

"I'm seeing guys I haven't seen since the tracks closed here," he says. "This is fantastic. If I never win again at least I'll save $40 a week in gas."

The Kid is in the middle of a bad stretch. The meet at Saratoga is killing him. Most people think of Saratoga and see the elegance, the splendor, the essence of the Sport of Kings. The "Kid" sees hot weather, long lines at the windows, and Angel Cordero Jr., the jockey who year after year seems to own Saratoga afternoons.

"With all the studying I do, I think I've been making about three cents an hour recently," he says disgustedly. "It's ridiculous."

"Who do you like?" asks a small guy in a white short-sleeve shirt.

The Kid shrugs. There is uncertainty in his eyes.

"The first race I wheel Cordero and he runs out," the small guy says with a snort. "This race I don't bet him and he'll probably win."

"I didn't bet him either," the Kid says.

The small guy snorts again, starts walking away. The Dog watches him go.

"Everyone wants to tell you their hard-luck story," the Dog says, "but they don't want to listen to yours. I wish I had a fin for every guy who tells me that their dog would have won from here to

China if he didn't get bumped. That's what they all say. From here to China. Don't ask me why. That's just what they say."

He looks up at the TV screen to see the horses approaching the gate.

"I always liked the horses better anyway," he says. "I just bet the dogs to win money. But the other day I was here and they had the dog races, plus races from Rockingham and Saratoga. It's like, 'Which one do I watch?' Like I'm losing over there, but I'm alive over here."

He shakes his head at the apparent incongruity of it all, a man who has seen the future and it bewilders him.

"What has this come to?" he asks. "What will they do next? Simulcast crap games from Las Vegas?" The horses are off at Saratoga, brought here to Lincoln by the wonder of simulcasting, horse racing's answer to the Global Village. A group of men stand in front of the TV. They yell at the screen as if they were there at the track, not a different world away.

"Come on, you eight," comes a voice.

"I can't believe this pig," comes another.

The air is thick with smoke and anxiety as the horses are in the back stretch. The tension is palpable.

"Now, now," yells a voice. "Make a move now."

There is no move, of course. Cordero brings Timeless Elegance home, an easy winner. The man yells an expletive to the heavens. We have all lost.

"I told you he was a pig," a guy says to the Kid.

The Kid shrugs, the resignation of man in the middle of a bad streak. The Dog rips his tickets and tosses them into the air. They seem to flutter to the floor, like confetti after some long-gone parade.

TOMMY GIOIOSA AND PETE ROSE

2/3/1991

*"All he had to do was get one message to me and I
never would have said Pete Rose bet baseball. I would
have taken that to my grave with me."*
—TOMMY GIOIOSA

PENNSYLVANIA — It seems an unlikely place to come looking for someone from New Bedford, someone who once lived in
Pete Rose's house, someone who once thought he was living in the
middle of some adolescent fairy tale.

It's called the McKean Federal Correctional Institute, and it's a
modern federal penitentiary in rural northwestern Pennsylvania,
just a few miles from the New York border. But it's here, in minimum security, where Tommy Gioiosa has been since June.

Once Gioiosa drove a Porsche, hung out in major league club-
houses. He was on life's fast track. That was 10 years ago, back when
Rose was the biggest name in baseball, and Gioiosa was privy to a
world he had previously fantasized about. On this morning Gioiosa
has just returned from driving a snowplow, his job here at McKean
after getting a five-year sentence last February for conspiracy to dis-
tribute cocaine and for two charges of income tax evasion.

The rent came due on the fantasy.

"When I heard the sentence the blood went out of me," he says.

He was led down a tunnel in handcuffs last February 1. He was met
by TV cameras and reporters. The night before he had been asked by
a reporter if Pete Rose had bet on baseball, and had Rose bet on the
Cincinnati Reds? Yes, Gioiosa said. Rose had bet baseball, and yes, he

had bet on the Reds. Then he asked the reporter to hold off on the story, just in case Rose came to his sentencing the next day. It was a question Gioiosa had been asked endless times before, and always had refused to answer. But now it had been five months since his trial and still he had not heard from Rose. He felt alone, abandoned.

Once Tommy Gioiosa had walked down another tunnel. That was in 1979, in the middle of the baseball season in Philadelphia. The tunnel was from the clubhouse to the dugout. He was wearing a uniform with "Rose" on the back. It was a couple of hours before a game; and as he walked out on the field at Veteran's Stadium, he looked around at the expanse of seats and was in awe. He headed toward the outfield and people, thinking he was Rose, cheered. When Rose came out of the dugout, he motioned to Gioiosa to play catch with him in front of the dugout. It's a moment he has thought about often, a personal snapshot of the good times.

Now he was walking down another tunnel, this one leading to jail. He was facing five years of jail time, and there was no sign of Rose at his sentencing.

"Run the tape," he told the reporter.

That night the story went out on ESPN.

The rest? Major League Baseball eventually bans Rose for life.

"What hurt me the most was that Pete never tried to get in touch with me," Gioiosa says. "Because I would never do anything to hurt Pete Rose. He was my idol. He was like a father to me.

All he had to do was get one message to me and I never would have said Pete Rose bet baseball. I would have taken that to my grave with me."

He is sitting in a small conference room at McKean. He is only 5-foot-5 but well-built, his chest defined by years of weight-lifting and steroids. His brown hair is short on the top and sides, but long in the back. At first glance he looks like a smaller version of Rose.

"Do you ever think that if you went to the movies and saw this story, you wouldn't believe it?" I asked him.

"No one would ever believe it," says Tommy Gioiosa with a wry smile.

He grew up in the north end of New Bedford, the old whaling town immortalized in literature by a great white whale. He was a good athlete as a kid, but had never seen Rose play. Then, one day his father told him that, "If you play baseball like Pete Rose plays baseball you'll make the big leagues." Gioiosa finally watched Rose play one night on TV in the All-Star game and then began to imitate him as a player. They were both small. They both hustled to compensate for a lack of natural talent. Tommy Gioiosa looked in the mirror and saw Pete Rose. He spent winters swinging a leaded bat at the local YMCA. He didn't drink. He didn't smoke. He lived for baseball.

"I wanted to go to college and I knew that the only way to get out of New Bedford was to get a scholarship, or I was going to work 8 to 5 the rest of my life for no money."

As a junior, he was co-captain of the baseball team, was named to the All-Regional team by the New Bedford Standard-Times. The next year, he was his team's captain, led the state in hitting for a while, was named to the All-State team. There was even a small blurb in a local newspaper that a Cleveland Indians' scout was looking at Tommy Gioiosa. Then it ended. Just like that. His high school career was over. There were no scholarship offers. No college. He went to work with his father. It was the fall of 1976.

"I didn't know what to do," he says.

A friend, Dave Clark, who had played baseball for Durfee High in Fall River, was going to Massasoit Community College in Brockton. One day Gioiosa went to see the coach, and was told that Massasoit had an indoor batting cage, and they also took a Florida trip every spring. That was enough for Gioiosa. He enrolled for the second semester, and that spring went to Florida with the Massasoit baseball team. They stayed in King Arthur's Hotel in Tampa, the same hotel the Cincinnati Reds used.

One day he was sitting around the pool, still wearing his baseball glove. Most of his teammates had gone out bar-hopping. He had stayed behind, his mind on baseball, when a kid about eight or nine approached him.

"Do you want to play toss?" the kid asked.

"Sure," Gioiosa said.

They played catch for a while, then Gioiosa asked the kid if he wanted to come to the Massasoit game the next day and be the team's batboy. The kid, whose name was Petey, said sure. The kid enjoyed being the bat boy. Gioiosa liked having him there. It was almost like having a little brother, someone who rooted for him, cared how he did in the game. On the bus returning from the game, the kid said he was Pete Rose.

"Yeah," said Gioiosa, "and I'm Babe Ruth."

"No," said the kid. "Pete Rose is my father."

"Sure," said Gioiosa, "and Babe Ruth is my father."

When the bus returned to the hotel, the kid took Gioiosa to meet his mother by the pool. Indeed, she was Karolyn Rose, wife of Pete Rose. Gioiosa was in shock. Here he was, a poor kid from New Bedford, and he was talking to the wife of his idol.

"Don't worry," Karolyn Rose said, reassuring him. "We started out just like you did."

Then he saw Rose himself walking up the sidewalk. He couldn't believe it.

"You call me Pete," Rose said to Gioiosa.

"I went back to my room and called my mom," Gioiosa recalls. "She thought I'd been drinking."

A couple of days later, Rose was washing his Porsche in the park-ing lot. Gioiosa went over to help him. When Rose left to take a phone call, Gioiosa kept washing the car. Rose returned, saw what Gioiosa had done, and said, "That just shows you work hard. If you work hard and give 110 percent, you'll make it."

It was the biggest thrill of Gioiosa's life, one he treasured for the next year. If that had ended up being his only association with Pete Rose, Gioiosa would have been eternally grateful. How many kids ever get to meet their idols, never mind get to spend some time with them?

But when he returned to the King Arthur Hotel the next spring with the Massasoit baseball team, there was Petey Rose to greet him, as if no time had elapsed. Later, Rose invited him over to his room, encouraged him, told him that you don't have to be big to play major league baseball. Before he left, Karolyn Rose gave Gioiosa the family phone number in Cincinnati, told him to keep in touch.

"Tommy was a nice kid," says Karolyn Rose, "and Petey liked him."

The following Christmas, he was invited to the Rose home in Cincinnati. He saw the World Series trophies. He saw the opulence. That first night, he went with Rose to the race track, watched while Rose bet $500 as if it were a nickel. Afterwards, Rose gave him a $100 bill.

"I never had had a $100 bill in my hand before in my life," Gioiosa says.

When his visit was about over, Rose asked him to stay. Live in the house here, he said. Drive Petey to spring training in my car, he said. Become part of the family.

"But I don't have any clothes," Gioiosa said.

Rose took him into a closet, took out some shoes.

"Now you have shoes," he said.

He took out some shirts, handed them to Gioiosa.

"Now you have shirts," he said.

Gioiosa had his own room. Rose gave him money. He gave him expensive warmup suits and silk shirts. He ran errands for Karolyn. He picked up Pete's laundry. He washed Rose's car. He drove Petey to school in Rose's high-priced cars.

"I went from being a poor kid riding a bicycle in New Bedford to riding around in a Rolls Royce," Gioiosa says. "I felt like the 'Fonz.' It was like I was dreaming."

It's difficult to pinpoint just when everything began getting complicated for Tommy Gioiosa. He continued to live in Rose's house, filling many roles. Man-Friday. Surrogate son. Companion. Friend. At the race track, he went to the window and placed Rose's bets.

"People thought I was his son," he says. There was even a strong rumor in Cincinnati that Gioiosa was Rose's illegitimate son.

In the spring of 1979, he drove Rose's Porsche to Florida, transporting Petey. He had his own locker in the minor league camp, with his name taped over it. He took batting practice in a Phillies' uniform, right along with guys like Ozzie Virgil and Lonnie Smith. When spring training ended he went back to Philadelphia to begin the baseball season with one of the biggest names in baseball.

"This was even better," he says. "I was there with Pete Rose. I'm coming to the ballpark in a Porsche with Pete Rose. I thought I was blessed."

The next year he went to the University of Cincinnati on a "Pete Rose Scholarship," donated by the player. By this time Rose was separated from Karolyn and was living in a Cincinnati condominium. Gioiosa went with him. Every day he commuted to the University of Cincinnati, driving one of Rose's sleek, expensive cars. He would bring teammates over to the condo to meet Rose. He continued to do whatever Rose wanted him to do — wash the car, pick up the dry cleaning, cash winning tickets at the race track.

Whatever.

Rose had a variety of girlfriends at the time, and Gioiosa often was used as a cover-up; Rose claiming a certain girl was Gioiosa's friend whenever it was convenient for Rose to do so. During the offseason, he would go to the batting cage with Rose and load the balls for him, standing there hour after hour, watching Rose hit.

In 1981 Rose arranged for Gioiosa to get a tryout with the Baltimore Orioles' Class A team in Hagerstown, Md. Gioiosa thought he had died and gone to heaven. Shortly before the season started, Gioiosa was released.

"I cried," he said. "I didn't know what to tell Pete."

He went back to Cincinnati, not knowing what to do. Rose was at spring training in Florida. One day Gioiosa went to Gold's Gym in Cincinnati. He couldn't lift 80 pounds. All around him were guys lifting 400 pounds, guys who looked like Greek Gods, their bodies a bas relief of muscles. How do you do it, he asked. Easy, they said. Steroids.

So it began.

The guys in the gym gave him bottles of steroids. They encouraged him. In less than a year he was addicted to steroids. He took Equipoise, which explains on the bottle that it is for horses only. He took steroids called Parabolin, Decca and Primobolin, injecting them in the fleshy part of his buttocks.

"Most people cycled their steroids," he says. "On eight weeks. Off eight weeks. I never did. I was overdosing on them."

They made him feel strong. More importantly, they made him feel invincible.

"I had a dream, and if this could do it, I would do it," he said. "I was taking every steroid I could to be a better baseball player. Within a year and a half, I had gone from 160 pounds to 210. I forgot about baseball. All I wanted to do was lift weights. To hang out with guys who lifted weights. I had a dream and they took advantage of my dream."

Gioiosa says that steroids changed his personality. That they made him violent, insecure, jealous. These are some of the side-effects of heavy steroid use, but he didn't know that at the time. He became a bodybuilder, hung out at Gold's Gym with a group that drove expensive sports cars and wore gold chains and other flashy jewelry. He could be loud and arrogant. He also became more outrageous. One night, after a friend's car was bumped by another driver, he followed the other driver through the streets of Cincinnati in his steel blue Porsche with "Gold's" on the license plate. He stopped him, picked a fight with him. Gioiosa was charged with assault, a case that later was settled out of court.

He was known to come into Gold's wearing a Rambo costume. He wore muscle shirts, often carrying money around in his socks because he had no pockets. Everyone knew he was Pete Rose's friend, and he always seemed to have money.

Rose's great career, which had begun in 1963, was ending. In 1984, after a year with the Phillies in which he only hit .245, he went to the Montreal Expos. He was 43 years old, and the only question was whether he could hang on long enough to break Ty Cobb's all-time hit record. That summer he was traded back to the Reds and was named player-manager. The next year he finally broke Cobb's record, guaranteeing him baseball immortality.

It was during this time that Gioiosa was doing a lot of gambling with bookmakers in the Cincinnati area, the time that now has become part of the public record of the Rose case, the time that eventually would make Tommy Gioiosa a national figure. He says that at the time, he never thought Rose had a gambling problem. Rose had gambled ever since Gioiosa knew him. The few times Gioiosa mentioned the subject, Rose casually dismissed it, as if the rules didn't apply to him.

"Betting baseball for him was no different to me than washing his car," he says. "Gambling was no big deal. It was just a way of life."

But his relationship with Rose was changing. Some of it was due to Rose's new wife, Carol, whom he had married in 1984. Carol Rose was trying to start a life with Rose, and the last thing she wanted was to have Gioiosa, Man Friday, around. A few years later, Rose and Carol were spending a lot of time with Paul Janszen and Janszen's girlfriend. Gioiosa had introduced Janszen to Rose in 1986, first bringing Janszen to Rose's house to watch a National League playoff game on television. Janszen also was a bodybuilder at Gold's Gym, one of the people who had turned Gioiosa on to steroids. Now it was as if Janszen had replaced Gioiosa in Rose's life.

"I felt I had become the outcast," Gioiosa says.

Gioiosa stopped taking steroids in 1987, largely because a

girlfriend at the time convinced him it was a good idea. He went to San Diego and managed a health club for a while. In 1988, back living in New Bedford, he met Rose at a baseball card show in Boston.

"All he talked about was gambling," Gioiosa says. "I knew then that he had a real serious problem."

In March of 1989, after reports of Rose's troubles with the baseball establishment became public, Gioiosa called Rose from the North Dartmouth Mall. Rose was in Plant City, Fla.

"I'm your friend to the end," Gioiosa said.

"I know that," Rose said.

"What do you want me to do?" Gioiosa asked.

"You'll be okay," Rose said.

A few weeks later, Gioiosa was arrested coming out of his parents house in New Bedford. He was charged with conspiracy to sell cocaine — specifically that he had transported a bag of cocaine from Florida to Cincinnati four years before. The bag of cocaine had been placed in his gym bag. He had been turned in by Don Stengler and Michael Fry — two of the owners of Gold's Gym — as part of their own plea bargaining.

"I didn't know what was in the gym bag and I didn't want to know," Gioiosa says. "A friend asked me to do a favor for him and I did it. I didn't ask any questions. That's another thing that happens when you're on steroids. It makes you feel bigger than life, that nothing can happen you."

He also was charged with five counts of income tax evasion. The principal charge was failing to report income from the time he cashed a Pik-Six ticket at the race track for Pete Rose.

Gioiosa refused to testify against Rose. He refused to cooperate with major league baseball's investigation of Rose's alleged gambling. While the others implicated in the Rose case turned state's evidence, Gioiosa, in his words, "stood tall to the end." All the while, Rose distanced himself publicly from Gioiosa, saying he had trouble remembering who he was, even once referring to him as "Tony Gioiosa," as if Gioiosa had become a pariah.

On Aug. 24, 1989, Gioiosa went on trial in federal court in Cincinnati, the same day that Rose was banned from baseball. The trial lasted nearly three weeks. Gioiosa's defense was steroids, that the drugs had caused him to act irrationally. After a two-day jury deliberation, he was found guilty, both on the cocaine charge and two counts of income tax evasion.

That was 18 months ago. Three weeks ago Rose began his community service as an assistant gym teacher at at an inner-city Cincinnati elementary school. He recently was released from federal prison, after serving five months, and he now lives in a halfway house.

If Pete Rose's world is different, so is Tommy Gioiosa's. Since he walked down the tunnel in handcuffs in that Cincinnati court house last February, he's been to prisons in Boone County, Ky., El Reno, Okla., Allenwood, Pa., Mountour County, Pa., in the main prison at McKean, and now in minimum. He has been handcuffed and shackled and put in holding cells and subjected to all the other indignities that come with being a prisoner.

"I don't know what happened to Tommy," says Karolyn Rose. "I just think he got caught up in everything. But I always say my prayers for all the people I used to know, and Tommy is included in that. His mother sends me cards every Christmas and Easter. I can't say enough about that woman."

Gioiosa is allowed to leave McKean during the day to work with a forestry ranger in the Bradford area. He also has been allowed to go to a local school to give a talk about the dangers of steroids, telling kids how steroids first changed his personality, then changed his life. He hopes to go on tour when he gets out of jail, to spread the word about steroids. He would like to write a book. He has things to say.

"The biggest mistake of my life was steroids," he says. "Steroids changed me psychologically. They made me more quick-tempered. They hurt my relationship with Pete. They made me think that I didn't need him, didn't need anybody. If I never got involved in steroids, none of this would have ever happened."

He says he couldn't watch the Cincinnati Reds in the World Series last October. He was at McKean, and all around him people were talking about the Series. He couldn't watch. He knew what Rose must have been going through. The Reds were too personal.

For the irony is that Gioiosa still idolizes Pete Rose, even with all that's happened. He continually defends Rose, though he recognizes Rose's gambling addiction was a sickness that ultimately got out of control, just as his own steroid addiction also got out of control. He feels guilty that it was he who first introduced Rose to Janszen, the man who ultimately brought Rose down.

And as he sits at McKean day after day, plowing snow, working out and just generally waiting for time to pass, he invariably wonders about the inexplicable twist of fate that now has him in federal prison in the woods of rural Pennsylvania, a long way from the New Bedford of his youth. It is all so unbelievable to him, how he met Rose, lived with him, and everything that's happened since.

But he also knows he and Rose are linked together forever. This past summer, when he played softball at McKean, the other inmates called him Pete.

"I think our paths will cross again," says Tommy Gioiosa. "Somewhere along the way."

KATHY SWITZER

4/21/92

*"...I was very proud of being a woman and being
in Boston to strut my stuff."*
—KATHY SWITZER

BOSTON — She remembers the day that changed everything as cold and raw.

She was a junior at Syracuse University at the time, here in New England to run the Boston Marathon. She had registered as "K. Switzer" because she had literary pretensions at the time and used her initials a lot. And because the day was cold, she had been at the starting line in Hopkinton with her long hair tucked up under her cap, and a gray sweatshirt with No. 261 on the front of it.

"I was very excited," says Kathy Switzer. "I felt like I was going to Mecca.

I wasn't a great runner, by any means, but I was very proud of being a woman and being in Boston to strut my stuff."

What she didn't know was she wasn't supposed to be in the marathon. What she also didn't know was that by the end of the day her life would be changed forever. So, in a sense, would the Boston Marathon.

It was April, 1967, and the world was a different place.

The Vietnam War was in its sixth year, with more escalation, more casualties. Only a few days before, 250,000 people had protested the war in Central Park, the largest anti-war protest yet. Muhammad Ali, still called Cassius Clay, was refusing to be inducted into the Army. There was a burgeoning counterculture, a sense society was volatile, alive with change.

And the Boston Marathon was for men only.

Only Switzer didn't know that. She had registered. The Boston Athletic Association had given her a number. She had gone to the starting line. She had started. She didn't think she was breaking down barriers. She was simply running a race she had dreamed of one day running in. After four miles, her hair fell down from under her cap. It was apparent she was a woman, a fact that no doubt caused marathon officials to think the sky was falling. One of the them, Jock Semple, came out on the course and grabbed her.

"I was very scared," she said. "He grabbed me by my shoulder and spun me around. He grabbed my shirt, was trying to rip my number off, his face totally contorted."

Running with her were a few guys from a track club in Syracuse called the Harriers. One was her boyfriend, a 230-pound hammer thrower. He put a body block on Semple. She kept running.

"I was humiliated," she said. "But I vowed to finish the race on my hands and knees."

As she kept running, through the streets of Wellesley, up Heartbreak Hill, then through the Back Bay, through Kenmore Square, her humiliation turned to anger. Why couldn't she run in the marathon if she wanted to? Why couldn't women run? Why weren't there other women here? Why weren't there women's teams like there were men's? Why were women only supposed to be cheerleaders? Why was there such a two-tiered reality when it came to sports?

Until then, she considered herself a normal enough female college student. She knew some others at Syracuse who were considered "women's libbers," but she wasn't a part of that group. She liked to get dressed up and wear nice clothes. She liked being feminine. She didn't understand a lot of their rhetoric. She certainly didn't consider herself political.

But she had been raised in suburban Washington, D.C., in a family that treated her and her older brother the same, had come of age believing that there was nothing she shouldn't be able to do simply because she was female. She trained with the men's cross country team at Syracuse. She ran with men all the time. And now she had been told she couldn't run in the Boston Marathon, for no other reason than she was a woman.

"It radicalized me," she said.

When she crossed the finish line she was met by only a handful of reporters. It was cold. It was raining. It was four hours after she had begun running in Hopkinton. Most people were long gone. She had no idea she had become a cause celebre. Another woman named Roberta Gibb also had run the race, joining it 302 yards in. She also had run it the year before. But she had not been officially entered, as Switzer had been. She had not been grabbed by a race official. She did not have her picture in virtually every paper in the country.

That night, driving back to Syracuse, Switzer stopped at a roadside restaurant. A Boston tabloid already had a post-marathon edition on the streets. There on the cover was the picture of her being grabbed by Semple. It was a picture that went around the world, one of those that seemed to symbolize the changing times. An Associated Press story that ran the next morning came under a headline: "Girls Crash Boston Marathon Again."

"I'm terribly disappointed that American girls force themselves into something where they're neither eligible or wanted," said Will Cloney, the race director. "All rules throughout the world ban girls from running more than a mile and a half."

Whatever, Kathy Switzer had become famous. And radicalized. Her slight at the marathon became the impetus that turned her into a world-class marathoner, an achievement she earned in 1975 when she ran a 2:51 marathon, sixth best in the world at the time. More importantly, she became a sort of tent evangelist for women's running. If she could become an outstanding runner, a lot of women could, she reasoned. All women needed was the opportunity. But back in 1967, that was all a novel concept when it came to women and sports.

In 1978 she went to work for Avon Cosmetics, essentially organizing international races for women. A decade later she started covering women's running for ABC. A few years ago, she married Roger Robinson, a New Zealand marathoner in the master's division, and now divides her time between New Zealand and New York City. But it was that cold, raw day in April of '67 that changed everything for her.

"After that, I just assumed some responsibility," she said, "and started doing what I could to change things."

Eventually, the Boston Athletic Association came to realize the world was changing and there was nothing they could do to keep women from running the Boston Marathon. Women were officially sanctioned in 1972. Now the women's race gets almost as much attention as the men's. Now the top women runners are recognized as world-class runners. Now it's hard to envision a Boston Marathon without women runners, or a world when women were called "girls" in print.

She is 45 now, and yesterday Switzer was here in Boston covering the Marathon for WBZ-TV, this same race where everything started for her 25 years ago. She is proud she's a pioneer in women's running, proud that that long-ago afternoon where she was the center of attention ultimately transcended her. She has come to see that she has a legacy.

Seven years ago, back before she was married, she was depressed one day about the idea of maybe never having children.

"Don't be," her mother told her. "You have all those women who got into running because of you. You have 100,000 children."

REGGIE LEWIS

7/28/93

"...all sorts of unanswered questions."
—BILL REYNOLDS

BOSTON — When Lenny Bias died in June of 1986 of cardiac failure, only two days after he had been the Celtics' No. 1 draft choice, Larry Bird said it was "the cruelest thing I ever heard of."

The death of Reggie Lewis is crueler.

This is not someone who dies of cardiac failure after a night of cocaine use. This is someone who collapses inexplicably, is examined by some of the leading cardiologists in New England and is essentially told by a doctor at one of the most prestigious hospitals in the country that he can continue to play professional basketball. This was the Celtic captain in the prime of his career, someone who was living out a personal dream that had begun in the asphalt playgrounds of inner-city Baltimore.

Cruel.

It is a tragedy when anyone dies before their time, of course, but somehow it seems all the sadder when he's an athlete in the prime of his career. Because athletes, in many ways, live out our fantasies, symbols of strength and physical prowess, forever young. They are not supposed to collapse on the parquet floor in the Boston Garden, a chilling reminder that no one is exempt from life's ugly curve balls, not even 27-year-old superstars. They are not supposed to die shooting baskets on a summer afternoon at Brandeis.

Especially not Lewis, someone who epitomized a great sports story, a guy who seemingly had come out of nowhere to achieve

NBA stardom, a playground dream come true. He had been the sixth man on his high-school team, famed Dunbar High of Baltimore, had spent his high-school career in the shadow of the more celebrated Reggie Williams, David Wingate and Muggsy Bogues. He had gone to Northeastern, a school with no college basketball glamour, one of those faceless kids who play in a league without television, without a whole lot of exposure. One of those kids who had spent four years here in New England playing college basketball and, except for basketball junkies, was relatively unknown.

When the Celtics made him their first-round draft choice in June of 1987, there was not a lot of fanfare. He played sparingly in his rookie season. That summer he played in a semipro game at the West Warwick Civic Center, signed a few autographs, but certainly was not treated as a celebrity. That would come later.

But the Celtics vaunted trio of Bird, Kevin McHale and Robert Parish were aging, the team's glory days seemed all in the past tense. Then Lewis emerged as the cornerstone of the future, a young player who had become one of the most explosive scorers in the league. And all of a sudden Reggie Lewis, the sixth man on his high-school team, was an NBA all-star. This past fall he was named the Celtic captain, succeeding the retired Bird, a symbolic move that declared emphatically that there was a new era in the Garden and Lewis was at the center of it.

So when he collapsed April 29 in a playoff game against the Charlotte Hornets, it was more than just the tragedy of an athlete whose career was suddenly in jeopardy. It was a major blow to a franchise that already was in transition from its great past to an uncertain future.

We all know the sad history. How Lewis was first taken to New England Baptist hospital in Boston after the game, but left after three days and checked into Brigham and Women's Hospital in Boston. How the tests done at New England Baptist were examined by a team of 11 cardiologists, and Lewis was told he had a serious heart ailment that would endanger his life if he continued to play bas-ketball. How he then got another opinion from a team of doctors headed by Dr. Gilbert Mudge, which essentially said Lewis had a comparatively benign neural condition that could be successfully treated with drugs and allow him to continue to play.

There are all sorts of unanswered questions. And it will be awhile before there are sure answers, maybe a long while. But that's for another time. For now, Reggie Lewis is dead, and all the medi-cal controversy seems like empty words written on old parchment. Now Reggie Lewis is dead at 27, after collapsing in the Brandeis gym on a summer afternoon, and it seems like a tragedy of immense proportions, one of the saddest moments in the long history of New England sports.

SAM JETHROE

5/28/93

*"They always said Boston was a racist town,
but I saw nothing when I was here. The fans
were always nice to me."*
—SAM JETHROE

BOSTON — He remembers it as a drizzly day, the day the Red Sox
had a chance to break baseball's color barrier. It was the spring of
1945, and he had been invited to Fenway Park to try out for the Red
Sox. With him were two other players from the Negro Leagues, a
guy named Marvin Williams and someone else named Jackie Robinson. Joe Cronin was the Red Sox' manager that year, but he wasn't
there.

It probably wasn't a coincidence.

In a sense, the Red Sox had been pressured into the tryouts, both
by the national Negro press and a Boston city councilman who, as
the story goes, had told the Red Sox they wouldn't be permitted to
play Sunday baseball at Fenway Park unless they gave some black
players tryouts. So there were the three black players — Williams,
Robinson and Sam Jethroe — two years before Robinson would
break baseball's color barrier, being worked out by a couple of Red
Sox coaches.

This story has long fed the perception of the Red Sox as a racist
organization, the gist being that the tryouts were basically a sham
since the assistant coaches didn't have the power to sign the Negro
League players. The folklore surrounding that day includes someone

yelling, "Get the niggers off the field." Also, that the players were dismissed as "sandlot players." Sam Jethroe doesn't remember that, but he does remember knowing he had no chance to be signed that long-ago day.

"I never even thought about the outcome," he said. "That way, I wouldn't be disappointed. I don't think it ever dawned on me that I was going to play in the major leagues."

"So you weren't nervous?" he was asked.

"Nervous? No. About what?"

"So it didn't bother you that you weren't being allowed to play in the major leagues even though you knew you were good enough to play?"

"It didn't bother me," he said. "I guess it wasn't the right time."

"It had been my dream to have Boston be the city to break the color barrier," said Mabray "Doc" Kountze, former editor of the Boston Guardian, a black newspaper at the time. "But Sam Jethroe is 100 percent right. He had no chance at that tryout."

Jethroe was at Fenway yesterday, at a press conference in the Diamond Club that paid homage to the Negro Leagues, a part of baseball that's always existed on the periphery. There was a certain irony about the Red Sox' honoring the Negro Leagues this week-end, given the Sox' unfortunate racial history. Everyone knows the Sox were the last team in baseball to integrate, a legacy that's haunted them for decades. This image has started to change, a cleansing of the past. Yesterday was just one more example.

The sad thing is Red Sox history could have been so different if someone in the organization had realized what they had on the field that day in the spring of '45.

Jethroe had grown up in East St. Louis in the '30s in an essentially segregated world, playing baseball not for fame or money, but for the love of the game itself. There were two kinds of baseball then — white baseball and "colored" baseball. Not surprisingly. Baseball always has mirrored society, and back then it was no different. By the early '40s Jethroe was one of the rising young stars in the Negro League, mostly with the Cleveland Buckeyes. By the time he came to Fenway Park for his so-called tryout, he was a star. The major leagues were not something he went to sleep dreaming about. Sam Jethroe knew how the world worked.

But change was in the air.

The next year Robinson signed with the Dodgers and was sent to Montreal, a year of prepping before he came up with the Brooklyn Dodgers. Jethroe went back to the Negro League. There was talk of the Cleveland Indians signing him, but supposedly the Cleveland Buckeyes wanted too much money. The Indians signed Larry Doby instead. In August, 1947, Doby became the first black to play in the American League, only a few months behind Robinson.

Jethroe was signed by the Dodgers the next year and was sent to Montreal. Two years later, he was in Boston with the Braves, the first black baseball player in Boston. He would become the rookie of the year, stealing a major league-leading 36 bases. He was 29 years old. He was out of the major leagues four years later, amid speculation that he was older than he said, and the feeling that his best years had been spent in the relative anonymity of the Negro Leagues.

"I've lived and I've learned and I always liked Boston as a place to come home to," he said yesterday.

"They always said Boston was a racist town, but I saw nothing when I was here. The fans were always nice to me."

It all seems so long ago and far away now. We see the salaries and the magic carpet ride that major leaguers live now. We see that many of today's sports stars are black. In this day and age when history is all too often what happened last year, it's sometimes easy to forget how different it once was. Jethroe is 71. He runs a bar in Erie, Pa., and says he's just trying to get by. He was wearing a gray suit and he stood up at the press conference yesterday, one of baseball's pioneers, an emissary from a long-ago world.

And how has that world changed since then?

"Money," said Sam Jethroe with a smile.

"So do you ever think you were born in the wrong decade, the wrong era?" he was asked.

"I don't think," he said. "I know."

STEPHANIE PERRY

11/14/93

*"She said I was off the team, and I said I didn't care.
I just wanted to come home."*
—STEPHANIE PERRY

PROVIDENCE — I was in a downtown store the other day, and she was working as a security guard.

The all-time leading girls' basketball scorer in the R.I. Interscholastic League: Stephanie Perry.

"Do you ever still play?" I asked.

"No," she said. "That's all behind me now. Those days are over."

She is a name out of the past, a name that once danced through the sports pages, maybe the closest thing we've ever had around here to a female basketball prodigy. It was the early '80s, a time when girls' high-school basketball was starting to come into its own in Rhode Island, and there was no bigger name than Perry. She averaged more than 30 points a game for three years, was All-State three straight years, scored more than 2,000 points.

I saw her in a playoff game at a community college during one of those years, and you didn't have to know anything about basketball to see she had the magic. She was so clearly superior to her competition, you knew she had the talent that one day would take her out of Rhode Island.

When she graduated from Central High School in 1984, she had been recruited by most of the name women's basketball programs. She settled on the University of Maryland. Chris Weller, the Maryland coach, said that "as far as I'm concerned, Stephanie can be the

Cheryl Miller of the East," a reference to the best women's player in the country at the time. Her coach at Central, Jim Robinson, was quoted as saying, "A player like this comes along once in a lifetime."

But when she went to Maryland, it was as if she fell off the planet. She was just one of those names that seem to belong to a different time.

"How long did you last at Maryland?" I asked.

"Two years," she said.

She paused, looked away.

"Everyone expected great things from me," she finally said. "I felt like I had to please everyone. People here thought I was the greatest thing in the world, but they've never been out of Rhode Island. It's a big world. There are thousands of Stephanie Perry's out there."

She is 27 now, no longer the young kid who danced through the sports pages.

She grew up in Wiggins Village, a housing project on Providence's West Side, the youngest of seven children. Her mother, Carol, was a Hazard, the South County family that's produced a lot of athletes for South Kingstown High School through the years, so she had the athletic bloodlines. Stephanie began playing basketball at age 10. From the beginning, she had ability and played against boys in playground games. By her sophomore year at Central, she was a bona-fide superstar, a scoring machine. And with that came the attention. Interest in girls' sports was growing; she became one of the obvious focal points.

"I was put on a pedestal too soon," she said. "I wasn't ready for all the attention. I was a shy kid. I didn't know how to talk that well. People were talking about college, and I didn't know anything about college."

In retrospect, it was probably inevitable that it wasn't going to work out at Maryland. She had never really been out of Rhode Island. Never been on her own. Never had to play against other talented players every day. She thought college was going to be like high school. Maybe it all came down to this: It's a long way from Wiggins Village to the University of Maryland.

She started some games her freshman year, then missed the first semester of her sophomore year for academic reasons. All the while she wasn't getting along with her coach, a personality conflict that started virtually from the beginning and just got worse. One day at Clemson it exploded. One of Stephanie's sisters had just died, and it was a traumatic time for her. The last thing she felt she needed was some coach on her case. There was an ugly argument.

"She said I was off the team, and I said I didn't care," Perry related. "I just wanted to come home."

That was seven years ago. Cheryl Miller went on to become a television analyst, still one of the most visible names in women's basketball. Stephanie Perry came home to a succession of jobs — bank teller, data processing, driver, jewelry-factory worker, customer-service rep — jobs usually subject to the vagaries of the Rhode Island economy.

For the last couple of years, she's been a security guard. She helps raise her sister's child. She tries to get on with her life, to put the past into some old footlocker and shove it under the bed, out of sight.

Still, that's difficult. She is Stephanie Perry, and people remember. Both the good and the bad, the fame she once had in high school and how it all seemed to disappear in a puff of smoke when she went away to Maryland. It's the price everyone pays for fame, even a high-school star who never wanted fame in the first place.

"My sophomore year in high school was the best," she said. "No one knew me. I just went out and played. After that there was too much pressure. They could have eased up on the girl a little bit."

She seems to alternate between defending her reasons for leaving Maryland after just two years, a decision that ended her career, and stating that basketball was good to her, gave her experiences she never would have had without it, as if she's still trying to sort out what happened, put it in some personal place where she can deal with it.

She seldom plays basketball anymore. Once in a while, she will pick up a ball and shoot around, but really nothing more than that. Occasionally, someone wants her to play in a league, or play for a team, but she always says no, that part of her life is all behind her now.

But is it?

Can it ever really be?

"I still polish my trophies," said Stephanie Perry.

ED COOLEY

2/20/1994

*"It was like walking into a blizzard
and the blizzard was a white world."*
—ED COOLEY

PROVIDENCE — Once he was an All-State basketball player at Central High School in Providence. He led the Knights to back-to-back state titles. He was recognized as one of our elite local high school basketball players. Now he's a senior at Stonehill College, the inspirational leader of a young team that's struggling to find itself.

But this really isn't about basketball.

It's about the courage to try and change your life, the power to transcend your background, the ability to grow. And, most of all, it's about love. Oh yes, it's certainly about love.

It's the story of Eddie Cooley, and it begins back in South Providence in the late '70s, on one of those nondescript streets near the old Roger Williams housing project where poverty seems to hang over everything like a layer of dust. He never knew his father. His mother was on welfare. He was the sixth of nine children, and it was a childhood out of some contemporary Dickens novel, complete with sugar sandwiches because there was no meat, corn flakes with water because there was no milk.

He was only 9 years old when he already knew something was very wrong, knew he wasn't getting enough food or attention, knew instinctively his mother couldn't cope with the grim reality of her situation.

As fate would have it, Cooley had a friend. His name was Eddie

Searight, who lived a few blocks away, and one day Cooley started going home with him. By the time he was in the ninth grade he was living with the Searights. They had four kids of their own, and Eddie Searight Sr. worked three jobs to keep food on the table. Still, Cooley became part of the family.

"Outside of my four biological children, I couldn't ask for a better child," said Gloria Searight. "He just became one of the family."

"It was hard for me growing up in South Providence," Cooley said. "I was an outcast. I never had good clothes. I never had any money. I was kind of 'bummy.' "

Nor were sports any real salvation back then. He was big, but he also was clumsy. He didn't run very well. He didn't jump very well. He certainly wasn't very graceful. But he used to hang around the South Side Boys Club, playing ball, dreaming his dreams, starting to get better.

The Searights were the ones who got Cooley out of the vocational program at Central and into courses that provided an opportunity for college. They were the ones who fed him and made sure he had the right clothes. They also showed him the possibility of a future that transcended the neighborhood.

"They gave me everything in the world, and the most important thing they gave me was love," Cooley says simply. "They've been my driving force."

It was at Central that Cooley first started to get recognized, not only as an athlete but as a person. Off the court, he had teachers who encouraged him. On the court, he teamed with current Providence College star Abdul Abdullah to lead Central to back-to-back state titles. He started getting letters from colleges, but didn't have the necessary SAT scores. So it was arranged he would go to New Hampton, a New Hampshire prep school, complete with a mountain outside his window.

And Ed Cooley's life changed again.

"It was like walking into a blizzard," he says, "and the blizzard was a white world."

It was a long way from South Providence and the only world he knew. The first few days he wanted to leave, go back to the cocoon of the neighborhood, the familiar. But he adjusted. Just as he did when he went to Stonehill the following year, lured there by Ray Pepin and Dave Kenney, two men he had known when he was in high school. He didn't know much about Stonehill, other than it was Division II, and it, too, was an all-white world.

"When I first came here another student wanted to touch my skin, touch my hair,' he said. "He didn't know any better."

Cooley adjusted.

It's now five years later and in basketball terms he's been a success. He's been a four-year starter, though he missed one full season because of back surgery and has played in pain this entire season, often having to miss practice. Still, he has tried to be an inspiration to the younger players, to dive on the floor and play hard, showing that if he can do it with his back problems they can do it, too.

For he knows he has things to teach his younger teammates, lessons that transcend basketball.

"When he is healthy he's one of the ten best players in this league," said Pepin, Stonehill's basketball coach and the former coach at Hendricken. "He's been what we expected him to be, and off the court he's been more."

Off the court.

Off the court, Cooley's come a long way from the South Providence of his childhood. He has worked hard as a student and now has dreams of one day going on to get a masters and a PhD in education. He has been a student-teacher at a high school near Stonehill. He's been on a couple of Stonehill's presidential commissions. He tries to write a poem every day. He has become a student leader.

In short, he has become the embodiment of what we want student athletes to be, someone who used basketball to get into college and then used college to change his life.

"Stonehill gave me the opportunity to change," he said. "The courage to try and other things."

Most of all, it's given him the means to pursue his vision, one that began back when he was a kid, fueled by the Searights' love and some teachers who went out of their way to help him.

For Eddie Cooley didn't grow up with dreams of one day playing professional basketball. He grew up with the dream to one day be a teacher, to go back to the neighborhood of his youth and tell the kids some of the things he's learned. How they don't have to be afraid to want to change. How it's all right to have dreams that transcend the neighborhood. How you don't have to live out a script that was written for you when you were a child.

"That's why I got into education," he said. "To give back what people gave to me."

For Eddie Cooley also knows that without the Seawrights and some special teachers his life would be very different now. So maybe it was only fitting that the other night, minutes before his last home game at Stonehill, on a night when the seniors and their mothers were being honored, Cooley hugged Gloria Searight to the left of center court.

POSTSCRIPT: *Ed Cooley became head coach of the Providence College Friars men's basketball team in 2011. In 2022, he was named Big East Coach of the Year as well as Naismith College Coach of the Year. In 2023, he left PC to become head coach at Georgetown University.*

ROB PHELPS

5/23/94

*"People who come from my neighborhood
are always told what they can't do.
They are never told what they can do."*
—ROB PHELPS

PROVIDENCE — Sometimes the best sports stories have nothing to do with sports. Sometimes in sports, words like dedication and commitment have nothing to do with what happens on the playing field.

Consider Rob Phelps, who graduated yesterday from Providence College.

I first met him in December of 1991. I was doing a magazine story then on what it means to be a basketball player at PC, a black kid in an overwhelming white world, and Phelps became the focal point.

He was a sophomore then, had grown up in the Bedford–Stuyvesant section of Brooklyn, one of the worst ghettos in the country, a place where dreams go to die. He had seen one of his best friends shot dead in a dispute over a hat. He had seen 14-year-olds walk down the street with automatic weapons under their coats. He had seen so much of the violence and daily pain that's become so much of life in the inner cities. He was 20 years old at the time and, in a sense, he already considered himself a success because he was still alive and many of the kids he'd grown up with weren't.

"So this is a long way from home?" I asked one morning.

"A long way," he smiled.

Making his adjustment more difficult was that Phelps had arrived at PC as a Prop. 48, the result of his failure to make minimum SAT requirements established by the NCAA. So in his first season in college, one which many kids find difficult, basketball had been taken away from him. Complete with the stigma that goes with it. The one that says that anyone who can't score at least 700 on the SAT doesn't belong in college. That anyone who doesn't score at least 700 can't possibly do college work. The labeling of 17-year-olds by one test.

This was the baggage Phelps arrived at PC with, and it was heavy. On the basketball court, he had to go through the difficult adjustment of high school superstar to Big East player, more difficult for him because he had come to PC with a big rep, the second-leading scorer in New York City basketball history. More importantly, he had to prove he not only belonged in college, but that he also could do college work.

"People who come from my neighborhood are always told what they can't do," he said. "They are never told what they can do."

So Phelps set out to prove everybody wrong. He fit into the structured academic world of a PC basketball player, the daily study halls, the tutoring. He never missed a class. He studied. He worked at his academics with the same diligence and dedication he worked at being a basketball player.

But then again, maybe no one should have been surprised. It was not the first time Phelps had proved a lot of people wrong.

In the ninth grade back in Brooklyn, he had left his neighborhood school to go to Nazareth, a Catholic school, a much more demanding school academically.

"Many people thought he wouldn't be able to make it academically," said Ted Gustus, his high school coach. "He was a kid from Bed-Stuy and Nazareth was a different world. It took until his junior year before he didn't fail at least one course, but when that happened you would have thought he had scored 50 in a game. But that didn't surprise me. Because he had worked so hard to improve, had so much discipline, that I knew he'd succeed."

While he was at Nazareth, his mother moved back to Florida, leaving Phelps to live with the parents of a friend, who eventually became his legal guardians. Somehow he survived it all. By the time I first met him there was a certain maturity about him, a certain focus, as if he knew what he wanted and he was willing to do what it took to make that happen.

One incident stands out.

We were in his dorm room one morning and I noticed his bed was made, often a rarity in a college kid's room.

"I always make my bed," he said. "It was the way I was brought up."

I remember thinking back then that Rob Phelps was not going to have any problem getting through college, Prop. 48, or no Prop. 48.

"Graduating — and doing it on time — this just proves that SAT test doesn't mean anything," Phelps said. "Because a lot of people said I wouldn't be able to do it. But I proved them wrong. I accomplished something that was very important to me. It was one of my dreams to graduate from college."

He said this with a lot of pride in his voice, justified pride. He has come a long way from Bed-Stuy, and it has nothing to do with basketball, nothing to do with the fact he came on strong at the end of his senior season, making all-tournament at the Big East Tournament as the Friars won for the first time ever. He is the first person in his family ever to go to college, and now he has graduated. He says it sends a statement to all his nieces and nephews that they can do it, too, that you can rise above your background, above your neighborhood. That dreams can come true.

You just have to want them badly enough.

ROLAND MARS

9/24/95

*"My mother always told me, 'You are not black.
You are Indian.'"*
—ROLAND MARS

CHARLESTOWN, R.I. -As I was reading a newspaper story about a fire that had destroyed the Narragansett Indian Meeting House in 1993, I came across the name Roland Mars. And all of a sudden it was 1958 for me, when I was in junior high in Barrington and the best high school team that came into town to play the high school was South Kingstown.

Not only were they the best, they also were unique. In the small world of Rhode Island Class C basketball then, South Kingstown was the only team with black players. The team had three of them, or so I thought at the time. They were Paul Fry, Joe Harris, and Rollie Mars. Fry was the scorer, one of the best players in the state. Harris was the clever point guard. Mars was the center, a strong 6-foot-5 kid with black hair worn in a sort of '50s pompadour.

Even at 12 years old I knew there was something different about this team. Now the newspaper story piqued my curiosity. What happened to Rollie Mars? How had a high school basketball star ended up being the pastor of the Narragansett Indian Church and one of the spokesman for the tribe in these tumultuous times? What was it like to grow up in what was then a small rural town, to come into all those little Rhode Island school towns to play high school basketball in the late '50s?

"On federal forms then there were three check marks — black, white, other," Roland Mars said. "I always checked 'other.' My mother always told me "you are not black. You are Indian.' But back then in the eyes of the world you were either white or colored."

We are sitting at a coffee shop in Charlestown on this gray September morning, a couple of miles away from where he lives on the border of the Narragansett Indian reservation. He is 55 now, a large man with skin the color of coffee au lait and voice deep enough to boom out over a pulpit.

"I can remember we used to come into all those white towns to play," he said, "but I never felt any real discrimination, any prejudice, growing up. There weren't very many of us, and we knew there were sections of town we probably couldn't live in, but everyone got along. South Kingstown was Hometown, USA."

And his roots ran deep in it. His mother could trace her ancestry back to Samuel Niles, the first pastor of the Narragansett Indian Church. His father, Harold Mars, had begun his ministry in Kingston in 1934, later was the pastor of the First Church of God on Allen Avenue in Peace Dale, as well as being a carpenter. That was where Mars grew up, on the road that led from Wakefield to Peace Dale, two villages within South Kingstown. He was one of four children.

When Mars was 11 the family moved to Rochester, N. Y., where his father took over a church and the family lived in what essentially a black world.

"But Wakefield was our home," Mars said. "We came back every summer."

And the Narragansett Indian reservation in Charlestown was their spiritual home. It was the ancestral burial ground. It also was where the annual powwow was held every summer, run by his father, two days of family days, a celebration of the past, a return to the roots.

"There was a Native-American community here then," he said, "and it was totally self-sufficient. We had carpenters, plumbers, everything. There were only about 100 of us, but we never felt deprived of the important things. We had woods and two ponds. We had our heritage. But my parents raised us to live in two worlds."

Sports were one of the bridges between the two worlds. And within sports Rollie Mars was a hero. He returned to South Kingstown High School in the fall of 1957, immediately became an all-state end in football, then the center on the basketball team where his cousin Paul Fry was the team's star. The coach was Warner Keaney, whose father, Frank, had been the famous coach at URI in the late '40s, the man credited with inventing fast-break basketball.

It was a different era. There was one state high school basketball tournament then, and in 1958 South Kingstown was only minutes away from being the first Class C team to win the state title. The team had beaten two large Class A schools to get to the finals. Now they were leading Westerly by double figures in the fourth quarter, so close they could touch it. But South Kingstown blew the lead, got beat by a basket. Instead of a little slice of Rhode Island immortality, it became just another team that lost, ultimately forgettable.

It also was a different era in that Rhode Island high school sports were seldom seen by college recruiters, especially in Class C. Especially non-white kids, many of whom were not even taking college courses in high school back then. So they finished their high school careers, then usually faded away into anonymity, like some comet that burned across the nighttime sky only to disappear just as quickly.

That's essentially what happened to Paul Fry and Joe Harris. They both briefly went to small black schools down South, only to come back to South Kingstown.

"Both of them were great athletes," said Mars. "But they never got the opportunity."

Mars was a little luckier. An acquaintance in Rochester guided him toward a football scholarship to Michigan State.

"You know the movie Rudy? How he comes up the tunnel the first time at Notre Dame and can't believe how big it was? That was me at Michigan State. It was too big a jump. I was just a boy from South Kingstown High School."

He quickly got into academic trouble, panicked, and left after the first year. He went into the Air Force instead. He went halfway around the world, played basketball on Air Force teams. And it was when he was stationed in Florida, in the still-segregated South, that he first encountered the realities of prejudice.

"It flattened me. My father always had warned me about it, but it still flattened me."

When Mars he got out of the Air Force he came back home to Wakefield, got a job in the post office. He would be there for 31 years. He was 39 when he got the call to preach. One day he was walking on a path near the Indian church and knew then it was his destiny to become a minister, like his grandfather and father.

That was 16 years ago and Mars has been preaching ever since. And if the Narragansetts haven't had a church building in nearly two years, Mars' voice hasn't been quieted.

"I guarantee you gambling is coming here," he said. "Our whole society is based on the dollar bill and with gambling the money is like water. But I am totally anti-gambling, anti-casino. I see it as very negative."

He looks at the Mashantucket Pequots in nearby Ledyard, Conn., people he's known all his life, and said "they may be rich, but they're a lost people." He looks at people in prisons and youth centers, people he's counseled for years, and says "their dreams are all about money.

"I've lived here all my life and now I see people I've never seen before. A dramatic change already has taken place. Now there are people here just waiting for the money. We used to have 100 people. Now we have 2,000."

He sees it all changing, the Narragansett Indians, the town of Charlestown, the life he's known. And none of it for the better.

"I have a very comfortable and happy life," said Rollie Mars. "But if the casino is built do me and my wife stay? And if we go, where do we go? This has always been my home."

He turns away, looks off to his right, off in the direction of the reservation, the land that's always been at the center of his life. And when he turns back his voice is softer, seems to come up through layers of regret.

"Our generation is the last of the Narragansetts. We are the children of the people who lived the heritage. Because now it's all going to change."

POSTSCRIPT: *Roland Mars died in 2015. In addition to being an outreach minister for several churches and ministries, he worked for the Postal Service for 31 years.*

CLARA LAMORE WALKER

2/5/1995

*"I have friends my age and all they want to do
is go to lunch. I don't want to go to lunch.
I want to go to the pool."*
—CLARA LAMORE WALKER

CRANSTON, R.I. — She has quietly become one of our very best sports stories. And it's not just that she now holds an amazing 98 world and national swimming records. Or that she now holds more records than any other masters swimmer in the world. Or even that this spring she will be inducted into the International Swimming Hall of Fame, the first woman masters swimmer in the world to be so honored.

It's more than that.

It's that Clara Lamore Walker, who once grew up in Providence and now lives in Cranston, should be an inspiration to all of us.

She is 68 now, but you'd never know it. She weighs 108 pounds, 40 less than she once did when she was decades younger. Six days a week she goes into the pool at Providence College and trains for more than two hours. Not just swims. Trains. Back and forth. Speed work. Interval work. Over and over. Day after day.

She swims with paddles on her hands. She swims using kickboards. She does laps and more laps. At 68 years old she both trains and competes as a serious athlete, showing both the quiet determination and iron will that all great athletes have, regardless of the sport, regardless of their age. Forget swimming for a moment. Hers is a story about second chances, and dreams that don't die, and staying the course. Most of all, it's about the essence of sports, about participating as a way of life. Not for money or headlines or recognition, but simply because it's at the core of who you are.

"I have friends my age and all they want to do is go to lunch," she says. "I don't want to go to lunch. I want to go to the pool."

In a sense Clara Lamore Walker has always gone to the pool. It all began when she was 12 and a friend dragged her to the Olneyville Boys Club pool, even though she couldn't swim. Four years later she won her first national championship at a meet in Chicago. It was the tail end of the Depression, a time of grim economic realities. With both her parents working, and her older brother away, her world became bordered by the pool's boundaries.

She was coached by Joe Watmough, who also was the Brown swim coach. Swimming became her passport into a world that would have been out of reach without it, a world of private clubs and out-of-state meets, a world of possibilities beyond Olneyville.

"Swimming was everything," she says. "I did nothing else. My coach wouldn't even let me date."

She was Clara Lamore then, and for a while in the '40s she was an unabashed phenomenon. During a five-year stretch, she never lost a race. Indoors. Outdoors. Freestyle. Backstroke. 100 meters. 1500 meters. You name it, she won it. For five straight years. She set two U.S. records and won five national championships. And in 1948 she closed out this storybook career by swimming in the 1948 Olympics in London.

Then she quit.

"I swore I'd never do it again," she says. "I was 22, I had been training for 10 years and I had had enough."

That was nearly 50 years ago. And for years, swimming was just something she once had loved, something that long ago had gotten stashed away in some foot locker. She worked for the telephone company for a while. She spent seven years in a cloistered religious order. She became one of the first female graduates of Providence College. She married Donald Walker, a Naval officer, and traveled through Europe with him for seven years. Then, after he died unexpectedly in 1970, she came back to Rhode Island and began teaching in Cranston. Later she became a guidance counselor at Western Hills Junior High School. And through all the years, and all the changes, she never swam.

Then, in 1981, when she was 54 years old, she discovered swimming again. She had hurt her back while pushing her car during a snowstorm. A doctor told her she should swim for therapy. For a few months she swam three times a week, nothing serious, just moving through the water. Until one day Win Wilson and Jim Edwards, two of the guiding forces behind the rise of masters swimming in Rhode Island, talked her into competing again.

She swam in the 50-54 age group, and in her first meet she broke a national record for that category in the 50-yard breaststroke. Then she left the meet to go to the movies.

But that was the beginning.

It was as if all the years away didn't matter. It was as though she were a kid again, back in the Olneyville Boys Club, her world defined by the borders of the pool. Once again, swimming became everything to her. She's been swimming competitively ever since. She does 35-40 meets a year, all over the country. She swam in Japan. She swam in Canada. And wherever she swims, she wins. She holds every world and national record in the 65-69 age group, except the butterfly. Also in the 60-64 age group. As well as many records in the 55-59 age group.

"I've been very lucky," she says. "I've never been sick, and I've never had a serious injury."

She also knows that she's come along at the right time, has been one of the pioneers of masters swimming. She knows all her records ultimately will be broken. Masters swimming is a rapidly growing sport as more and more people begin to realize that competing in sports doesn't have to have any age limits. This is the reason masters swimming is finally being recognized by the International Swimming Hall of Fame, the reason Clara Lamore Walker is finally being recognized for her unbelievable accomplishments over the past 14 years.

"I feel awestruck," says Clara Lamore Walker. "I never could have imagined this."

She's retired now, but she still counsels pregnant teenagers. She keeps busy. And she goes to the pool. Every day. It long ago became a part of her life.

The other day she saw a picture of herself, back when she was 18. She was at the Olneyville Boys Club, in a cotton swimsuit and a plastic cap with strings that tied under the neck. Back in a different era. Back before goggles and swimsuits that seem paper-thin. Back before lane lines and starting blocks. Back when both she and swimming were very different. The picture was a visible symbol of how far she's come from that pool at the Olneyville Boys Club, a lifetime of laps that now have taken her to the pinnacle of her sport. All the way to the International Swimming Hall of Fame induction in May.

So call this a lifetime achievement award.

For a life we all can learn something from.

ANGELO PAZIENZA

6/10/94

"How proud am I of Vinny? The dictionary is not big enough for the words to describe how proud I am."
—ANGELO PAZIENZA

CRANSTON, R.I. — I am standing with Angelo Pazienza. He is showing me a picture. It is one of his son Vinny at age seven. In the picture Vinny is wearing large headgear and he is in a boxing tournament.

"I knew when he was a little kid that one day he was going to be big in sports," says Angelo, with his Italian accent. "I didn't know it would be boxing. But I knew it would be something. Because he always had the desire."

"But you didn't want it to be boxing, did you?"

"No," he says firmly. "I wanted him to go to school."

He hesitates a beat, as if running all the years through his mind, a lifetime of choices, roads not taken, opportunities lost.

"I didn't want him to end up like me," he says finally. "To do some of the things I had to do. I wanted him to have more opportunities."

We are standing in the Father and Son gym on Laurel Hill Avenue, just a few blocks away from where his grandparents once lived. The gym is a shrine he built to his son's career, the past on the walls in pictures, the long incredible story that's been the Vinny Pazienza saga: the kid from Cranston who once saw Rocky and bought the entire myth, then set out to make it all come true.

It is a few minutes before Vinny's last press conference in Rhode Island before he goes to Las Vegas for his fight later this month against Roberto Duran in the MGM Grand Hotel. And maybe nothing illustrates just how far Angelo Pazienza has come than the fact that this has now become his life, too, this glittering trail of press conferences and resort hotels, this life spent in the spotlight that now follows his son's career.

For he's always there, of course, part of the entourage that's the public life of Vinny Pazienza. He is at the press conferences, talking to the press, pulling no verbal punches. He is at the fights, part of the procession that leads Vinny into the ring. He is at the post-fight press conferences, part bodyguard, part guard dog, defending his son at the slightest hint of any umbrage.

He can be loud. He can be crude. He wears his emotions on his sleeve. Sometimes he seems as though he stepped right out of a Martin Scorsese movie by way of Damon Runyon. But no can ever say Angelo Pazienza isn't an original. Or that he hasn't taught his son some important lessons along the way. Lessons that Vinny Pazienza carries with him every day of his life, in the ring and out.

"In your wildest imagination could you ever have envisioned how your life turned out?" I ask Angelo.

"Having a son who is a world champion? Never in a hundred years," he says quickly, the words all but tumbling over themselves in an attempt to get out of his mouth. "A hundred years? A million years. Never in a million years. I'm reliving my youth."

In a sense, it's the youth he never had. He was born in Providence in 1919, but his father died four months before he was born, dead of influenza at 27. Two years later, Angelo and his mother moved back to Italy, to a small town called Frosinone, 20 minutes from Rome. As a child, his sports were soccer and skiing and he says he was good at both of them, a love of sports he would one day hand down to his son.

Angelo was 18 when he came back to the United States, back to the Silver Lake section of Providence. It was the mid-1930s, the middle of the Depression. He knew no English, and it wasn't easy to learn because virtually everyone in his neighborhood spoke Italian. He was a mechanic for a while. Then a carpenter.

"Wherever there was more money, that's where I went," he says. "But it was never easy. When I first got here, I was a dead fish."

Later, he had a barbershop in East Providence for 12 years, then a small clothing store. But always it was a hustle, scratching here, clawing there, trying to make a living, trying to give Vinny and Vinny's older sister a better life than he had had.

In the beginning, he thought Vinny was going to end up as a baseball player. Then came the boxing. At first, Angelo was dead set against it. Boxing was too much of the old world he had always tried to get away from, of scratching and clawing, of hitting and being hit. Hadn't he raised his son so he wouldn't have to get hit for a living?

All that was many years ago. Vinny is 31 now, no longer the young kid chasing a dream. There have been too many fights, too many mornings-after to really ever be young again. Angelo is 75. In many ways, the real battles have all been fought. Still, they both persevere in this toughest of sports, seemingly as hungry as they've always been.

"How proud am I of Vinny?" Angelo asks rhetorically. "The dictionary is not big enough for the words to describe how proud I am. You know how many times I've heard people say my kid wasn't going to make it? A million times. At first, I used to try and fight them. Now I just laugh."

Vinny is finishing up his press conference, saying how he's going to bring a lot of pain into Roberto Duran's life. How he no longer really cares how much money he makes for a fight because "I'm really happy with my life and you can't put a price on happiness." He handles the press conference expertly. Sometimes it's easy to forget that beneath all the hype and all the show, Vinny has emerged as an articulate, self-assured public personality, someone who always has handled his celebrity very well. His career has become a testimony to heart and desire, all those intangibles that have been there ever since he first began the improbable quest to be a world champion boxer from Rhode Island.

So just where did these qualities come from?

"My father," he says.

"What's the biggest lesson your father taught you?" I ask.

Vinny pauses.

"I used to watch my father when I was a kid. How he put his heart and soul into everything he did. How much desire he had. That's what I'm all about, and I learned that all from him."

He turns and looks at his father across the room. Angelo is excitedly talking to someone, arms waving, vintage Angelo. And, when he starts to speak again, Vinny Pazienza is smiling.

"The apple doesn't fall too far from the tree, you know," he says.

JOHN CALIPARI

2/21/96

"All being realistic does is put restraints on you.
I tell my team to be unrealistic."
—JOHN CALIPARI

PROVIDENCE — He is the new college basketball wunderkind, the hot young coach with the salesman's smile, complete with the perception that everything he touches turns to gold.

John Calipari.

Hotter than Georgia asphalt in the noonday sun. Profiled in national magazines. Romanced by the Celtics last spring. His team ranked first in the country virtually the entire year. The one Dick Vitale all but sings nightly hosannas to.

And it's not without a certain irony. For only a decade ago Calipari was just another wannabe, one of those gung-ho, talk-a-dog-down-from-a-meat-wagon assistant coaches, complete with the hunger and ambition that all but dripped off him. He was at Pittsburgh then, just another young assistant with his big dreams, just another young coach in a business where fate and circumstance eventually chews up so many.

Even when he got the UMass job in 1988 he didn't figure to put down a lot of roots. For UMass was the end of the basketball earth back then. No interest. No success. No tradition. No nothing. Merely a place where too many coaching careers had gone to die. A place where the best a young coach could hope for was to do well enough to get a better job somewhere else.

What were the odds then that in the winter of 1996 UMass would be the No. 1 team in the country?

Please.

So the obvious question yesterday afternoon as Calipari was leaving an afternoon practice at the Civic Center: "Are you surprised this has all happened?"

"I used to dream about it," Calipari said. "I'd be jogging and I'd be day-dreaming about being ranked first in the country, winning big games, going to the NCAA Tournament, being interviewed afterwards.

But then I've always been like that. I'll be hitting a tennis ball against a backboard, but in my mind I'll be beating Ilie Nastase. Or else I'll be thinking about playing Larry Bird one-on-one and beating him. They were just daydreams.

"Even when I was thinking about being ranked No. 1 in the country, it wasn't realistic. It was never realistic. But you know what? I tell my team not to be realistic.

All being realistic does is put restraints on you. I tell my team to be unrealistic."

Unrealistic, indeed.

For don't kid yourself. A few years ago Calipari couldn't ever have envisioned UMass being ranked first in the country, never mind anyone else. The thinking then was that Calipari was one step away from a truly big-time job, the kind of job that conceivably gets you ranked No. 1 in the country. A glamour job. The kind UMass could never be. But a funny thing happened on Calipari's way to his next job. UMass became it.

"I was fortunate," Calipari said. "It wouldn't have happened at a lot of schools — it didn't happen at URI with Tommy Penders — but UMass 'made this my next job. It made it so I didn't have to move. After we started having some success I think UMass started thinking we can't afford him, but we can't afford to lose him either."

No question.

For what Calipari has done in his eight years at UMass is slightly short of unbelievable. Who else is even comparable? Who else built a national program from the ground up at a place with virtually no glamour, no tradition? Al McGuire at Marquette? Jerry Tarkanian at UNLV? Not too many others.

Not only did he have to create interest at a place where there was virtually none, he had to entice players to spend their college careers in the basketball wilderness disguised as Amherst, Mass.

Selling ice boxes to Eskimos might have been easier.

But no one ever said Calipari couldn't recruit.

Even when he was just beginning to make a name for himself in the business and a lot of the old guard were saying he was too ambitious, too controversial, too something, no one ever thought Calipari was going to fail. In the beginning, he did it with a lot of hard-nosed kids who had been overlooked by the more glamorous schools for a variety of reasons. He made them burn for success and recognition just as he did. Kids he was able to convince to be unselfish, team-oriented and play with all the grit and intensity of Marines charging up San Juan Hill.

Refuse to lose?

Long ago it became more than just a slogan at UMass.

For that's always been the thing that's overlooked about Calipari. It's easy to see the "Coach Cal" image, the big salary, a freeze-frame of the '90's coach, and think Calipari has done it all with mirrors and a salesman's con. Nonsense. He is one of the very best coaches out there. His teams are controlled, intense, and never beat themselves. In a sense they're a throwback to a more fundamental era.

And they also mirror him. This man who used to daydream about being ranked No. 1 and being on top of the college basketball mountain and has now seen all those dreams come true. This onetime basketball frog who dreamed of being a king and has now become one.

POSTCRIPT: Calipari has been head coach of the University of Kentucky's men's basketball team since 2009. He was inducted into the Basketball Hall of Fame in 2015.

LOSERS' CAFE

10/29/96

"Losers, sir. We never seem to run out of them."
—Waiter at the Losers' Cafe

LOSERVILLE, USA — It was late Saturday night, minutes after the Yankees had won the World Series, and I was sitting in the Losers' Cafe.

You know where that is.

Go down Bill Buckner Boulevard, take a right on Mookie Wilson Way, go about a 100-yards down Lonely Street and there it is, right next to Heartbreak Hotel.

Losers' Cafe.

All dark wood, dim lights and a lot of guys crying in their beer. Literally crying. Loud wails of anguish. The kind of place where you go to tell your troubles to someone who has more than you do. Loserville, with a capital "L."

A fitting place to be for a Red Sox fan Saturday night.

I was there to do penance. Saturday morning I had written that "if there's a God in Heaven it will be the Braves in seven." Saturday night I had received my answer. Or as Ken "Jersey Red" Ford — Fall River's resident Yankee fan who isn't very subtle — had said minutes after the Yankees won, "Yes, you nitwit, there's a God in Heaven and his name is Babe Ruth."

Who was I to argue?

"How long have you been open?" I asked the waiter. He looked like George Steinbrenner having a bad hair day. The same kind of smugness. The same kind of supercilious manner.

Since 1919, sir," he said. "But every year we seem to do more business."

"Why's that?" I asked.

"Losers, sir," he said pointedly. "We never seem to run out of them."

Ouch.

On one wall was a picture of the ball going through Buckner's legs in '86, a freeze-frame of Red Sox frustration. On another was a picture of Bucky Dent's fly ball going into the screen in '78, another one of those daggers that never seems to get extricated from a Red Sox fan's heart. On the wall were big blown-up pictures of all the Yankees through history that had punished the Red Sox, a rogues' gallery of dream-killers. Seventy-eight years of reminders. And hovering over everything, like some cruel God overlooking a barren landscape, was a huge picture of Babe Ruth.

The original sin of the Red Sox. From the time the Red Sox sold Ruth to the Yankees in 1920.

The Curse of the Bambino.

"In a few days we're going to have another picture," the waiter said.

"What's that?" I said. "A picture of the 12-year-old kid who robbed the Orioles of going up two games to none?"

"See," said the waiter haughtily. "That's the trouble with you people here. You don't lose with class. And you would think you'd be able to by now. Because you've had so much practice."

"What's with this you people stuff?"

"Well, sir," the waiter said, with all the arrogance of a Yankee fan secure in the knowledge that the Bronx Bombers have now won 23 world titles since the Sox won their last one. "This is the Losers' Cafe. Accent on Losers."

Was it ever.

You could almost reach out and touch the gloom. This was one big room full of fans confronting their worst nightmare. Bad enough this was another lost season for the Sox, one more in a long list. But the Yankees' winning? That wasn't just rubbing salt in the wounds. That was sprinkling in some gasoline and throwing in a match.

Bad enough the MVP of the Series was John Wetteland, the same John Wetteland who once was coming to the Sox before the labor dispute and the deal was voided. But there on the big-screen TV, just minutes after the game had ended, was Wade Boggs parading around Yankee Stadium on a horse.

Could it get any worse than this?

No, this was Bucky Dent all over again. This was arguably the most selfish player in Red Sox' history now acting like he had been born in pinstripes. This was the epitome of why the Red Sox haven't won in Almost 82 years, someone who was a virtual non-entity in the postseason, acting as if he now cares more about the team than his own stats.

Can it get any worse?

Forget the "Braves in seven," I thought. If there's a God in Heaven the horse is going to toss Boggs off. Please horse, I begged. Toss Boggs. Give me a little consolation prize. Make my day.

But not on this night.

Not here in the Losers' Cafe.

"Your order, sir," the waiter said, suddenly reappearing with a gleam in his eye.

"But I didn't order anything," I said.

"It's the specialty of the house," the waiter said. "Everyone here at the Losers' Cafe gets some. But we made up a big helping tonight. Especially for you. Especially for people like you who write gibberish like, "if there's a God in Heaven it will be the Braves in seven."

The food lay across my plate looking big, dark and unappealing, like an old Richie Gedman catcher's mitt that had been charbroiled.

"What is it?" I asked.

"It's crow, sir," the waiter said. "One big order of crow."

BOB LOVE

4/29/1996

"I used to go home and pray. 'Please, Lord,
let me find a way to speak.'"
—BOB LOVE

PROVIDENCE — On the surface he had a life out of some playground fantasy.

He was an NBA star. He was the leading scorer on the Chicago Bulls for seven straight years. On the surface, he was leading the kind of life that so many others look at with envy, the kind of life that he once had only dreamed about, back when he was growing up poor in rural Louisiana, so poor that he had to take coat hangers and make them into a basketball goal.

On the surface.

Beneath the glittering surface, away from the cheers and the glamour, Bob Love had a secret life, one governed by frustration and failure.

"I couldn't talk," he said.

His stuttering problem was so extreme he couldn't be interviewed after games. Nor did he ever get any of the speaking engagements or endorsements that are the perks of NBA life. His speech defect was so crippling that it even interfered with his personal relationships, a private shame that seemed to color his life, taking much of the joy out of it.

"I used to go home and pray," said Love. "Please, Lord, let me find a way to speak."

For he really never could. As long as he could remember, he stuttered, the words that others spoke so freely becoming prisoners in his throat. He grew up one of 14 children, raised by his grandmother in a tiny house with only two bedrooms. But it wasn't the all-encompassing poverty that crippled him. It was his speech defect, the stuttering and stammering that had come to define him. He would sit in school every day of his life afraid that the teacher would call on him and reveal for all to see the depths of his shame.

"On Sunday mornings my grandmother would tell me to put three marbles under my tongue, then go into church and I wouldn't stutter," smiled Love. "Every Sunday morning I'd swallow two of the marbles, till I eventually told my grandmother: I'm up to my neck in marbles and I still stutter."

Eventually, he hid behind basketball. He was 6-foot-8, with fluid moves and a slithery jumper, and eventually those moves took him to Southern University in Baton Rouge and then on to the NBA. Moves so good that no one cared that he couldn't talk. He had come so far from the tiny little house of his childhood, all the way to the biggest basketball arenas in the country.

But his speech defect went with him, too.

He was called "Butterbean" then, a childhood nickname he'd gotten from always eating a vegetable indigenous to the South. Bob "Butterbean" Love, one of the top scorers in the NBA. For years he led the Bulls in virtually every offensive category. But the interviews always went to somebody else. The endorsements always went to somebody else. One night, at an awards ceremony, he was coerced into saying a few words and when he got to the podium he found he couldn't say a word. Not one. He went outside to the privacy of his car and cried.

"My dream was to be able to get up in front of a room of people and just talk to them," he said. "I thought about it all the time. That was my dream."

It would be a while before it got actualized. A long while and a lot of hard road. For when Love retired from the Bulls in 1977, he quickly discovered a painful lesson: Basketball had been the easy part. No longer was he Bob Love, basketball star. No longer could he hide behind the game. Now he was Bob Love, who stuttered so badly he became virtually unemployable. His wife left him. He lost all his material possessions. For seven years he had a succession of jobs that went nowhere, until he eventually found himself working as a dishwasher and busboy in Nordstrom's in Washington state.

"I would hear all the whispers and see all the stares," Love said. "But you know what? I decided to see it as an opportunity. I decided to become the best dishwasher I could be. I decided that I wasn't going to let myself be a victim. That I was going to take the first step."

That was Love's message yesterday at URI's College of Continuing Education. Love was the main speaker at a ceremony rededicating the school's student center in the memory of Janice Paff, the former director of student services. It was a powerful one, especially at a school that deals with so many students who are coming back to education after years away, so many coming back in quest of dreams that got deferred.

For Love is convinced his life never would have turned around if he had not taken the first step himself, if he'd continued to play the role of victim. Certainly his hard work as a busboy, and the attitude that it conveyed, paid off for Love. After six months he was rewarded with a better job at Nordstrom's. More importantly, the company sent Love to speech therapy. He was 45 years old, and for the first time in his life he finally was dealing with the one thing that always had been his albatross.

That was six years ago.

Love is now director of communications for the Bulls, and says he's the happiest he's ever been in his life. In addition to serving as a spokesman for the Bulls' organization, he regularly speaks to schools and community organizations, speaks about the travails of his own life, and about not giving up on your dreams, and how you have to take the first step to attain them. Speaks about how once upon a time he couldn't utter a single word without stuttering and how free he now feels, the words no longer prisoners in his throat.

"You know," said Bob Love. "I can't remember the first basket I ever scored in the NBA, nor can I remember the last. But I can remember every speech I've ever given."

JEREMY KAPSTEIN

12/20/98

*"Outside of my family and friends, the joy
I have received in the streets is the greatest gift
I have ever received."*

—JEREMY KAPSTEIN

PROVIDENCE — The voice on the other end of the phone is from another place, another time. It belongs to Jerry Kapstein, and once upon a time he was one of the biggest agents in sports, a Jerry Maguire before Jerry Maguire.

He was the kid from Providence's East Side who did the stats on Providence College basketball broadcasts with Chris Clark, then grew up to become one of this state's all-time successful sports stories. In 1990 he even ran the San Diego Padres.

And then he disappeared.

Just like that.

"For the first time in my life I had both the time and the means to do something different," he says. "For the first time I had the opportunity to truly examine where my life was, and what it was about."

He was 47 years old.

Now it's eight years later and Kapstein has surfaced again. Only now he's living a life that no one could have ever predicted. Certainly it's light years away from what he was doing in 1976, back when Kapstein was a major player in a scenario that probably changed baseball forever.

Ironically, some of it happened here in Providence. Kapstein rented an office on the fourth floor of the Hospital Trust Tower and the fun began. He represented some of the biggest names in the game: players like Joe Rudi and Bert Campaneris, Don Gullett and Gene Tenace. There were 24 players eligible for free agency that year and Kapstein had 11 of them.

"It was never about the money," he says. "The focus was about getting a fair contract."

Nor was it something Kapstein planned. He had never set out to be an agent, had no idea of where the baseball business was going to go. It was 1972; he was getting out of the Navy, and the question was: What to do? He already had been to law school and a friend asked him if he would help a young Baltimore Oriole player named Bobby Grich negotiate his contract.

In the beginning he represented Don Baylor, Johnny Oates and Dusty Baker. Kapstein says they all shared a similar vision, one geared around the concept that for too long the player had been the indentured servants of the game, and it was time for a change.

"Some players were making something like between $12,000 and $14,000 a year and then they'd go in to renegotiate and the clubs would try to cut them $500," Kapstein says. "It was so one-sided."

So began a whirlwind time for Kapstein. He traveled extensively, worked around the clock, kept adding more clients. He was in the right place at the right time, free agency having come to baseball with a vengeance. By '76 he was as big as big could be. In a way he was the prototype for what the sports agent was to become.

And if he was based on the West Coast, it was Providence that he returned to in November of '76 where he put his personal stamp all over baseball. Providence, which for a short time became the center of the baseball universe, complete with free agents hanging around Haven Brothers downtown and executives flying in here with brief-cases overflowing with money. The Providence of his youth.

He had grown up on the East Side. His father was Sherwin Kap-stein, a former teacher-coach who later became the Rhode Island head of the National Education Association. He went to Hope High School, where he was the fullback on the football team. Then in the fall of 1961 he went on to Harvard.

He already had a certain sliver of local fame, though. When he was 15 years old, Kapstein approached Clark and asked if he wanted someone to keep the stats on PC basketball broadcasts. Clark said yes, and a career was born. For 10 years Kapstein did the stats for Clark. And not just kept them. But read them over the air. In a state that was in the middle of a love affair with Providence College basketball, in the days when radio often was the lifeline, it seemed like Jerry Kapstein had the best part-time job of all.

Certainly that's how Kapstein remembers it.

"It was a wonderful time," he says. "To be involved with such great people like Chris Clark and Joe Mullaney. To be a part of that era, even if it was in such a small way, is something I've always treasured."

Kapstein also remembers the Rhode Island of his youth very fondly.

"I grew up around teachers and coaches who were very instrumental to me," he says. "People with big heads and hard noses. People you want in the trenches with you. People who were very loyal. I was lucky. This was the environment I came out of."

Eventually, Kapstein would have as many as 50 clients, some of the biggest names in baseball.

In 1988, though, his life changed. He had married the daughter of Joan Kroc, whose husband, Ray, had owned both McDonald's and the Padres. Joan Kroc asked Kapstein if he would run the Padres for her.

"It was a family decision," he says.

The team was sold in 1990, and Kapstein was faced with a major decision. He could go work for another major-league club. He could go back to being an agent. He could really do anything he wanted.

What to do?

For the first time in his life he had the time to sort it all out. He also was going through a divorce, and one senses it was a traumatic time for him. He had worked and worked and worked, living out of suitcases, a frenetic life that never seemed to slow down, a life that often had been so consumed by his clients. He had been on a merry-go-round for years, one that, on the surface anyway, had taken him from the Providence of his childhood to the American Dream. He had obtained the world and all of its gold, and somehow it wasn't enough.

"I looked at my bookcase and the book I took out was the Old Testament I'd had since I was 13 years old," he says.

He began reading Scripture, and the more he read, the more he kept coming back to a theme that seemed to run through all the prophets: You can't just say it, you have to do it. You have to go into the world and help people. Kapstein's search eventually took him into the streets of San Diego, far away from the glittering world of a sports agent.

It's a journey that continues.

For the past eight years he has worked with the homeless in San Diego. He has done this anonymously, without fanfare, without publicity. Almost every day he goes into downtown San Diego, sometimes alone, sometimes with a couple of friends, and functions as an unofficial advocate for the homeless. He takes people to shelters. He helps people get food. He is their friend.

"Outside of my family and friends, the joy I have received in the streets is the greatest gift I have ever received," he says. "I feel blessed."

He says he's not a preacher, not a rabbi. Nor does he believe that everyone should do what he does; everyone must decide the course of their own life in their own way, he says. He even downplays what he does, says that he's just fortunate he's had the time to be able to do it. He also says he's not doing anything that different from the way he was raised, that he was raised in a family that had a social conscience "based on a strong religious base," and his work with the homeless is merely an extension of that.

And does he ever miss being a big-time agent?

"I'm thankful for it," he says. "But it's a chapter that's closed."

Two years ago he was named to the Padres' board of directors. He had been reunited with Padres president Larry Lucchino, whom he had known years ago. One thing led to another and Kapstein became an unofficial consultant to the Padres, then a member of the board. He says his only payment is that the Padres must set aside some tickets for inner-city kids.

"It's gotten me back into baseball and I love that," he says. "I feel very fortunate."

But the real focus of his life is still the work he does in the streets of San Diego, this world he's created for himself that's so very far from what his world used to be, back when he was one of the biggest agents in all of sports, one of the all-time Rhode Island sports' success stories.

"It's the best thing I've ever done," says Jerry Kapstein. "It's the focal point of my life. And when I'm doing it, I feel like I'm home."

ARMAND BATASTINI

10/18/1998

"Every year the balls get heavier."
—ARMAND BATASTINI

NORTH PROVIDENCE — He walks into the small gym carrying a big blue bag full of basketballs, just like always. He puts a whistle in his mouth, just like always. His players respond to his words as if they're a Sermon on the Mount, just like always. It's 6 o'clock on an October evening, at the start of another season, and Armand Batastini is again coaching his CYO team.

Just as he's done for 48 years.

Roll that number around on your tongue for a while.

Forty-eight years.

Nearly a half century.

Think about it. Batastini started coaching CYO basketball before

rock 'n' roll, before the Kennedys, before Vietnam, before comput-
ers, before Civil Rights and feminism, before so many things we've
come to associate with life in America. Back when Harry Truman
was in the White House, and the second half of the 20th century was
still a blank slate.

And he's done it all with his own unmistakable style.

"If you're on time what are you?" he asks one shaggy-haired 12
year old.

"Late," the kid says.

"Right," Batastini says. "If practice is at 6, I want you here at 5:45
getting ready."

He has coached boys. He has coached girls, including his youngest daughter Christina, who now plays at Stanford. He has coached
high school kids, junior high kids, elementary school kids. Year after
year.

Decade after decade. For no money, and no fame.

He's volunteered his time over innumerable hours and seasons
that have come and gone. Nearly five decades now. One of the true
unsung heroes of sports — selfless people who coach for the essence
of it, not the tangible rewards.

It was 1950 when his parish priest in the Elmhurst section of
Providence asked him if he would coach the St. Pius CYO team.
He was 20 years old at the time, a self-described "sports nut," and
figured why not? Once he had gone to Brown to play basketball,
only to get into a beef with the freshman coach and transferred to
Providence College, back to the neighborhood he'd grown up in.
His own basketball dream was over. He would now coach others.

That was 48 years ago.

"Every year the balls get heavier," he mutters, the words coming
out of the side of his mouth.

Yet if the basketballs seem heavier, Batastini is still the same. He's
not simply "old school." It seems like he invented "old school." Part
Damon Runyon, part dictator with a whistle. All Armand.

Like the way he won't allow parents to watch practice. ("Parents can't walk into a classroom, can they?" he says. "What's the difference?") Like the way he tells kids that it's "not recess, so pay attention." Like how he says that his new team is still "a little afraid of the Big Bad Wolf and that's me." For there are a thousand Armand Batastini stories, all told by the people who once played for him, the fiction sprinkled in with the truth to the point that it's all part of the legend. The throwing of chairs. The kicking of basketballs.

"You know all that stuff about me yelling and screaming and throwing chairs?" he once said three years ago with a sly look. "That's all a myth. Never happened."

Of course not.

He's a product of the era that shaped him, one in which the coach is the absolute ruler, and there's only one way to play basketball: the right way. No showboating. No playground primer. Simply basketball out of some musty old textbook, as fundamental as a two-hand chest pass, as timeless as a layup drill.

His other message: do things right. Be on time. Be persistent. Overcome adversity. Don't quit. Things he considers the life lessons.

"All the cliches," he says.

These are cliches that became the article of his faith a long time ago. For nothing has really changed. Not even the kids he coaches.

"Everything has changed around them, but the kids haven't changed," he says. "They still have the same expectations they always had."

Nor has Batastini changed. Not really. The obsession with basketball is still there. The sense of satisfaction he gets from kids learning the game is still there. The relationships that began in small gyms and continue to this day are still there. The rewards he gets from his coaching are still there.

Yet he never set out to coach for 48 years. He was just taking it year by year, until one day he looked up and the years had added up. Through his job as a truant officer in the Providence school system.

Through his 14 years as a state representative. Through raising four children with his wife Mary. Through all of it.

On this night at the start of still another season, his team is lined up before him. They are CYO Midgets, ages 10–12, and when he says "Jump," they ask "How high?" They will go through drills without a ball, what Batastini calls his "phantom drills." They will do a succession of drills, all run to the letter, no nonsense.

It is all a basketball workshop, taught by he and his assistant John Riley, who played on Batastini's first St. Pius team in 1950. After a while it's all timeless. Close your eyes and it could be 1957. Afterwards, he is asked the obvious question: why keep doing this?

"It's a part of me," says Armand Batastini. "It's just something I have to do."

He pauses a beat, lost in thought somewhere, as if all the years and all the kids have become a newsreel running through his mind, an assembly line of memories, nearly half a century of a personal love affair.

"How do you replace something like this?" he finally asks.

But Armand's got it all wrong.

MO VAUGHN

6/2/98

"We would tell him that he has a history,
one of black achievement."
—LEROY VAUGHN

BOSTON — Today is Father's Day. So this is about the father, and the lessons he taught his son.

The son is Mo Vaughn.

The father is Leroy Vaughn.

And as John Gray, who once taught with Leroy in Norwalk, Conn. says, "If you go back to that area and ask around, it's not Mo Vaughn people talk about. It's Leroy Vaughn."

It was the late 1960s when Gray, now principal at Barrington High School, taught with Leroy Vaughn. It was a time of tumultuous social change, when race relations often were combustible in a high school that was roughly 20 percent black. Leroy Vaughn was a chemistry teacher at Brien McMahon High School then, also the assistant football coach. More importantly, he was the voice of reason.

"He had the respect of everyone, staff and students alike," says Gray. "Leroy Vaughn was one of the most respected people in the community. He was a real leader."

Leroy Vaughn had grown up in Baltimore, near where Camden Yards is now. Baltimore was still a segregated city then, and Vaughn went to all-black Carver High School. In fact, he lived in such a segregated world that he says he never really experienced much racism.

Yet he says that there were kids he grew up with who never made it out of that insular world.

"Thank God I was able to get out of the ghetto back then," he says.

Sports were the big ticket out. His sports were football and basketball, and he played in high school against the likes of Elgin Baylor and Maury Wills, who were both from nearby Washington, D.C. His coaches and teachers were his role models, people who had escaped the ghetto and the future that stopped at next week.

"I wanted to be like them," he says.

Eventually it was sports that led him to Virginia Union, where he met his wife, Shirley. Then sports led him to the Baltimore Colts, where he was on the "taxi squad" in 1955. The Vaughns moved to Norwalk in 1958, because Shirley Vaughn had family there. Leroy Vaughn went to work as a teacher, first in the middle school, then at Brien McMahon High School, where he eventually became an assistant principal. During his career there he also coached football and basketball. For years he spent autumn weekends playing quarterback for the Stamford Golden Bears, a local semipro football team.

So it's not surprising that Mo, who has two older sisters, grew up with sports. And not just baseball. There was also hockey, and even swimming in YMCA meets. He also played recreational basketball, even went to Calvin Murphy's basketball camp as a kid, Murphy being from Norwalk.

But Mo's childhood was more than sports. A lot more.

"We would tell him that he has a history, one of black achievement," says Leroy Vaughn.

Mo was told about black leaders, people who had lived the struggle. About Jesse Owens. About Willie Mays and Hank Aaron. About people who had come before, the pioneers. And maybe most of all, about Jackie Robinson, who lived in nearby Stamford then. Jackie Robinson, whose house Leroy and Shirley had been to parties at.

So it's not simply coincidence that throughout his career Vaughn always has worn number 42, Robinson's number. It's the legacy of all those dinner-table conversations, a childhood spent learning that there were people who had come before him, people whose journey had something to teach him. It's not simply coincidence that from his rookie year Mo Vaughn always has exhibited a sense of baseball history, unlike so many other players whose sense of history seems to go back to their first contract.

It's also not coincidence that Mo Vaughn has exhibited a significant social conscience in his stay in Boston, his commitment to kids and youth organizations as much a part of his Red Sox tenure as home runs. He's always given off the sense that a professional athlete should give something back to the community, that those who have been blessed with talent and fame have a debt, too. That he should be a role model to kids, the way teachers and coaches once had been to his father back in segregated Baltimore.

These, too, were the lessons he grew up with.

His father was a strong presence in the community. Shirley, also a teacher, was forever bringing kids home for the weekend, kids who needed some sort of life raft. She also tutored kids for free. She was a teacher who didn't believe that the school day ended at 3 o'clock.

"You only pass this way once, and you have to make your mark," Leroy Vaughn says. "That's the way we raised all our children."

Mo Vaughn has said his parents taught him about having character, having respect. That if you're going to do something, do it right. That his parents set standards for him, and he was expected to meet them. No excuses. No nonsense. Just go out and do your job. Do what you're expected to. And in times of adversity, do it harder.

He has said that the toughest time for him was 1992. He was a highly touted prospect then, thought he was ready for the big leagues, but he flopped, was even sent ignominiously back to the minors. He had doubts about his ability, even thought about quitting. But those time-honored lessons from his youth wouldn't let him.

Three years later he was American League MVP.

Leroy Vaughn is retired now. He and his wife live in Virginia, near Virginia Union. Yet they almost always are at Fenway Park during home games. They even sometimes travel to away games. Mo's two older sisters also are at virtually every Red Sox home game. They're all there because Mo wants them there.

"You never know what your kid observes in you," says Leroy Vaughn. "But we did a lot of teaching back then."

Lessons Mo Vaughn carries with him to this day.

Lessons from his childhood.

Lessons a father passed down to a son.

PART THREE
2000-2010

BILLY PERRY

6/18/2000

"I had to be hard, just to survive."
—BILLY PERRY

PROVIDENCE — He sits at a table in Amos House, where he eats breakfast every morning, because you have to leave the homeless shelter on Prairie Avenue at 7. It is 8:30 and already the day is beginning to stretch out like a forced march across a desert.

What to do?

Does he go downtown to Traveler's Aid, to another day of sitting there waiting for something to happen, waiting, waiting, like waiting to win the lottery even though you never buy any tickets? Does he go over to Broad Street where he often hangs out across from the Bell Funeral Home until the police come along and tell him to move?

What to do?

There is too much time in the day. Too many hours with nothing to do. Too many hours until the shelter opens up again at 6 p.m. and he has somewhere to go. Too many hours to fill up, a daily fight against boredom and frustration, and the awareness that somehow, some way, his life got off track.

He rubs his hands over his face. It's a face that now shows his 43 years, as if the street and the years have taken their toll.

"That's what I think every morning when I walk out of Amos House," says Billy Perry. "What do I do now?"

Once, he knew.

Twenty-five years ago, Perry was a member of what might have been the best high school basketball team ever in Rhode Island. He was the point guard for Central, one of four great high school players who carried the school to back-to-back state titles. Michael Hazard. Willie Washington. Dobie Dennis. Billy Perry. Even now, so many years later, they have their sliver of local immortality.

"We were ghetto stars," Perry says with a laugh.

But ghetto stars can burn out quickly, a lesson Perry has painfully learned. He has done two brief stints in the ACI relating to drug possession and is currently on probation. He has seen his long-time girlfriend die of cancer, leaving him with their four children. He once spent six months in a drug rehabilitation center. Since September he has been homeless.

That's the condensed version, but it doesn't tell the whole story.

For this is a story of a basketball life when the game is over. When the cheers have stopped and the dream has died. It's a story of poverty and ghetto life, and the toll they both take, dragging everything down, coloring everything a drab shade of gray, eventually nudging a life off track.

It's also, curiously enough, a story of hope.

And like all stories it begins in the beginning, with a little kid and a blank slate.

Perry was 5 when he first came to Providence, moving from Delaware into the Roger Williams Housing Project because "the Lord told my mother to come to Providence." He was the third of five kids. He never knew his father. His mother couldn't read or write.

"I really didn't have any older brothers watching over me," he says. "No cousins. No extended family. I was always getting beat up, picked on.

Right from the jump things were tough. It hardened me. I had to be hard, just to survive."

By the time he was coming of age, though, he was on a fast break to trouble. The rule was simple in the projects: either do what everyone else is doing, or be a chump. He wasn't going to a chump. By his early teens he was breaking into houses. By 14 he was in Family Court, thinking he was headed for the Training School. He got probation instead.

He also got basketball.

Basketball was the life raft in this turbulent urban sea. He played in the projects. He played at the Southside Boys Club. He played on youth teams and won trophies, and after a while he no longer was Billy Perry who didn't have any extended family to watch his back, he was Billy Perry who could play some ball. From an early age basketball was more than just a game to him. It gave him an identity. It gave him a certain status.

It also gave him a dream.

It was the ghetto dream of one day being a professional basketball player, one that flames like an open fire in inner cities across America. Basketball as nirvana. In the early '70s Marvin Barnes had come out of South Providence all the way to a fat professional contract, a real-life fairy tale, and every kid in South Providence wanted to be Marvin. With Perry, it was even more pronounced. It was almost a calling.

"I really believed that because my mother was so religious her gift from the Lord was going to be that I became a pro and could take care of her."

So what if he was only 5-foot-8? So what if the odds of getting to the NBA and the big money are the about the same as winning the lottery? So what if Perry had no clue about college, or the courses you have to take in high school to get to college, or any of it? So what if he didn't have a backup dream? He was going to one day play in the NBA. He was convinced of it.

"I used to shovel the snow off the court," he says. "That's how bad I wanted it."

The letters from colleges started arriving during his junior year at Central, some from schools he had never heard of.

"Every day I would get letters," he says. "I just figured I could pick where I wanted. Like a game show."

When he was a senior, URI came calling but he didn't have enough credits. Instead, he and Dobie Dennis went to small Connecticut prep school. It went bankrupt in December. So he went to another one in the woods of upstate New York, but it was a long way from Prairie Avenue, and one day he came home.

The next year he went to CCRI, where it was old home week, a Central class reunion. Reunited with Dennis, Hazard, and Washington, Perry starred on teams that won two New England junior college championships, two trips to the national JUCO tournament in Hutchinson, Kan.

That was the public Billy Perry. Beneath the surface, however, real life was a little more grim.

He already had a child with a girl from the neighborhood. Eventually, there would be two more children with her. He was still living in South Providence. CCRI might only have been a few miles down Route 95, but to Perry it might as well have been on the far side of the moon.

"I had no funds for a ride," he says, "so I had to catch a bus to go to school. If I missed the bus I missed school. Here I was supposed to be this big basketball star, but I had holes in my clothes. I used to be embarrassed."

Once his eligibility ran out, he never went back.

The basketball dream still lived, though.

It lived through a job with a small construction firm in South Providence where he learned how to work with concrete; lived through a stint in the National Guard, until he eventually didn't like being ordered around and dropped out; lived through a job working at McDonald's in downtown Providence. Through it all, he still clung to the belief that he was going to be a professional basketball player, that somehow he was going to be discovered, his mother's reward from the Lord.

He played in local leagues. He played in the North Providence Summer League. In the mid '80s he tried out for the Rhode Island Gulls in the United States Basketball League. When he failed to make it, the dream finally lying in tatters at his feet, he started to drift.

"Basketball has been my life," he said back in 1985. "Without it, I'm kind of lost."

Amos House, which feeds about 600 people a day, is in South Providence, a jumper away from Broad Street, a few blocks away from Central. In the middle of what's always been Perry's world. Most days, this is where Perry eats breakfast and lunch, the centerpiece of his day.

"This is home," he says.

He's been living in the Urban League shelter on Prairie Avenue since September when his mother died. It's a descent he says started in 1995 when his long-time girlfriend Cindy Johnson died of cancer. Until then he was living in the Manton Avenue Projects on Providence's west side with her and their four children. He was a member of Local 40, a cement and plasterer's union.

"Things were good," he says. "I didn't owe anybody nothin'. I had a job, a family, money."

Then Cindy Johnson died.

"That was the start of the downfall," he says.

For two and a half years he tried to raise the four kids by himself. He says it was the hardest thing he's ever done. He cooked. He cleaned. He was Mr. Mom. He had been laid off, and the family lived on welfare and food stamps. Eventually, the money ran out, and "I started slinging a little bit," his euphemism for selling drugs.

His drug use had started roughly a decade earlier, shortly after he'd been cut by the Rhode Island Gulls. He started sniffing cocaine. In a sense it was part of the street scene: get high, forget about life for a while. He says he never really had a serious drug problem, but who knows? Where do you draw the line? He also says the selling was only to either get money to get high himself, or buy his kids things. In fact, things were going smoothly until the night the police came into his apartment and arrested him. He was charged with possession. Soon after, Perry was in the ACI.

"It was like I knew everybody," he says. "It was like being back in the projects. Everyone standing around watching me play ball."

He did two short stints, and maybe they were the lowest times, daily reminders of how far he'd fallen. When he came out his children were either living with relatives, or in foster homes. All his possessions were gone. Pictures of his children. His furniture. His clothes. All gone.

There were times he wished he were back in prison, for at least there he would have a place to go. All he really had were one bag on one shoulder, one on another. Hanging on Broad Street, doing nothing, like doing time on some nowhere ward. As bleak as bleak could be. Then last Thanksgiving, at a meal in a South Providence church, he was approached by a man named John Edes.

"Aren't you Billy Perry?" Edes said. "I used to referee some of your games."

One thing led to another. Edes, an investment broker, has become a mini support system for Perry. As has Dick Dannenfelser, the former chaplain at Brown, who volunteers at Amos House, and is known as "The Rockin' Rev." They have gotten him back in the union. They are trying to get him work.

Perry is like many people who drift in and out of Amos House, people seemingly stuck on the carousel of poverty and frustration, one that goes around and around, but so rarely forward. There are few safety nets in the inner city.

"We deal with a lot of people on the edge here," says Adrienne Marchetti, the assistant director of Amos House. "They can go either way. But I've known Billy for years and he's got a good heart. He helps the older people. He's good with kids. And I know he doesn't like the street life anymore. He's gotten too old for it."

"Billy has stayed alive and that's no small thing," Dannenfelser says. "I have no question about his heart, and like anyone in recovery, he needs to take things one day at a time. But he has skills. He can work with cement. He's had stretches in his life when he's had a steady job. To use a sports metaphor, I guess you could say he needs playing time. That and a good team around him."

Says Perry: "I thank the Lord for John Edes and the Reverend D. Because of them I'm back in the game. I have hope."

Some days he tries to investigate job leads. Some days he goes to a place that pays by the day, a sort of migrant work for laborers. That means leaving the shelter at 5 in the morning, walking downtown, then taking a bus up to North Main Street. Some days there is work. Some days there isn't. Even when there is, it doesn't pay a whole lot, $38, out of which he must buy his breakfast and lunch.

Spend any time talking to Pery and it's immediately apparent that he wants to change his life. Interestingly, his fantasy is the most traditional one. He envisions himself coming home from work, to the home he shares with his family, eating a nice meal, then maybe going to out to coach a kids' basketball team. It is the most American of aspirations, a home, a family, a life.

"All I want is an opportunity," he says. "I know I can turn things around. When I was playing ball I was always a winner. I just have to win again."

The other day he was walking by Central, and the memories came flooding over him, all those good times, back when Central was the best high school team in the state and his basketball dream burned as bright as a harvest moon.

"I got chills," he says.

Most days, though, he's looking for something to do.

"People see you hanging on Broad Street and they think you're either a crack addict, or you're dealing drugs," he says. "But they don't know my story. I'm out there because I've got nowhere else to go. I would rather be working, going home to my family. But I'm homeless."

He says this one minute, yet the next he is remarkably optimistic. He doesn't blame anyone for his misfortune. He knows now that basketball was too important, blinded him to school. Knows now that the ghetto dream of the NBA is a siren song, leaving crushed hopes in its wake. He knows he made some bad decisions.

Yet he still believes opportunity is within his sight, like a clear path to the hoop.

"I'm down, but I'm not out yet," says Billy Perry. "The Lord is standing over me and he's counting. But before he gets to 10, I'm going to get up."

PEDRO MARTINEZ

6/8/2000

"It's like I see myself when I was younger.
The way I wanted to be."

—JUAN ARIAS

PROVIDENCE — Sometimes, sports are more important than just sports.

Take Pedro Martinez, for example.

To most of us, he is the best pitcher in baseball. To most of us, he is the reason the Red Sox are now neck and neck with the Yankees in the American League East. To most of us, he might just be the best thing that's happened to baseball in Boston in a long time.

To Juan Arias, he is more than that.

"I can't begin to tell you how important Pedro is to us," says Arias. "There are no words."

Arias grew up in the Dominican Republic, in a place called Barrio Rey Cristo, where the hungry dogs ran in the streets and the poverty seemed to hover over the city with the afternoon clouds. Grew up with his own baseball dreams that he put in a small suitcase and brought here with him. Grew up hearing about Juan Marichal, the great pitcher who once had left the Dominican to that magical land of Oz known as the big leagues, the one "who put us on the map."

Arias was 15 when he came to Providence, arriving here with his summer clothes for the same reasons people always have come to this country — the promise of a better life. As a senior at Central High School in 1976, he was an All-State pitcher. He eventually was signed by the Red Sox for $1,000 and spent a summer in rookie ball in the New York–Penn League, on the same team with Bruce Hurst and Wade Boggs.

So when he watches Pedro pitch, it's almost as if he sees himself, the way he once fantasized his own baseball career playing out. Back when he didn't realize that a different language and a different culture could be more difficult to face than any hitter. At the time, the Red Sox had two bilingual instructors who floated through their minor-league system. Much of the time, in that summer long ago, Arias felt isolated, a prisoner of a different language. He was released at the end of the year.

"I think I know what Pedro's thinking on the mound," Arias says.

"It's like I see myself when I was younger. The way I wanted to be."

But his appreciation of Martinez is more than simply seeing someone else living out his baseball fantasies. So much more. Arias now is 43, has been in this country since he was 15. But when asked whether he considers himself a Dominican or an American, he admits it's a tough question.

"I think I consider myself an American," he says. "I met my wife here. My two kids were born here."

Still, his roots are strong.

He says how there's a large Dominican community in Rhode Island, and how much of his life here revolves around it. He goes to a Dominican church in Providence. Every summer he goes to the big Dominican festival in Roger Williams Park, where the guys stand around and talk about baseball, about Pedro and Sammy Sosa and the other Dominican players who make everyone so proud. He follows the elections in the Dominican. Last year he played in a Hispanic basketball league in Providence, the same league in which one of Pedro's cousins played.

"I still follow my fellow countrymen," Arias says. "I follow what's going on politically. I follow the winter league in the Dominican. I follow the prospects."

So maybe it's not surprising that Pedro has been like a godsend to Arias and so many of the other Dominicans who live here. As if his success is their success. As if his validation as a great pitcher is their validation as a people trying to make their way in this country. And it's not just Pedro's great ability. It's that he's humble, that he gives back to the people in the Dominican, and remembers that he comes from a small country where the dogs run hungry in the streets.

It's also the fact that Pedro seems to handle himself so well, his command of English apparently as dominant as his command of his pitches. For Arias knows how difficult the cultural adjustment can be. He knows it's not just about baseball and getting hitters out; it's also about all the things that nobody ever tells you when you are just a kid and professional baseball seems as far away as Heaven.

"It took me a lot of years to learn to speak English," says Arias. "When I first came here, I was frustrated. I couldn't understand anybody. I didn't know how to read a sign. I didn't know how to buy a lollipop. I thought the other kids were making fun of me."

Arias works for the Providence School Department now. For a while he was the assistant baseball coach at Hope High School, a team that was almost all Hispanic, half of whom spoke little English. Now he is an umpire and also coaches a kids' team. Baseball is still important to him, even if it's been 23 years now since that summer in the New York-Penn League, his own chance at the baseball dream that Pedro Martinez now lives.

"I get pumped up when Pedro pitches," he said. "Sometimes I'll go to a friend's house. Sometimes there will be more people there. We all root for Pedro. We yell and scream. What's he doing? Why'd he throw that pitch? We live and die with every pitch. I'm on the edge of my seat. I get nervous. Almost like I'm pitching myself."

Arias pauses a beat, as if searching for the words. And when he speaks again, you can hear the pride in his voice, the unmistakable sense that sometimes sports are more important than just sports.

"Pedro represents all of us when he pitches," says Juan Arias. "He's not just pitching for himself. He's pitching for the country."

GARY "TIGER" BALLETTO

11/2/2002

"I want to be a world champion."
—GARY "TIGER" BALLETTO

PROVIDENCE — The cheers were gone.

The "Tiger" chants were gone.

The crowd was gone.

It was Friday night, about 15 minutes after he had lost a split decision in the biggest fight of his life, and now was the tough part for Gary "Tiger" Balletto. The part you don't see on ESPN. The part you don't see on the highlight films. The hard part.

He sat in a small enclosed space in the back of the Convention Center, his nose broken and disfigured, his face looking like he'd just been in some horrible accident. He had a cut over his left eye that was going to need stitches. The knuckles on his left hand were bruised and swollen. He was waiting for the ambulance to take him to the hospital, and the air smelled of failure and regret.

The day before he had said he had to win the fight, that "this is my whole career here," as if his other 32 fights no longer mattered. He had said this fight was everything he had worked for, as if all the workouts and all the sparring sessions and all the long hours that nobody ever sees, all the times he couldn't eat because he had to maintain his weight, all the monotonous drudgery that's so much a part of being a professional fighter, had led him to this night.

Now he had lost.

"I tried," he said softly.

Did he ever.

No one could have tried any harder. Fighting 10 rounds after he'd broken his nose. Constantly swallowing blood. His face covered in blood through much of the fight. And still, Balletto kept coming at Goyo Vargas, the Mexican fighter now ranked 16th in the world, taking the fight to him, as if he could will himself to win on the size of his heart alone.

For Friday night was going to be Balletto's official coming out party, the local kid fighting in his hometown, on national TV no less. A boxing fantasy come to life. The plan was for Balletto to use last night the same way Vinny Paz once had used his fight against Joe Frazier Jr. in the Civic Center in the late '80s, the one that had not only jumpstarted Paz's career, but made him a Rhode Island star.

Certainly, Balletto is already a great Rhode Island story, one that cuts across time, one that's about the generations and a family's name, and maybe about a family's redemption, too. Hardly a week a week goes by when someone doesn't ask the fighter about his grandfather, George Balletto, who was gunned down in a Federal Hill gangland shooting in the '50s. No matter that Balletto never knew his grandfather, wasn't even born until 1975. Or that it's not fair for anyone to have to explain his grandfather's life. Balletto knows he can't escape his family's past, that it's part of his résumé whether he wants it to be or not.

Maybe that's because this is Rhode Island, where everyone seems to know everyone. Maybe it's because George Balletto was called "Tiger," too, just as Gary Balletto's father was called Tiger, and Gary Balletto's 10-year-old son is called Tiger, too.

Tiger.

The family nickname.

And maybe it's because George "Tiger" Balletto was one of those mythic names that came to define Providence then, back when its image as a mob town was as real as Raymond Patriarca's office on Federal Hill, back when the Hill really was the spiritual center of the New England Mafia, and not just a quaint place where yuppies go to eat. A time that, in some ways, is now looked back on with a certain romanticism. Even now, so many years later, if you are of a certain age George Balletto's legend endures. Local promoter Jimmy Burchfield says he was one of the toughest guys who ever came out of Rhode Island.

Whatever.

Gary Balletto grew up hearing some of the stories, the fiction sprinkled in with the facts, so that the truth got blurred a long time ago.

"I know my grandfather did some bad things," Balletto said Thursday. "But he did some good things for people, too. I'm proud of where I come from."

It's become part of the Balletto mystique that he was born in Federal Hill, as if that somehow links him to the time when the Hill was sacred ground to so many Rhode Islanders of Italian descent, but truth be known his early years were spent in Providence's Silver Lake neighborhood. Then, when he was 10, his father died of cancer, and his mother took him and his brother to live in Florida.

It was there he began boxing. At first it was because some kid on his Little League team was saying he was a boxer, and Balletto figured he could take him easy, so maybe that meant he was a boxer, too. And maybe, just maybe, it was in his blood. Hadn't his grandfather boxed? Hadn't his father done some amateur boxing? Hadn't he always believed that one day he would be a boxer, too? Soon he and his brother were boxing in the basement. That was the beginning.

Kurt Reader, who once worked with Vinny Paz and now trains Balletto, remembers the first time he met him.

"One day this skinny kid walks in the gym and he's got this mullet haircut and he's wearing plaid shorts and there's no one in the world who would have thought he was a fighter," Reader said. "Then he gets on the bag and everything changes."

Two and a half years ago Balletto met with Burchfield, the man who arguably does more for boxing in this state than anyone. Until then, Balletto had been fighting on his own, changing promoters all the time, a young career that seemed to lack direction.

"How serious are you?" Burchfield asked.

"Very serious," Balletto said.

"What do you want to accomplish?" Burchfield asked.

"I want to be a world champion," Balletto said.

So it began.

Maybe more importantly, Burchfield quickly grew to respect Balletto. How he's a good family man. How he owns his own construction business, his own gym. How he shoehorns his workouts around working for a living.

"So many of the young fighters have personal lives that are in disarray," Burchfield said. "Gary's not like that. He's a worker. He really wants to take care of his family."

That's not the only thing that seems different about Balletto. There's nothing flashy about him, no sense he's hooked on the fast life, the one that's become almost a cliché of boxing. He's married to his high school sweetheart. They have two young children. He says he doesn't want to be in boxing for the long haul, that it's no sport to grow old in. In a sense, he's in boxing because he's good at it. That, and the fact he got into it early, and one step simply led to another step.

At least that's what Eric Scott Latek thinks. He's 27, a Providence filmmaker, and for the last year he's been doing a documentary on Balletto. It's called Sweet Dreams, and it's an attempt to not only record Balletto's career, but also some of the Italian-American culture Balletto comes from.

"Gary's not in this to be a star," Latek said. "It's something he got stuck into."

Which is why Balletto is at a certain crossroads.

There's little question he's come so very far from that day nearly a decade ago when Reader first saw him, come so much further than most kids who ever put on a pair of gloves. He's won a lot of fights. He's one of New England's most exciting prospects, arguably the best fighter to come out of Rhode Island since Vinny Paz. He went into Friday night as International Boxing Union lightweight champion, which in the alphabet soup of boxing titles puts him on the cusp as a legitimate world-class fighter.

But he's also 28, not old certainly, but no longer young either. So there are questions. Does he end up in boxing's rarefied air where the real money is, or does he remain an opponent for the elite fighters? Does he keep going in this cruel sport that takes few prisoners, or does he walk away, just put the dream in the closet, and go back to his wife and kids and his business, sure in the knowledge that he took it as far as he could?

All of that was in play Friday night, questions that floated over the ring like suspended smoke. And now, in the small space where Balletto sat waiting for the ambulance to take him to the hospital, the questions were still unanswered. The day before the fight, he had said that if he got beaten badly he would probably walk away, "get out of this rotten sport." As if he was already tired of the time it takes away from his family, the prison of never being able to eat what you want. But he had not been beaten badly.

Outside, in the hallway, Burchfield was talking to a small group of reporters, saying Balletto "became a legend tonight. No one who ever saw that fight will ever forget it."

A few minutes later Balletto started walking across the Convention Center floor. He walked slowly, almost gingerly. Next to him was his wife, Christine, and a couple of friends. He was wearing a midnight blue velour warmup suit that said "Team Balletto" on the back.

He walked slowly, not to the victory party he had so hoped he'd be going to, but to the ambulance that was going to take him to the hospital and the other side of the cheers.

THE SPORTS DETECTIVE

6/25/2002

*"Hey, I'm not Dionne Warwick. I'm a Sports Detective.
I look for clues, sift through evidence, and the evidence
after the first three months of the season is the Red Sox
are as good as anyone in baseball."*

PROVIDENCE — The guy came into the office, complete with a Red Sox hat, a heavy heart, and a look on his face like he had a stomach ache.

"Are you the Sports Detective?" he asked.

"No, I'm the Welcome Wagon," I snapped.

Always put the mooks on the defensive. Let them know right from jump street who the alpha wolf is.

"What's up?"

The guy looked confused. He looked at the half-eaten pizza strips that lay on my desk like little animals that had died. He looked at my feet up on the desk. He looked at the tired furniture that screamed Salvation Army. He didn't look confident.

"I'm not sure I came to the right place," he said.

"Depends what you're looking for," I said, giving him my best Bogey imitation. Either that, or Jim Rockford doing Bogey. Being a detective these days is all about nuance. That, and attitude, of course.

"But you're the Sports Detective, right?"

"That's me, always on the case, 24-7," I said. "But the clock's running."

"I don't know what to do," the Red Sox cap said, the anguish running through his voice. "Three weeks ago, we were the best team in baseball. I was planning my vacation around the celebration in City Hall Plaza, and…"

"You were what?"

"You know, the celebration in downtown Boston," he said. "When the Sox finally win it all. It will be the biggest day in the history of Boston sports, and…

"Whoa, buddy," I said, putting up my hand. "You're killing me."

That's the great thing about the sports detective business, I told myself. You never run out of nitwits.

"But this is supposed to be the year," the Red Sox cap said. "This is the year we're supposed to win it all. But now we just had a 3-6 road trip, we've lost first place to the Yankees, and it's all falling apart. It's beginning to look like SOS — Same Old Sox. Raise our hopes, just to break our hearts."

He stopped to take a breath, then continued, as though he couldn't get the words out fast enough, as though he's been waiting for decades to say them.

"Three weeks ago, everything was as great as the bases loaded and Nomar at the plate," he said. "Now we don't seem able to hit, Manny's in Pawtucket, we're life-and-death to get a win, Oakland and Anaheim are back in the wild card picture big time, and what am I supposed to do?"

"Chill," I said, in a calm voice. "Think big picture."

"I don't understand," he said.

No kidding, I said to myself. That's why you're paying the Benjamins to talk to me.

"Nothing's changed," I said. "This is still the best Sox team in memory. Still a team that's as good as any in baseball. A team that just traded for a quality left-handed setup guy, and if Pedro stays healthy, it's a team with two great starters. All this, and Manny's coming back, too."

"So you think I'm overreacting?" Red Sox cap said.

"What did you think, we're going to play .700 ball all year?" I asked.

"I guess not," he said. "But it's like we can't beat the good teams."

"Well, you're in luck," I countered, "because pretty soon you won't be playing all that many of them. You'll be back playing all those teams that can't play dead. You'll win a lot of games. They'll be doing the wave at Fenway. Everyone will be scoreboard-watching the Yankees. Everything will be good again."

"You really think so?"

"Hey, I'm not Dionne Warwick," I said. "I'm a Sports Detective. I look for clues, sift through evidence, and the evidence after the first three months of the season is the Red Sox are as good as anyone in baseball."

"But you've done this a long time, right?" he said.

What to tell him? That I have seen innumerable mooks just like him come through this office through the years, all waving their Red Sox pennants, wanting answers, wanting sure things when there are none. Wanting guarantees when the key to being a fan is there are no guarantees. Just hope and faith, and a heart strong enough to survive being broken. What to tell him? That the seasons change, but the anxiety never does.

"So you think it's going to be all right?" he said, the hope back in his voice.

"Yep, I do," I said. "This is just a bump in the road."

Tell them what they want to hear, I always say. That, and send them the bill. Not that I'm planning my vacation around a celebration in City Hall Plaza. My mama didn't raise any fool. But I didn't tell the guy in the Red Sox cap that. Let him dream all he wants. Isn't that what being a Red Sox fan is all about? Dreams and heartbreak, round and round.

"Any last words of advice?" he said.

"Yes," I said. "Close the door on your way out. And keep away from high places during losing streaks."

DEAR GRADUATES

6/13/2004

*"The dirty little secret of sports is that none of us
are ever as good as we wanted to be..."*
—BILL REYNOLDS

Dear Graduates;

You have heard the commencement speaker, the one who tells
you how bright the future is, how you can be anything you want
to be, the one who talks about the limitless possibilities. Call me the
anti-speaker, the one who is here to talk about the past, namely the
high school athletic careers you've just concluded.

For the overwhelming majority of you have played your last real
game. You're not going to ever play professionally. You haven't
gotten a college scholarship. Odds are, there will be no more seasons
to get ready for, no more cheers, no more teams. The story's over.
Roll the credits.

What to make of this?

First of all, I want to commend all of you who played a sport in
high school. That, in itself, is a major accomplishment. You don't
believe me? Think about all the 10-year-olds who set out to play
sports, all the innumerable ones who fell by the wayside along the
way. All those who set out to do what you have done, had the same
dreams, and never saw them realized.

You are the ones who survived. The ones who didn't quit. The
ones who didn't give up. The ones who overcame a lot of odds. The
ones who went much further up the athletic ladder than most people
ever go. You should be proud of that.

And if you didn't see all your sports dreams come true, then stand in line. So very, very few ever do. The dirty little secret of sports is that none of us are ever as good as we wanted to be, even the select few who go on to play beyond high school. This is maybe the most painful of sports' lessons; almost no one is exempt. It's not the only lesson, of course. Sports are full of lessons, some obvious, some subtle.

That's why I am here talking to you today. To tell you what you've learned, even if you didn't always know you were learning it.

At the most obvious level, sports taught you how to be on time, to show up every day, even on those days when you didn't want to. That's not a big deal, you say? Wrong. It's a very big deal. Too many people don't show up every day. Too many people have 101 excuses why they don't show up. You know what they are. We've all heard them. It's too hard. It's too boring. It's too something. It's very easy not to show up. It's been said that 90 percent of life is about showing up, about coming to play every day, regardless of what arena you play in. You have learned that.

Lesson number two. Sports taught you how to be on a team. To depend on others. To be responsible to others. To be part of something larger than yourself. And, sometimes, to subordinate your own interests for the common good. This, too, is no small thing. Not in this Age of Entitlement, this society in which too many of us are raised to think we are a planet unto ourselves, with the moon and the stars revolving around us. Being on a team, with its inherent message that you are a part of something, is an incredibly valuable thing to know at any age.

But maybe most importantly, sports taught you how to lose. Maybe there is no greater lesson to be learned. We are not supposed to lose. Not in America. Not in a Darwinian society where calling someone a "loser" is one of the worst pejoratives. Winning is supposed to be our birthright, right? But sports taught you that failure is part of life, the unwritten lesson that every time someone wins, someone else loses. Sports taught you to fail and then show up the next day to play again. And that's not easy, especially today, when far too many people can't deal with any kind of failure.

For we all lose, in many ways. We lose when our dreams die. We lose when we don't get what we want. We lose when life beats us down. Losing is a fact of life, and not to realize this is delusion.

But it's what we do with that losing that counts. Do we quit? Do we give up? Or do we continue the struggle, find new dreams to replace the ones that died, new goals, new ambitions? That's the challenge. One you are better prepared for because you played sports.

Sports also taught you that life is not always fair. That, too, is invaluable. There are coaches who don't always see things the same way you do. There are referees who make bad calls. There are things that don't go the way we want them to. Sometimes things are simply not fair, and that's just the way it is.

And maybe most of all, dear graduates, I am here to tell that as the years go by, the fact that you played a sport in high school will be more important to you than it is now. I am here to tell you that someday, you will appreciate it more, savor the memory more. And it won't matter then how many games you won, or even how you did personally. It won't matter that you lost the big game, or weren't as good as you wanted to be, or any of the things that might seem so important now. What will matter is the people you played with, the things you shared, both the good and the bad. What will matter is the bond you always will feel with the people you played with, even if life pulls you off in different directions.

What will matter is that you played.

That, and the fact you are better off for having done so.

'73 FRIARS

5/16/2004

"Hey. We always were a team."
—MARVIN BARNES

PROVIDENCE — Outside on Smith Street, it's 2004.

Inside Little Chopsticks, it's 1973. Consider this exchange:

"I had sprained my ankle that afternoon, and you bailed us out against URI," Ernie DiGregorio says to Marvin Barnes. "Remember?"

It's apparent Barnes has no recollection. But he counters quickly. Then again, Marvin always was quick.

"I did that all the time," Barnes shoots back. "What's the big mystery?"

DiGregorio laughs. Barnes laughs. Everyone laughs. Just like they laugh when someone remembers how fans at Boston College once threw rubber hot dogs on the court at DiGregorio. And how Barnes was once so disgusted when a little-used reserve dunked on him one day in practice that he took off his sneakers and walked off the court.

Just like they laugh when, after DiGregorio says how it's amazing how generous the Mashantucket Pequots have been to him in his job as a celebrity host at Foxwoods, Barnes asks, "How about you tell them that an even more amazing thing would be for them to be generous with one of your old teammates?"

But Barnes knows better.

"I know Ernie's got that casino thing locked up," he says.

How's that?

"Look at him," Barnes says. "He's become an Italian Indian."

He pauses.

"Ernie would always pass the ball, but he won't pass the buck."

Then everyone laughs again.

For here in the backroom of this Chinese restaurant on this after-noon, just a jump shot away from Providence College, where glory once caressed their shoulders like the warm sun, are five members of the 1972-73 Friars team that went to the Final Four. It was the greatest college basketball team to ever come out of Rhode Island. The one that had Memphis State beat in the national semifinals until Barnes got hurt and it all changed. Ernie D. Marvin Barnes. Kevin Stacom. Assistant coach Jimmy Adams. Coach Dave Gavitt.

This is the Friar team that's remembered the most, the one that achieved a slice of immortality in that long ago winter, even as so many other teams have come and gone, the seasons running into each other. There are reasons, of course. It was the year the Civic Center, now the Dunkin' Donuts Center, opened. It was the first time the Friars went to the Final Four, back when no one cared about the Patriots, and college basketball was king around here. Maybe more importantly, the two stars were local, the Italian kid from North Providence and the black kid from South Providence, teammates in an era when race relations could be like flash-paper.

Which might have been Gavitt's greatest gift. He's got many, that's for sure. The founder of the Big East. The coach of the 1980 Olympic team. One of the pooh-bahs in USA basketball. One of the game's power brokers. But it was his ability to take a collection of disparate egos and give them a common purpose that might have been his greatest coaching gift. His ability to make Ernie and Marvin see that, as great as they were, they needed each other.

"I took Ernie down to South Providence one day because all my boys are saying Ernie was overrated," Barnes says, the pride in his voice. "They were always telling me PC builds him up, protects him. That he's just another little white boy, that he's not that good. So I take him into what's now the Davey Lopes Center and he spanks all of them."

Barnes looks away for a second, as if running some personal news-reel through his head. Then he points at both DiGregorio and Stacom.

"We always had it covered," he says. "Irish. Italian. Black. We had it all covered around here."

They have been getting together four or five times a year for a few years now, little unofficial reunions. Mark McAndrew is a regular. So is Tommy Walters, who had been a reserve guard on that team. Charlie Crawford used to be, until he moved away.

"If they are not here, we get them on the cell phone and pass it around," says Barnes.

One time they did that with Fran Costello, who essentially has been living in Europe for 30 years.

"I always thought you hated me back then," Barnes said to him.

"I did," said Costello.

The talk turns to Nehru King, now a teacher.

"Thank God my kids are out of school," quips DiGregorio.

And everyone laughs again.

The players are all in their fifties now. The Civic Center is no longer shiny and new. Gavitt is in his late sixties. Adams retired a few years ago after being the coach at Rhode Island College. PC is different. The game is different. Everything is different. Except the memories. The memories are the same.

That and the bond.

That's the most apparent thing. The years have come and gone. Their lives have taken them in different directions. DiGregorio, Barnes, and Stacom all played in the NBA, but in many ways basketball never was as good for them as it was in that winter of 1972-73 when they caught a state's fancy, when it was all like first love, something that never can really be replicated, no matter how much money you make or how many big arenas you go on to play in. Back when there was an innocence to it, before the cocoon broke and they all went out into the world.

So, it doesn't matter that they haven't been young in a long time.

Or that outside on Smith Street it's 2004, with its pressures, its realities. Around this table it's all timeless. The jokes. The one-liners. As if nothing is sacred, nothing taboo.

"Kevin was Dave's adopted son," Barnes says. "Everyone knew how it went. Ernie was son number one. I was son number two. Kevin was the adopted son."

Gavitt just smiles and shakes his head.

Or as DiGregorio says, "Thirty years later and we're still laughing."

Yet it's more than just the laughs and the memories. It's a testimony to the emotional pull of a team. Like men who once went to war together, a team binds people together in ways few other things do. There's no question they are all linked together by that one winter so many years ago, the winter that gave them a certain immortality around here.

"I think these guys have been great for Marvin," says Gavitt. "It helps keep him connected."

The same Marvin, who once asked me if cocaine killed brain cells.

"I don't know Marvin," I said. "That's what they say."

He had paused then, before saying:

"Then I must have been a genius when I started out."

He is someone who has peered into the abyss and lived to tell about it. The troubles he's had have been well-documented, the incredible journey through the horrors of addiction, which led to too many jail sentences and too many rehab centers, so far away from those cheers in the Civic Center. It's different now. He's been back here for a couple of years now, has his own foundation, gives talks to kids, a powerful message of what happens when you walk down the wrong roads.

"You know you all could be standing by my grave site now," he says, "and you all would be saying, 'Oh that, Marvin. He sure could rebound... Too bad he can't rebound his way out of this one.'"

But then Barnes turns serious, says how Stacom is the godfather of one of his children, how DiGregorio once spoke up for him at a parole hearing. The things that endure, right there with the memories. Not that we should be surprised. Didn't he say they always had it covered, Irish, Italian, black?

"Hey," says Marvin Barnes. "We always were a team."

They still are.

Three decades later.

1972-73 FRIARS' HIGHLIGHTS

- The Friars were 16-0 in the Civic Center in the first year the building was open.
- Down, 19-2, to Brown in their last Civic Center appearance of the season, the Friars stormed back to win by 13 and finish the regular season at 24-2, the two losses coming to Santa Clara in the Utah Classic and at top-ranked UCLA.
- Ernie DiGregorio scored 30 points before fouling out, as the Friars beat fourth-ranked Maryland to advance to the Final Four.
- The Friars were up on Memphis State in the national semifinals, but Marvin Barnes got hurt in the first half and Memphis State caught up in the second half and won, 98-85.

KANSAS CITY, HERE I COME

3/19/2004

"Going to Kansas City, Kansas City here I come.
They've got some pretty little women there and
I'm going to get me one."
—SUNG BY WILBERT HARRISON

KANSAS CITY — It is morning, and I am here in search of what Wilbert Harrison once came here looking for. Not the pretty little women, but the Kansas City of legend Harrison was looking for, when he said he was going to stand on the corner of 12th Street and Vine "with my Kansas City women and my bottle of Kansas City wine."

Or something like that.

When I was a kid, this was my only image of Kansas City. Not the Royals. Not the Chiefs. Not the stockyards, where Kemper Arena now sits. Not the downtown Municipal Auditorium where Wilt Chamberlain and Kansas lost in 1957 to North Carolina in three overtimes, one of the greatest NCAA final games ever. But this fifties song that was all over the radio back when I was in junior high school, a song about promise and expectation, about Kansas City as some midwestern Valhalla. A song that's lived in my head ever since.

"I might take a plane. I might take a train. But if I have to walk,
I'm going to get there just the same."

So I am here trying to walk in Wilbert Harrison's footsteps, here to look for what this city once had. What this city had that would make ole' Wilbert walk here, if that's what it was going to take.

The only problem is I can't find 12th Street and Vine. The interstate seems to go right through where it should be.

Once upon a time it didn't. Once upon a time the corner of 12th Street and Vine was one of the symbolic centerpieces in one of the most significant black neighborhoods in the country, a cultural stew of music, clubs, barbecue joints, after-hour clubs, boogie-woogie bars, shoeshine stands, pawn shops, more clubs with their neon signs winking through the darkness, gambling joints and anything else you can think of. One of the spawning grounds of jazz. Part of a nine-block stretch that in the 1920s and '30s was one of the places that changed the culture, back when this old cow town was called "the Paris of the plains."

Kansas City was a wide-open place then, and its soul was in this neighborhood just east of downtown where, in the words of one of the habitues back then, "Kansas City on a Saturday night was like trying to walk through Harlem when there's a parade. Everybody who was anybody was at 18th and Vine."

Ah, 18th and Vine.

It's still there, even if it's all about memories now. On one corner is the Blue Room, where once upon a time jazz greats like Big Joe Turner and Charlie "Bird" Parker made music that tried to talk to the gods. Across the street is the Gem Theater, an old Art Deco palace that's been here forever. A storefront church that speaks of yesterday is around the corner.

What keeps the area alive are two museums. One is the American Jazz Museum, the other the Negro League Baseball Museum. For Kansas City was one of the spiritual centers of the old Negro Leagues, home base of the Kansas City Monarchs, the place where Satchell Paige pitched and Buck O'Neil played, the place where Negro League baseball was as much a part of old Kansas City as the jazz that spilled out of the clubs on Vine. It is all here, the photographs, the posters, the history, the tangible reminders of another time.

And to walk through the baseball museum is to get a crash-course in American history, to realize that the Negro Leagues were a parallel baseball universe. It had its own stars, its own fans, its own culture, with teams like the New Orleans Black Pelicans, The Chattanooga Black Lookouts, a way of life that lasted for decades. A way of life, born out of prejudice and discrimination. Until Branch Rickey signed Jackie Robinson and the world changed.

I was thinking of that as I left the museum. About how far we've come since that time. About how much this country has changed in the past 50 years. For I am here to cover the NCAA Tournament, here to cover a college sport that is played primarily by black players. Players whose opportunities were built by so many of those men who played in the old Negro Leagues, the ones who kept games alive in the most difficult of times, the athletic ancestors of these kids today who live in such a different world.

The guy in the gift shop tells me that Satchell Paige is buried six or seven miles from here. Behind the museum there is a community center named for Buck O'Neil. A few yards away is a statue of Charlie Parker, the local kid who eventually took his horn to New York and a certain immortality.

"Bird lives," says the inscription.

More than the neighborhood anyway.

Much of it is open space interspersed with a few housing projects. It's all quiet in the morning sunlight, the only sign of real activity being the cars going by on I-70, the highway that bisects the neighborhood, cars heading for Kansas to the west, St. Louis to the east. Everything else is just memories and old pictures, a time gone by. On the corner of 12th and Vine is a small park, and there's not a pretty little woman in sight.

And whatever happened to Wilbert Harrison, anyway?

POSTSCRIPT: *Wilbert Harrison was a black rhythm and blues singer and musician from North Carolina, who recorded "Kansas City" in 1959. The song was written in 1952 by the famous songwriting duo of Jerry Leiber and Mike Stoller. Harrison had a number of hits and recorded for a number of labels. He died at age 65 in North Carolina in 1994.*

YUDEHWEH GBAA

6/8/2003

*"I just thank God that he brought us
from a far place to this, right now."*
—Yudehweh "Peter" Gbaa

PROVIDENCE — It was late Thursday afternoon, track practice was finishing at Hope High School, and it had been raining for a while. A few kids came into the locker room, then some more. Soon there was only one kid left outside, running over hurdles in the rain and gloom, a junior named Yudehweh Gbaa, whom everyone calls Peter.

"So you don't mind practicing in the rain?" he was asked.

"No," he said. "I'm training for the States this weekend, and the better I do the more opportunities I will have."

Opportunities. To most kids that's just another word in the dictionary. To Gbaa, it's long been a way of life. In a sense, it's the only life he's ever known.

What's a little rain when you used to hear gunfire and see dead bodies? What's a little rain when you once spent four years in a refugee camp so far, far away from the practice field at Hope High? What's a little rain when you once lived with 11 others in only one room? What's a little rain when you now find yourself in the middle of a life you never could have imagined?

Gbaa already holds four Rhode Island records in the hurdles. A year ago, he won both the state title, and the New England title, and now he is the ninth-ranked schoolboy in the country in the 110-meter high hurdles. In the world of local high school sports, he already is an amazing success story, and has become national caliber.

But this is not really about that. This is about the incredible journey that brought him here. To this time, and to this place, and to opportunities that can come because he practices his hurdles in the rain. A journey that began on the other side of the world, in Liberia. He was the youngest of 12 kids, and as a young child a brutal civil war swirled around him. For a while his family lived near some military barracks, later in a missionary's house. Still, there was no escaping the war and its cruel realities. He heard the gunshots. He saw dead bodies. He was 7 years old.

Fortunately, his family fled Liberia for Ivory Coast. At least most of them did. Two of his older siblings stayed behind. He was in Ivory Coast for about a year, learning to speak French in place of his native African dialect, before they all went to Ghana, to a refugee camp that had been set up to deal with Liberian refugees, a place of barracks and tents.

"The camp kept getting bigger and bigger because more refugees kept coming," Gbaa said, "and sometimes there wasn't enough food."

He was in the refugee camp four years. In the meantime, one of his older brothers had made his way from Liberia to Chicago, and arranged for the family to join him. So one day in the dead of winter Gbaa landed in the culture shock of Chicago, to a new world that was cold and foreign and like nothing he'd ever experienced before. Arrived at O'Hare Airport with his summer clothes and no clue as to what lay ahead.

"I was like, 'Wow'," he said.

At first, they all lived in his brother's one-room apartment, while his father and mother went out looking for work. He went to school, where he struggled to learn yet another new language and his classmates teased him because he came from Africa.

"I hated it," he said.

Soon, though, the family moved to Westerly, coming to Rhode Island because his father wanted to start his own church there and he had a friend in Westerly. They were there for three years, one of the few black families in town. Gbaa and his brother were two of maybe six black kids at Westerly High School during the year he was there. But after Chicago, Westerly was like Oz, a magical place where he made friends and never had a problem.

He already was being called Peter, a name given to him as a child when no one could say Yudehweh. So Peter it became. As a freshman at Westerly, he played soccer, the only sport he had played in Africa, and was first introduced to track, participating in both the hurdles and the high jump. Then came last year, the year Gbaa's life changed. The year opportunity became more than just another word in the dictionary.

The family moved to Providence, where there is an established Liberian community, and where Gbaa's father's became the pastor at the Providence International Advent Christian Church. And Gbaa's high school coach at Hope became Tom Spann, one of the true unsung heroes in this state; a man who, for two decades, has taken innumerable inner-city kids and used track as a vehicle to show them the way to a better life; a man who also coaches Gbaa in the Providence Cobras youth track club, and has been known to pay some of his entrance fees, who helped shepherd him into track culture.

"None of this would be happening without him," said Gbaa.

What is happening is something just short of miraculous. By the end of his first year at Hope, in only his second year in high school, Gbaa won two events in the New England championships. To put that in perspective, his winning triple jump of 47 feet, 10 inches was better than the first-place finisher at the Atlantic 10 championships at URI last fall. And that's not even in his best event.

More importantly, he became a commodity, a slew of colleges writing him letters. How many?

"I don't even know, there have been so many," he said with a smile. "I didn't even know that could happen."

These are the opportunities he talks so much about, the realization that there's a big new world out there that his track ability can give him the ticket to enter. The realization that he can one day go to college for nothing. So he works hard as a student, though he says reading is a constant struggle. He works hard at track. Then again, he's always seen his parents work hard. In addition to his part-time work as a pastor, Gbaa's father worked as a tailor. His mother works in a nursing home.

And what is track if not work? The daily repetition? The constant testing of yourself, pushing of yourself? What is track if not a microcosm of life, you against your own potential, over and over again?

Last summer he went to the Junior Olympics. Last Month he participated in the prestigious Penn Relays, where he was the second American finisher in the triple jump. It's all so far from a refugee camp in Ghana.

Yesterday, in the rain at Brown Stadium, he won both the 110-meter high hurdles and the triple jump. In the hurdles, he set a State Meet record, almost as if he were running alone. And when he stood in the rain to get his medal, he put his hands over his head and applauded the other medal winners.

And maybe it's because of his past, and maybe it's because of what he's seen his family go through, but Gbaa doesn't take the concept of "opportunities" lightly. To him, opportunity is not just another word in a dictionary. It's what he's in search of, even on a practice session in the rain behind Hope High.

"I just thank God that he brought us from a far place to this, right now," Yudehweh Gbaa said softly. "That he brought us, 12 kids, through the war, through all the troubles, through everything, to this place, this moment."

RED SOX "SPECTACULAR"

12/9/2004

*"…why do men who make millions charge
big appearance fees to meet their fans?"*
— BILL REYNOLDS

PROVIDENCE — P.T. Barnum, who said "there's a sucker born every minute," once had an act where two midgets named Tom Thumb and Lavinia Warren were on display. This was in Bridgeport, Conn., Barnum's hometown, and as the crowds flocked to see what was billed as the smallest couple in the world, there was only one problem. People simply stopped and stared too long, thus creating long lines.

What to do?

So Barnum, according to the book Chase The Game, put a sign over the couple's head. It said, "See the Egress," with an arrow. The crowd followed the arrow, only to see another sign leading them to the "Egress," then another that said, "Approaching Egress." To one last sign that said, "At last, the Egress."

At which point the people went through a door that led them to the street, "Egress" being from the Latin word for exit.

I was thinking of that yesterday at the Rhode Island Convention Center, at something called "The Sox Spectacular," where a handful of Sox players — highlighted by Manny Ramirez and Johnny Damon — were on display. For a price. Or how does $175 for a signed ball sound? Or $250 for so-called premium items? After you pay the $20 entrance fee, of course.

This way to the Egress.

The obvious question is why do men who make millions charge big appearance fees to meet their fans? Why do men with rich and famous lifestyles feel the need to gouge the very fans whose allegiance ultimately pays for their lifestyles? The simple answer? Because they can. The other answer? Good ole' American commerce, I suppose. What the market will bear.

And there's no question there's a market. By all accounts Red Sox memorabilia is all but jumping off the shelves, as everyone wants to feel a connection to this team that won its first World Series title in 86 years. There's also a huge memorabilia business out there, one that's independent of the Sox winning the World Series. Combine the two and you have the "The Sox Spectacular."

Just don't forget to bring your wallet.

And yet there was something sad about yesterday's show. Like the woman who said she couldn't afford to get Johnny Damon's autograph for $175 and had to settle for Doug Mirabelli's, which only went for $30. Like the woman with two little kids in Manny jerseys who had forked over something like $460 for his autograph, and was still waiting at 2:15 even though Manny was supposed to have been there at 1 o'clock. Like the innumerable people who had to stand behind the cordoned off autograph area, nearly 50 yards away from where the players signed, if they didn't spring for the autograph fee.

For these are the people who make the Red Sox such a phenomenon, the ones who give their hearts to it, make these players the stars they are. It's the fans who made the Sox finally winning a world title such a wonderful story, the ones who are there year after year as the players come and go. The fans, and their long-suffering wait, who became almost as much a part of the story as the players themselves.

And yet yesterday the only thing that seemed to matter was how much? How much for Manny? How much for Damon?

How much? As if even affection comes with a price tag.

You could see that with Damon's appearance. He came out to

cheers, even if the size of the crowd shortly after 1 o'clock was only a few hundred people, far less than what I'd been led to believe. He sat down to sign, and the people who had bought the autograph ticket started going through the roped-off funnel that led to Damon, like parishioners on their way to Lourdes. The others stood behind the barricade. They waved. They took pictures. Occasionally, they yelled out to Damon. In the end, though, it all seemed about as intimate as trying to find a date on the Internet. And when Damon was finally finished, he stood up, waved a few times and disappeared through the curtain.

Couldn't he have walked along the perimeter and shaken some hands? Couldn't he have done something to acknowledge the people not in the autograph area before vanishing through the looking glass?

Guess not.

And maybe it doesn't matter. Certainly it doesn't when you are 12 and you're name is Aaron Granoff and you and your friend are here because you pleaded with your mother to take you. But then, you're 12.

And I know that no one's putting a gun to anyone's head to pay for an autograph. And I know you can make a case that the players are simply trying to cash in on a business in which someone is always trying to rip off their signatures. But take away Bronson Arroyo and these are the same players who couldn't find the time to come here when the Red Sox brought the World Series trophy to the State House lawn, back when there was no appearance fee.

So when I left the Convention Center yesterday I wanted to take a shower, anything to wash away the slime of naked commerce. To wash away the sight of overpaid players, who should get down on their knees and kiss the feet of the fans, instead of charging people who adore them too much. And the people who want to give someone who makes $20 million a year $195 for his autograph?

This way to the Egress.

JIM CALHOUN

9/11/2005

"I think Jimmy would have been happy being a high school coach forever."

—TOM CANNON, A COLLEGE TEAMMATE OF JIM CALHOUN'S

SPRINGFIELD, Mass. — This is as much a New England story as the Red Sox and Paul Revere's ride.

It's the story of a kid who grew up outside of Boston loving the Celtics, back when the names were Cousy and Russell and Heinsohn. A kid who grew up lusting after the game, just another kid in a world full of them, a kid whose father died when he was just 15, a kid who didn't have it easy, and has carried that reminder with him ever since.

That's the thing to remember about Jim Calhoun. It's what is beneath the two national titles and the building of UConn into a national power, the glittering résumé that Friday night got him inducted into the Basketball Hall of Fame and gives him his slice of basketball immortality. It's what is beneath the money and the celebrity, beneath everything.

For Calhoun always has been the kid whose face is pressed up against the window, the kid who had to work in a shampoo factory in Springfield for a semester before he could scrape up enough money to go to American International College. And when he came out of AIC four years later, and thought he wanted to be a coach, he was a nobody. So what if he had been a great player at AIC, one of those tough small college forwards who would all but bite your head off to get a rebound? He hadn't played major college basketball. He hadn't played for a name coach who could open doors. He was just another guy trying to be a coach in world full of them.

And one day he would be inducted into the Basketball Hall of Fame? Could anyone have predicted that back then?

Not likely.

"I think Jimmy would have been happy being a high school coach forever," Tom Cannon, a college teammate of Calhoun's, once said. "That's what he aspired to."

Three years ago, Calhoun had talked about the education of a young coach back then. How one night you could drive to Providence and see Joe Mullaney coach the Friars, and the next night go to Boston College and see Cousy coach the Eagles. How there was always a game somewhere, always some coach you could learn from. He was just a high school coach, but even then he knew New England basketball was one big smorgasbord he could sample from.

For that's part of this story, too. Even though the game was invented here, New England basketball often gets overlooked, trumped in the old days by New York City and later by the huge college programs that mushroomed across the country. But there's always been a basketball culture here, even if it existed in the shadow of the Red Sox, and the perception that so much of New England was hockey country. Even if much of it is largely gone, the result of the changing realities of college basketball that began with the formation of the Big East a quarter of a century ago.

It was one of small gyms and cold winter nights, of long bus rides to places like Orono, Maine, or going to the old Worcester Auditorium to see Holy Cross play the Friars, back when those games seemed to be life and death, long before big arenas and national television, everything bigger than big. It was one of summer leagues and playground legends, of people who kept the game alive, kept it moving forward. The sense that New England's basketball history was more than just that once upon a time James Naismith nailed a couple of peach baskets on a gymnasium wall.

These are the roots, and Calhoun always pays homage to them, even if he's moved so far from them.

The other day he talked to the Hartford Courant about going into Roxbury as a kid to play the local legends on some team called the Roxbury Royals and how they had a theme song called "School's Out." He said how he hoped he would represent all those guys, all those guys and came and went while he kept going, along with all the others who chased the game all over New England.

"I'm bringing in all of you who have spent hours and hours driving I-95 to play in the Memorial Day tournament in Plymouth, play behind the Quincy Y, behind Waltham High School, up in the Berkshires, at the park in Worcester," he said. "I'm bringing in everybody in that was a better basketball player or coach than I was. All of them are coming in with me."

The roots.

The ones he came of age with.

The ones he always carries with him.

So it was only fitting that at his induction ceremony he was introduced as someone who "climbed to the top of the basketball world without ever leaving New England." And it was only fitting that it happened in Springfield, the same city where he went to college and used to go to the old Hall of Fame back when it was on the Springfield College campus and stare at the exhibits there, to look at pictures of his heroes, a world that must have seemed as far away as the heavens. Back when he would have mortgaged his future just to get a high school job somewhere, never mind anything else. That's how far Calhoun has traveled, a personal odyssey that mirrors the incredible ride he's taken UConn on, joining Frank Keaney and Doggie Julian as the only three New England coaches in the Hall of Fame.

On Friday night he talked about how there is a certain purity to basketball, how it is a game that doesn't know race, doesn't know economic status, how basketball is a "language that unites us." How it is game that still grabs his heart the same way it once did when he was just 15 and his father had died and the game was one of the things he used to get past the hurt.

Even now, at 63, and with so many games won, so many miles walked, so far from how he started out, it's almost as though nothing has changed. No matter how talented, Calhoun's teams still play as if they have a chip on their shoulder, a mirror image of himself, as if there's still a part of him that has to prove it, always has to prove it, no matter what the record says. The core of his coaching style.

"He always told us to never forget where you came from," former player Ben Gordan said.

Calhoun never has.

A New England story.

FLOYD NARCISSE

7/8/2007

*"A lot of the schools we play around the state
have no clue of what we go through every day."*
—FLOYD NARCISSE

PROVIDENCE — Central High School basketball coach Floyd Narcisse heard on TV that Darren Reagans, one of his players last season, had been killed outside a Providence nightclub.

"My heart just stopped," he said on the phone.

There was a pause, and when he spoke again, his voice was soft, sounded almost wounded.

"The list goes on and on," he said.

He was talking about another senseless killing, another life ended way too soon, another family that will be changed forever. He was talking about another sad snapshot in the losing war that is kids living in the inner city.

And make no mistake, Narcisse knows of what he speaks. He is one of the unsung heroes in local sports around here, one of those people who coaches in the city, one of those people who tries to take boys and help turn them into men, even while there are so many opponents that are infinitely tougher than an opposing team. Opponents like fractured families and the seductions of the street. Opponents like drugs and violence and gangs and dreams that can turn to dust right in front of your eyes.

Narcisse is one of those people on the front lines of what all too often is this country's unseen war, the one that no one ever mentions when they talk about the Providence Renaissance.

"It's worse than it's ever been in the city," he said. "People don't fight anymore. They cut you. They shoot you."

He paused again.

"A lot of the schools we play around the state have no clue of what we go through every day," he continued. "No clue to the problems we face."

Take 18-year-old Reagans, for example. Darren Reagans had a number of arrests on small charges that eventually put him in the state's Training School. He spent time at Ocean Tides, an alternative school that works with at-risk boys. He is the father of one young daughter he had with his girlfriend, with another child due in five months. He was stabbed to death outside a nightclub when a fight broke out in line.

His older brother was also killed as a teen.

And Reagans was just one kid Narcisse coached last season. This is the terrain he deals with, and in a sense it's what he's been dealing with his entire life. He is 60 now, has been in Rhode Island for 20 years, but Narcisse grew up in New Iberia, La., coming of age in the segregated 1950s. Segregated schools. Riding in the back of the bus. Separate water fountains. Coming of age in what now seems like such a different America.

He was one of 10 children. His father wasn't around. And all around him was a closed, parochial world where prejudice and discrimination were as much a part of things as sunlight and summer, a world where the inherent message was that black kids didn't count.

"I was brought up in the South worrying about racism," he says, "but in many ways there's more friction now. Now we fight each other. People will shoot you for a pair of sneakers. You look at me wrong, I will knock you out. There is no 'no sir, yes, mam.' When I grew up in the South, you knew where you stood. Now it's more dangerous."

He moved to Springfield, Mass., when he was 13, where baseball got him to American International College and a world he never could have imagined as a little kid in New Iberia, La. But he's never forgotten the lessons he learned there, and in the two decades he's been in Rhode Island he's been a huge presence in his church, has been active in the John Hope Settlement House. And all the while he's been involved with youth basketball, from coaching AAU teams to high school, to unofficially mentoring kids, to doing so many little things that rarely get noticed. Even with a family of his own, he's always believed that black men have to give something back to their communities. He's always been a presence.

One of the first things he did when he became the coach at Central, almost a decade ago now, was to make his players wear ties when they traveled to other schools. Why? Because he wanted to teach his players it wasn't just about being basketball players; it was about being people.

"This is an inner-city school and these kids face those stereotypes every day," he once said. "You know the ones. That these kids are gang-bangers, hoodlums. That they disrespect people, scare people. Those are the stereotypes they fight every day, the stereotypes all inner-city kids face every day."

To Narcisse, a neck tie is a symbol. It says you are trying to be a responsible person; it says you're trying to play by society's rules. It's the reason he makes his players sign a contract, one that says that you must be on time, you must have passing grades, you must take care of school property, and you must respect people.

Why?

"Because I learned a long time ago that to be successful you have to be able to compete in the real world," he said, "not just the neighborhood."

Still, he's just a coach, and outside the gym walls life is more complicated than being on time to a basketball practice. Outside the gym walls is a minefield these kids walk through daily, a societal obstacle course fraught with potential peril. Narcisse knows this, too. In real life, he's a "behavior coach" for the Providence School

Department, dealing with kids who are in danger of falling off the earth, kids who need a lifeline before they're put on the street and it's too late.

And his message?

Stop blaming everyone else. You don't have a father? So what. I didn't have one either. You're poor and there's racism? So what. I've been there, too. Stop looking for excuses and start taking responsibility for your life.

"We have to be accountable," he said. "We have to take ownership of our lives."

This is his mantra, and it transcends how many games his team wins, transcends who makes All-State, or any the other traditional ways we measure success. This is his mantra, one he keeps preaching over and over, as the kids come and go, and the neighborhood gets worse, the violence continues, and one of his players dies outside a Broad Street nightclub the other night, and he hears it on the TV news and his heart almost stops. And the list goes on and on, another losing battle in a never-ending war.

"Every day this is my sermon," said Floyd Narcisse, whose voice seemed to come up through layers of regret. "Because this has got to stop."

DORIS BURKE

4/8/2007

"I couldn't even have dreamed this."
—DORIS BURKE

PROVIDENCE — Last Wednesday, she was one of several local women honored by the R.I. Women's Center at a luncheon at the Marriott. Her award was for being a trailblazer. It was extremely fitting.

It's easy to take Doris Burke for granted around here, even if she seems to be on television these days almost as often as Friends reruns, now doing roughly 90 basketball games a year for ESPN, from being the sideline reporter for men's college basketball, to doing color on WNBA games. She's been doing all this for so long and so well now, one of the few women doing men's games in the country, that it's easy to think she was somehow born into the job.

We shouldn't.

Burke's story is an amazing one, a testimony to many things, not the least has been her ability to climb to the top in a male world where the broken dreams all but lie scattered by the side of the road.

And the irony in all this?

Doris Burke never set out to be on television. Never set out to go on college campuses and have young women say they want to be her some day. And never set out to be a trailblazer, a word that to this day almost makes her cringe. Even now, she has little interest in her growing celebrity, finds it uncomfortable, as if that all belongs to someone else, some alter ego that has little to do with her.

No, all she wanted to do back in 1990 when she gave up college coaching was to find some way to stay around the game. For basketball always had been the safe harbor, the place where she went and hid from an unhappy childhood, the place that always had been her sanctuary.

"I was a very shy kid," she says. "I had bad clothes, bad hair, bad skin. I was socially inept. The only place I felt comfortable was inside the lines of a basketball court."

This was all taking place in the Jersey shore town of Manasquan, where she says she was the poor kid in a rich town, the youngest of eight kids. From an early age, basketball was her identity. So she would take her ball and go across the street to a park where it didn't matter that her life wasn't like a teen magazine.

Basketball became her passport to Providence College, a basketball scholarship the only way she was going to get to college. She was Doris Sable then, and she became an All-Big East player. And then it ended, and then what was she supposed to do? What do you do when the game is your sanctuary and now there's no more game?

She taught for a year in New Jersey, then was an assistant coach at PC for two years. Then she married Gregg Burke, now the interim athletic director at URI, and didn't think that college coaching and having a family could coexist very well.

"I figured I'd teach and coach at the high school level," she says.

Then everything changed. Not that she knew it at the time. She started doing color on PC women's games on local radio, even though she knew nothing about radio. One day an agent heard her, and said she should think about doing TV. A year later, she did a Division II women's final in North Dakota.

"I had zero knowledge about television," she says.

Nor did she even want to be on television. She just wanted to talk about games.

Then she got two huge breaks, the two things that, in retrospect, were launching pads to where she is today. The first was the time one of the broadcasters couldn't make a Big East men's game at the last minute in Hartford in the mid-1990s and she was called. The second? She was hired by the Atlantic 10 to be their lead analyst for their TV games.

Suddenly, Doris Burke had a television career.

And you know what?

When she talked about basketball, you realized she knew what she was talking about. Knew that she wasn't just some sideline reporter there as eye candy, someone who wouldn't know a pick and roll from a tuna roll, that all those hours she spent in the park across the street from her childhood home, a lifetime of playing and watching games, was all there in her voice.

And if she knows she's been extremely fortunate in the sense her career was aided by both the exploding interest in the women's game and the birth of the WNBA, she's also had to show she could be accepted by men. One symbolic moment happened about a decade ago when UConn coach Jim Calhoun, about as old school as you can get, said to Gregg Burke, "Your wife is excellent on TV."

Yes, she is.

She is 41 now, and there's no question she's become one of the recognizable names in sports television, juggling a career that had her all around the country and her family in North Providence. For four years now, she's worked with Dick Vitale and Dan Shulman, ESPN's main college basketball broadcasters. She was one of a handful of original broadcasters hired by the WNBA. She was one of the first females to do New York Knicks games.

And if she says that being a working mother is never easy, that there are times when she's in some gym somewhere and wonders what she's doing there, she knows how improbable her story is, how far it is from doing those PC women's games on local radio. She also knows that if she never went on television again that would be all right too, that it never was about that.

Most of all, she knows that none of this was ever planned, that she simply wanted to be around the game. The one that had gotten her through a difficult childhood, the one she had hid in for so long, the one that has now taken her to places that once would have seemed as far away as the moon back when she was a little kid and the only place she felt comfortable was within the lines of a basketball court.

"I couldn't even have dreamed this," says Doris Burke.

LAMAR ODOM

6/4/2008

"I was as lost as lost could be."
—Lamar Odom

KINGSTON, R.I. — Ten years ago I went looking for Lamar Odom's roots. He was about to play his first game for the University of Rhode Island, the most celebrated recruit in this state's basketball history, and already he had spent the previous year living in the middle of a media firestorm.

His destiny was to one day play in the biggest arenas in this country, to have the basketball world and all of its gold in the palm of his hand. It was a destiny that had begun in the spring of his sophomore year at Christ the King High School in Middle Village, Queens. He had scored 36 points in the city championship of New York and a grainy black-and-white photograph captured all of it forever, Lamar cutting down the net, a swarm of teammates and fans underneath him, Lamar at the top of his world, the next basketball wunderkind.

But was he ever going to get to his destiny?

That was the question in the fall of 1998. Back then, he had all but become a poster child for everything that was wrong with the sport, a basketball vagabond who had been to three high schools in his senior year and was rumored to be jumping to the NBA after high school. Then he had gone to summer school at UNLV, until his test score was questioned in a Sports Illustrated story.

So he had arrived at URI in the fall of 1997 because Jerry DeGregorio, with whom he had spent some time living the year before, was the new assistant coach to Jim Harrick. At the time Odom was

perceived as another inner-city athlete complete with all the stereotypes, another victim of no grades, a fractured home life and a
basketball subculture that had spun out of control. Another kid who
seemed to be up for bid, grist for the mill.

His first year at URI, he had not been a fully enrolled student,
thus was ineligible to play and had spent the year in a personal limbo.

"I was as lost as lost could be," he would later say.

On that November day I was sitting in his grandmother's small,
gray house is South Ozone Park, Queens, about a jump shot away
from the Aqueduct racetrack. Just down the street and around the
corner was a small playground. That's where he had gone when he
was 12 years old and had just found out that his mother had died, and
he went and shot baskets by himself, trying to use the game to ward
off the pain, basketball as balm.

Seven people lived in the small row house: his grandmother, his
uncle, two of his cousins and their children. When he went home,
he slept on the couch.

On this day his grandmother sat in the darkened living room.
Behind her, in the small dining room, were innumerable trophies.
Yet, she said that it wasn't Lamar's basketball success that interested
her, as much as it was his academic progress. She wanted him to be
in school.

"His academics are the main thing," she said that day. "You can
always have a job if you have knowledge."

There was a grace to her, the grace of an old woman who had
worked as a nurse and then, when her three children were grown,
went back and got her college degree. You could see that, too, with
Odom back then. He never came across as some street kid with all
sorts of attitude. He was polite, extremely likable.

"Lamar never had an attitude," said Bob Oliva, the longtime
coach at Christ the King, later that day. "Never. Lamar knows the
difference between doing things the right way and not doing things
the right way. He was just lazy. Like a lot of kids, he didn't like to

go to school. He was always looking for the easy way, and outside of here he wasn't pushed."

Christ the King, a tan brick school from which you can see the glistening buildings of Manhattan in the distance, is a no-nonsense place, one in which boys wear ties.

"Everyone loved Lamar," Oliva said. "His teammates. Teachers. Everyone. He was never a discipline problem."

So how did it all get so crazy?

Maybe it was the lack of direction, a kid whose mother was dead and whose father had never been around. Maybe it was the fact that it was all too much too soon, being talked about as a junior in high school as one of the best kids to ever come out of New York City, instant immortality. Maybe it was the lure of the NBA and all of its riches, the fact that you could now go right from high school to the league and not to have to worry about Western Civ and teachers with their dirty looks, ready or not.

Who knows?

Maybe it all went back to that night he had scored 36 points in the city championship as a sophomore in high school.

"After that, everything changed," he once said.

There was a fragility about Odom in the two years he was at URI, as if there were two sides of him. There was the public side, the size and skill and talent, the sky-is-the-limit potential, the siren song of the NBA constantly buzzing in his head. And there was the private side, a kid who wanted to be a kid, even if the realities of his life kept getting in the way of it. Could Lamar Odom be a normal college kid? He never had that luxury. He always was in the middle of a soap opera, the price tag he paid for all of the potential.

So it shouldn't have been a surprise when he vacillated about whether to leave URI after his one year as a player. Should he go? Should he stay? Hamlet as a basketball prodigy.

But wasn't this his destiny? Hadn't it been determined that night as a high school sophomore when he scored 36 points in the city championship and everything changed?

Wasn't it only inevitable that he was going to go off to where the big money and the big games were?

So he did.

He was the fourth pick in the 1999 NBA Draft, taken by the Clippers. Five years later, he landed back in L.A., this time with the Lakers, after a stint with the Heat. And if he was suspended for a while in 2001 after violating the league's anti-drug policy — rumored to be marijuana — and two years ago went through the tragedy of a young son dying in a crib death, Odom has found himself with the Lakers. This year, he averaged 14 points and 10 rebounds, the perfect complementary player to megastar Kobe Bryant.

Not that any of us who ever saw him play at URI should be surprised. It was never a question of talent with Lamar Odom. And as I've watched him compete during these playoffs, I keep remembering that day 10 years ago when I went looking for his roots, back when everything was so uncertain for him, and how very far he's come from that little gray row house in Queens.

He is now 28, in the prime of his NBA life, a key player on a team in the NBA Finals, so very far from where he was when he first came to URI, "as lost as lost could be." Here he is, right in the middle of his destiny.

Finally.

CLAY BUCHHOLZ

5/27/2008

*"Guys old enough to be my father will come up
and ask for autographs. It's sort of weird."*

—CLAY BUCHHOLZ

PAWTUCKET — I first met Clay Buchholz last August, a month
before he threw a no-hitter at Fenway Park and his world changed,
back before his life got showered in pixie dust.

But even then, he already was so close to his dream that he could
almost reach out and touch it.

Once it had been his father's dream, then passed down to Clay
like some precious stone, a dream that got nurtured on all the
parched southeastern Texas infields of his childhood. Consider the
story his father, Skip, told me a year ago.

Clay was about 10 and his father was hitting ground balls to him
in the sports complex of their hometown of Lumberton, Texas, a
place where there are seven or so fields. It was a brutally hot day and
his parents were working Clay out.

"What do you see?" Skip Buchholz asked his wife and son.
"When you look around, what do you see?"

They looked around and saw empty fields.

"That's why you're going to make it someday," Skip Buchholz
said. "Because you're the only one here."

So that was the dream that dominated his adolescence, the one
that was always sitting off in the distance like some magical won-
derland, a Baseball Oz, so far from the sandlot world he was coming
of age in on those dusty fields of southeast Texas. He was going to

make it. He was going to come out of a small Texas town and make it all the way to the bright lights and the big games. Forget the odds.

And by the time I first met him last August in the PawSox' club-house, it was as if he already could see those Fenway lights winking at him. Everyone said he was a "childhood dream all but jumped into his lap."

"Everything changed that one night," he said.

He was standing in the same spot yesterday in the PawSox' club-house, as he had been last August, here as part of a rehab assignment, having been impressive in four innings Saturday night. But that's the only thing that's the same as last August.

"I didn't realize the ramifications at the time of the no-hitter," he said.

How could he have? He had just turned 23, in only his second major-league start, and already he had his little slice of baseball immortality. At the most obvious level, it made him a celebrity in Boston, unable to go anywhere in obscurity anymore. Fans. Media. The general public. Buchholz is known now in ways that were almost unimaginable to him just a year ago.

"Guys old enough to be my father will come up and ask for auto-graphs," he said with a bemused smile on his face. "It's sort of weird."

That's the thing about celebrity. The organization can tell you all about it, can give you tips on how to deal with the media, and how to deal with the public, but until it happens to you it's all uncharted territory. So it is with Buchholz, who knows that one night last September, that one night when he became one of the best stories of last year's Red Sox season, made him cross a line from which there is no turning back.

"You're under a magnifying glass in ways you never were before," he said.

In a sense, he's in a strange place, still trying to prove he is ready to be an effective starter in the major leagues, yet someone who has thrown a no-hitter. Still trying to prove he can live up to all the hype that's surrounded him since he's been in the Red Sox' organization, yet a name that everyone knows, complete with two endorsements already, symbolic of a certain cachet.

He said he doesn't really feel any pressure, that there's always been a certain pressure, always were some people back in his small Texas town that said he would never make it. He says this matter-of-factly, as if it's long been part of his life, the price tag for having a dream when you're a kid, the price tag for everyone knowing your business and having an opinion on it.

But he's also come to learn that when you're pitching for the Red Sox and you're not pitching well "you are going to hear about it."

He is 2-3 in this young season, has had some excellent outings, some not so good. He knows he has to get more consistent, throw more strikes, go after hitters more. All things virtually all young pitchers must get better at, the things that come with experience. For it's not about talent with Buchholz.

"It's kind of a live-and-learn experience," he said.

Uncharted waters. Like his life has been ever since he threw the no-hitter last September and his world changed. Still, he also knows that he's right in the middle of his childhood dream, and how many people can say that?

"There's not a word to describe it," he says.

For this is the life he long ago mapped out for himself, the dream his father once passed down to him, the one he began chasing as a young kid and never looked back. The one that has now taken him to places he only used to fantasize about, bright lights and big games, a world that once upon a time must have seemed as a far away as the stars in the nighttime sky.

"We didn't have the luxury of having a lot of things when we were young," says Clay Buchholz. "This is a completely different lifestyle."

Yes, it is.

One in which your childhood dream all but jumps in your lap.

LIAM COEN

4/30/2009

"It makes you rethink everything."
—LIAM COEN

PROVIDENCE — This is the other side of NFL Draft weekend.

This is the other side of the attention and the interviews and all of the promise, all of the glamour of an event that's become a significant part of the American sports scene. The weekend when so many football dreams come true, all those dreams born on sandlots, dreams that are actualized with being drafted to play in the NFL.

This is the other side of the story.

A story about waiting for your cell phone to ring, waiting for your dreams to come true.

Liam Coen's story.

And like all stories, it started a long time ago, years before last weekend's draft, back when Coen was a youngster chasing the football dream, someone who could always throw a football, could always put it where he wanted it to go. It was an ability that took him to La Salle Academy, where he became an All-State quarterback; it got him boxes full of recruiting letters, and it got him a scholarship to UMass. He was going to play college football, and that always had been the dream.

But a funny thing happened.

He became better than anyone ever thought — himself included. Last fall, he ended his college career as the all-time passing leader in UMass history, the kind of numbers that jump out at you. In fact, you can make a case that he was the most successful quarterback to come out of Rhode Island in the last half-century, a great college career.

So he spent the winter at a workout facility in Pennsylvania, where he was one of about a dozen guys all preparing for the NFL. He calls it the hardest thing he's ever done, and by the end of it he had gone from 225 pounds to 215 and was in the best shape of his life. So by the time he worked out for NFL scouts, he thought he threw well, ran well, had done everything he could do.

Certainly, that was the feedback he was getting. Just keep doing what you're doing. That was the message. For he knew the negatives: A lack of size, at just under 6-foot-2. Not a great athlete. Someone who had played Division I-AA football. But he had strengths, too. He has shown he can run a team and put the ball in receivers' hands, someone who always put up impressive numbers. He went into last weekend figuring he might not get drafted, but that he was in the next group, referred to as preferred free agents, someone who figured to be quickly signed and invited to a training camp.

"It became an expectation," he said. "I felt it was probably going to happen."

His college success had changed the equation. If once the dream had been to one day play in college, the dream he had carried so close to his heart through those high school years at La Salle, now the dream had gotten bigger. Now it had become the biggest football dream of all, the chance to one day play in the stadiums of the NFL. Now there were higher expectations.

Until the phone didn't ring.

The reality is that only 10 quarterbacks were selected in the draft, creating a domino effect. The six or seven guys who expected to be drafted became the glamour free agents, pushing Coen and the others farther down on the list. So now he's in football limbo, waiting for the phone to ring, waiting for his agent to tell him some good news — waiting.

"What happens is you start to question everything you've done," he said. "Should I have gone to prep school and tried to play at a higher level? It makes you re-think everything."

He knew things were deteriorating for him in the seventh round when the names of too few quarterbacks had been called. He knew then that it was going to be more difficult to get an invitation to a training camp, knew then that the odds were growing longer.

So now what?

The one thing Coen knows is he's not ready to put the pads away for good, not with the echoes of all those college cheers all but ringing in his head. For how do you walk away from something that's been such a part of your life? How do you walk away from something that you've been doing since you were a little kid, your head full of all those sports dreams? That's the other side of the NFL Draft weekend, the one we rarely see. We see the ones whose names were called, the few whose careers get a chance to go on to the NFL, the anointed ones.

The others?

The ones who wait for that phone call that doesn't come? The ones whose dreams just got punctured like some big balloon poked by a sharp stick? We rarely see them.

"I'm going to give it a year," Coen said.

The best-case scenario, of course, is the phone will ring. He says he would consider playing in Canada. If not, there's the chance of being signed in the fall to what's called a "futures contract," football parlance for signing players for the next year. As of now, it's all a bit unclear, all mixed in with the hurt and disappointment, the reality that this is no longer about Saturday afternoon cheers. That this is now a business that can be as cold as a loan shark's heart.

"I can deal with it if I go into a camp and am simply overwhelmed by it," said Coen. "If I go into a camp and am simply not good enough, I can live with that. I just want a chance."

So the dream continues.

Even if it's more complicated now.

POSTSCRIPT: When his playing days ended, Coen turned to coaching, and he is now the offensive coordinator and quarterbacks coach at the University of Kentucky. He has also coached in the NFL, with the Los Angeles Rams, and at Brown University, UMASS, the University of Maine and the University of Rhode Island.

PETER MANFREDO, JR.

11/22/2009

"You don't choose boxing, boxing chooses you."
—PETER MANFREDO

PROVIDENCE — It was a strange place to come looking for boxer Peter Manfredo Jr., who once was a star on "The Contender," the popular TV show on which the camera seemed to follow him around as if it were a home movie.

It was late on a Saturday night two weeks ago, about an hour after Providence College had played Stonehill in an exhibition basketball game at The Dunk. And there was Manfredo coming in to work with the cleaning crew, something he's done for almost a year now. And you didn't have to be a screenwriter to see the irony: Peter Manfredo, who has fought many times in that building to adoring crowds and cheers that used to float through the building like personal arias, now helping to clean up the postgame litter.

But sing no sad songs for Peter Manfredo, Jr.

"I need something to do," he said. "I'm not financially set. I came from nothing. But I love to work. It makes me feel like a man."

He was apprehensive in the beginning. What would the other guys on the cleaning crew think? Would they see him as a failure? Would they accept him as just one of the guys, just another guy who needed a job, another guy with a wife and three kids and bills to pay, all those real-life things that have nothing to do with cheers and adoring crowds on fight night? They did, and on this night Manfredo is just one of the gang in an empty arena, this place that once rang with cheers for him. Back when his career was all in front of him, was always going to be about big fights and knockouts, about paydays and dreams that come true.

The last time I talked to him in The Dunk was five years ago, back when he had just taken a pound of flesh from Joey Spina in a fight called "Put Up or Shut Up." He was a kid on the rise, but even then he already knew professional boxing was a dance with the devil, or as he once ruefully said, "You don't choose boxing. Boxing chooses you."

It certainly had chosen him. He had been taken to the gym by his father when he was a small kid, trained to be a fighter from the time he can remember, coming home from the Holy Ghost school on Federal Hill. That was when he was in elementary school, and going to the gym every day was what he did because boxing was the family game and he was an apprentice in a sport that's all about sweat and pain, a sport that all but eats its young.

So Manfredo always knew he didn't want to fight forever, and had few illusions about what he did for a living. Now he has less. A year ago, he was knocked out in the third round of a title fight at The Dunk by Sakio Bika.

"I was crushed," he said. "I was done. I wanted to cry, but you're a man, so you don't. I was seeing stars after the first round. I had never been hit like that before."

He paused.

"It all comes down on you. That had been my third big fight and I had failed in all of them. I didn't know what I was going to do."

That's what the movies don't tell you, of course. They don't tell you what a fighter does when he loses the big fight and the crowds are gone and his world has blown up and now the doubt is right there in his head. They don't tell you what a fighter does when he's 29 years old and everything he's ever done in his life appears to be over, and what's the second act going to be?

It also was the little things, the ones no one ever tells you about. Like how your people look at you differently, as if you're somehow less than what you used to be. Like how you walk into a restaurant and it's not the same, as if the aura that always used to surround you is no longer there.

And the most important thing? How to change your head.

"It's like life after death," Manfredo said.

For isn't that what the end of a career is like, a little death? Isn't that what it is when you're going to be 29 on Thanksgiving and this is the life you know? He always had said that he didn't want to be fighting past 30. That really hasn't changed, even if he is back to boxing again. He's fought twice since that night last November when everything changed. He is back to being a middleweight, and the goal is one more championship fight, one more last hurrah.

"I want one more, big payday," he said, "and that would be it."

For he knows how difficult boxing is; he has always known it.

He's also come to know that it's all ephemeral — the fights, the wins, the cheers, all of it. He knows that it can all go as quickly as a punch to the head, a punch that makes you see stars, changes everything. Then again, he never was overly starry-eyed about boxing. It's what he does to put bread on the table. It was never about cheers.

"It won't be hard to walk away," he says. "You play other sports. You don't play boxing."

He says he likes working in The Dunk after everyone else has left, that he has no problem doing anonymous blue-collar work, even if it seems so very far from "The Contender."

"I've never forgotten where I come from," he said. "And I'm comfortable with what I'm doing. I love this kind of work. I wouldn't mind doing it for the rest of my life."

So sing no sad songs for Peter Manfredo, Jr.

"I'm fine," he said. "I have everything I ever wanted."

Can a prizefighter ask for any better epitaph?

Can anyone?

ADRIAN WILLIAMS

2/7/2010

"A lot of kids didn't know who he was but the teachers and coaches always knew."

—ADRIAN WILLIAMS

PROVIDENCE — He was in elementary school, maybe 5 or 6 years old, when one of his teachers gave him a copy of a Sports Illustrated with a picture of his father on the cover.

"That was the first time I realized it was a big deal," says Brown basketball player Adrian Williams. "The teachers wanted me to know that I was part of an important legacy."

But it was a few years later when he realized that his father's accomplishments were something he was never going to escape, whether he wanted to or not. He was playing youth football, and from the beginning he was "Doug Williams' kid." The same Doug Williams who was the first African-American quarterback ever to win the Super Bowl. The same Doug Williams who forever is a part of sports history.

"I didn't really like that," he says with a rueful smile. "I wanted to make my own history."

Complicating everything was that he didn't live with his father, had never lived with him. But he had visited his father's family in Zachary, La., many times, where the biggest thing in that rural town was a Wal-Mart. He stayed on Lemon Road, the dirt road where his father, three aunts, and grandmother all had houses. He spent a lot of time with his seven half-siblings. It was all one big extended family, and sometimes his father was there and sometimes he wasn't. Adrian lived in Atlanta with his mother, Lisa Robinson.

But there was no escaping his father's presence in his life, even when his father wasn't there.

It was there every time he went out for football and was given number 12, his father's old number, whether he wanted it or not. It was there when he played quarterback on youth football teams. It was there every "Black History Month" in the predominantly white school he went to, where Doug Williams' winning the Super Bowl for the Washington Redskins in 1988 tore down another one of the racist stereotypes, the one that said blacks didn't have the mental capabilities to play quarterback in the NFL.

Doug Williams, who had gone to college at all-black Grambling in Louisiana, where he finished fourth in the Heisman voting in 1977, was a 6-foot-4, 220-pound quarterback. He was taken in the first round by the Tampa Bay Buccaneers and led them to three playoff appearances and one NFC title game. Then he jumped to the USFL over a salary dispute, before coming back to the NFL and the Redskins in 1986.

A year later, he would make history. He was chosen by the 'Skins to be the starter in Super Bowl XXII. Against the Broncos and John Elway, he threw for 340 yards, four touchdowns and a place in history.

Adrian Williams was born 11 months later.

Over the years, Adrian would learn the specifics about his father's career, and everywhere he went it was a moveable feast that always went with him, whether he wanted it to or not.

"A lot of kids didn't know who he was," he says, "but the teachers and coaches always knew."

Through middle school, his relationship with his father was spotty, but he always was known as "Doug Williams' kid," even if his relationship with his father didn't exactly come from a greeting card.

"I never really knew anything but me and my mom," he says.

He played football through his sophomore year in high school. After that, he concentrated on basketball, and arrived at Brown in a strange way, all but recruited by his mother. Well, not really. But it was his mother who called an assistant coach at Georgia Tech, and that coach called Yale, Cornell and Princeton and essentially told them that Adrian Williams was a good basketball player and a good student and they should check him out.

"I had heard of Harvard and Yale and Princeton," he says, "but in the South, they're really not on people's minds. But my mother got it done. She got the Ivies interested in me. She somehow did it."

He is now a junior a Brown, and has been a starter the past two years. His father has been a coach for much of his life after playing, both in high school, and at Grambling. He now lives in Tampa, where he is the player personnel director of the Buccaneers. This past summer, Adrian Williams worked there as an intern.

"I think it strengthened our relationship," he says. "My father has really made an effort the past couple of years, which I appreciate."

Adrian Williams also has come to appreciate his father's legacy in ways he never really could when he was younger, has come to understand the historic significance of it. For it was only 22 years ago, as hard as that might be to believe, just a blink of an eye when it comes to history. Twenty-two years ago, the perception persisted that African-Americans were not cerebral enough to be able to quarterback an NFL team. Doug Williams changed all that in one game in 1988, the symbolic shattering of that particular glass ceiling.

Interestingly, Adrian Williams has never seen the Super Bowl game that gave his father his slice of football immortality, even if he knows the particulars. He's also seen the Super Bowl ring his mother has. For the game, and the ramifications of it, is always there, like an unspoken family secret.

"My father never talks about it," Adrian says.

But Adrian Williams now understands what those elementary teachers back there in Atlanta were trying to tell him when he was just a kid, that he is part of an important legacy. One that is his family's, and his country's, too.

PART FOUR
2010-2019

DAVE NYBLOM

11/20/2011

"He was like a son to me."
—DAVE NYBLOM

"Shoulder-high we bring you home,
And set you at your threshold down
Townsman of a stiller town."
—FROM "TO AN ATHLETE DYING YOUNG"
BY A.E. HOUSMAN

PROVIDENCE — The body of Laurence Young lay in an open casket in front of the altar in the Christ Temple Church off Cranston Street. On his chest was a gold basketball trophy.

Somehow it was only fitting.

Basketball had taken him very far from the South Providence of his roots, a place where too many dreams never make it out of the neighborhood. It had taken him away from a difficult situation, where he had ultimately ended up living with his grandfather and aunt, caring for his grandfather who was a double amputee. It had taken him away from an environment that all too few escape, had given him a life that must have seemed unimaginable back there in 1999, when he graduated from Hope High School, just another inner-city kid with a future that seemed to stop at next week.

Basketball had taken him to Rider University in New Jersey, a place where he found himself. And then it had taken him to play professionally in Brazil, where he played for several years, until he was recently hospitalized there after dental surgery. Until he died from what is being called a "generalized infection initially caused by a dental problem."

On Friday morning, he was eulogized in a packed little church, and one of the speakers was Dave Nyblom, who coached him at Hope.

"He was like a son to me," says Nyblom. "He always knew what he had to do."

For Young was never some childhood phenom, someone anointed by the basketball gods at a young age. Nyblom remembers him as a skinny 10th grader, someone who spent much of his sophomore year playing on the JV team. He went on to be a great player at Hope, second team All-State in 1999, but ultimately the high school cheers had become just faded echoes and Young had nowhere to go.

"It looked like I was going nowhere," he once said.

But Nyblom always was Young's advocate, this white man who grew up in South Kingstown and has spent his life teaching and coaching inner-city kids, this man who says he was taught by his father to never see color.

"He always believed in me," Young once said of Nyblom. "In the summers, he used to bring me to the URI camp when Lamar Odom and Cuttino Mobley were there. He was always taking me to play against better guys, telling me I could play with them."

The following spring, he played well in a big AAU Tournament in Providence and his world changed, a scholarship offer from Rider. He was thrilled.

"I've seen a lot of guys who could play that are back home doing nothing," he would say later, "so this is like a dream come true."

So was playing professionally in Brazil. He taught himself to speak Portuguese. He had a fiancée. He had a life he never could have envisioned on the streets of South Providence.

"He actually did what he wanted to do," Bishop Phillip Ferrara told the people inside of Christ Temple Church for Young's memorial service Friday morning. "A lot of people dream about they want to do, a lot of people have dreams. Laurence actually did them. He grew up in the ghetto. He had reasons to quit. But he never did. A lot of people talk about dreams. Laurence was living his."

And maybe the best thing about it was that he knew it.

He liked to say that he learned a jump shot at the curb and it took him around the world, and who would have ever thought that?

The church was packed, people standing in the small area between the front door and the inside of the church. People kept coming up to the front of the church to talk about Young, putting a human face on the body that lay in the front of the room in a casket, a gold basketball trophy on his chest.

Nyblom had known that Young was sick in a Brazil hospital, but then came the call that Young had died.

"I started crying," he said. "I couldn't do anything else."

And when it was his turn to speak, he talked about what a good person Young had been, the emotion growing stronger in his voice with each passing sentence. In the back of the church were Nybom's wife and mother, his father having died 20 years ago when he fell off a ladder fixing one of the basketball hoops at Old Mountain Field in South Kingstown. And when he came to the end, the tears were right there with the words.

"If there were two people I could see again, it would be my father and Laurence," he said, through the tears.

Could a coach give a player any better epitaph?

Could a player have any better epitaph than to know he lived his dream, one that took him from South Providence all over the world, even if it all ended too soon?

D.J. HERNANDEZ

10/23/2011

"…without my brother I wouldn't be here today."
—Aaron Hernandez

PROVIDENCE — You come looking to find out who Aaron Hernandez is, the New England kid who is starring for the New England Patriots.

You know all the obvious things. You know that he is a tight end who catches passes like a wide receiver. You know that he has made the transition from the University of Florida to the NFL.

You know he was special, whether it was once being the high school player of the year in Connecticut, or the best tight end in college football in 2009. You know that he has a Hispanic name, which makes him relatively unique in the world of the NFL. And you now that he's one of the incredible weapons Tom Brady has in his arsenal.

But who is Aaron Hernandez, anyway?

So you come into the Brown football office one morning to talk to his older brother, D.J., who once played at UConn and is now the quarterbacks coach at Brown. You've already been to Foxboro, already have stood in the Pats' locker room waiting to talk to Hernandez. But this is the Patriots, where young players have been well trained to treat the media as just another opponent. This is the Patriots, where players are either in meetings, or going to meetings, and just about the last thing they're going to do is tell you their story.

So Aaron Hernandez doesn't tell you that he went to Bristol Central High School, doesn't tell you that he was the Gatorade player of the year in Connecticut as a senior in high school, doesn't tell you that he set a state record for receiving yards, or that he tied the state record with 71 touchdowns. He doesn't tell you that he set a state receiving record, and a national record for yards receiving per game.

Nor does he tell you that a failed drug test for marijuana at Florida no doubt dropped him to the fourth round when he obviously was a first-round talent.

But maybe he tells you something better before he changes his shirt and is off to another meeting.

"I just followed my brother's footsteps," he said. "I just tried to follow his work ethic. Because he did everything the right way. He was always successful."

He smiles.

"I probably could have followed his footsteps a little better than I sometimes did," he says, "but without my brother I wouldn't be here today."

So now you are talking to his brother, who looks much like Aaron — close-cropped hair, someone whose father is Puerto Rican and his mother is of Italian heritage. You are talking to his brother, who played quarterback and wide receiver at UConn, as his father once had played at UConn before him, the father who died at 49 years old from complications after hernia surgery.

"I was 20 when he died and my brother was 17," D.J. Hernandez said. "It was tough. It was difficult for him."

So D.J. became the surrogate father, his brother's keeper if you will, even though they once had played on the same high school team in Bristol, D. J. as a senior star, Aaron as a freshman.

"He was horrible that year," laughs D.J. "He had size 13 feet and he was always tripping over them. But you could tell he was going to be a great athlete. He was dunking a basketball in the eighth grade."

D.J. Hernandez went off to UConn, while Aaron Hernandez became a supernova of high school football stars in Connecticut, committing to UConn before his high school coach sent a game tape of him to Florida and everything changed. By the time he was a sophomore, he led the Gators in receiving yards as Florida won the national championship. The next year he was a first team All-American.

Last year, his first with the Pats, he started the season as the youngest active player on an NFL roster. In the season's 15th week, he was the rookie of the week in the NFL.

Now?

Hernandez now has teamed with fellow tight end Rob Gronkowski to give the Patriots a two-headed tight end monster. Two weeks ago, against the Jets, he had five catches. Last week, against the Cowboys, he came back from a fumble to catch the winning pass with just 22 seconds left.

That is what we all see. What we don't see is the maturation of Aaron Hernandez, whose father died when he was 17 years old, and whose brother became his both his role model and his keeper.

"I'm always honest with him," says D.J. Hernandez. "And my message? Keep working hard and make the most of your opportunities."

For D.J. knows how far his brother has come from the practice fields of Bristol, Conn., to the bright lights of Gillette Stadium. And he knows that it takes more than just talent to make it all the way to the NFL, knows that it takes hard work and perseverance, all the lessons he's tried to tell his younger brother all these years, knows that in all the important ways his brother's success is his family's success, too.

"He would have made my father proud," says D.J. Hernandez.

As he's made his older brother, too.

DAVE GAVITT

9/23/2011

"We loved him, and he loved us."
—Kevin Stacom

PROVIDENCE — They were three of the honorary pallbearers Thursday morning and they led the casket as it moved inside the stained-glass grandeur of the Cathedral of SS. Peter & Paul. And just for a minute it was 1973 all over again.

The cathedral is only about a jump shot away from what used to be known as the Civic Center, back when Dave Gavitt was the Providence College coach and his three stars were Ernie DiGregorio, Marvin Barnes and Kevin Stacom. Back there in the best college basketball season in this state's history.

"We loved him, and he loved us," Stacom said.

It was a scene that cut through both time and memory, through history and enduring affection. There also was the sense that this was the symbolic end of an era, Gavitt's death on Sept. 16 coming at a time when the Big East Conference he once founded is imploding, a victim of a changing sports landscape.

But before Gavitt created the Big East Conference, before he became one of the most influential people in all of college sports, before he was the Olympic coach and became enshrined in the Basketball Hall of Fame, he was a basketball coach. That's all he ever wanted to do after a brief sojourn in the corporate world after graduating from Dartmouth in 1959, and that winter of 1973 was his crowning coaching glory.

Even now, so many years later, that season seems like a moment frozen in time. The Civic Center had opened just a few months before, a big new downtown arena, and a new college basketball world was beginning around here. As fate would have it, the two stars were local: DiGregorio, the flashy guard from North Providence, and Marvin Barnes, the 6-foot-9 center from South Providence, two kids thrown into fame's unrelenting spotlight in the middle of incredible racial tension both in the country and in Providence.

That was Gavitt's challenge back then. That DiGregorio and Barnes have remained lifelong friends is a testament to how skilled Gavitt was in dealing with people. That DiGregorio, Barnes and Stacom were pallbearers at Gavitt's funeral Thursday morning is a testament to the bond that he created in that long ago winter.

"He molded my life," DiGregorio said, his eyes stained with tears. "He was the one who let me be Ernie D."

In a sense, Wednesday had been the day for the national basketball world to pay homage to Gavitt, as the calling hours on the East Side had been packed with basketball royalty, everyone from former Celtics' greats Larry Bird and John Havlicek to Duke coach Mike Krzyzewski, along with a slew of college coaches, past and present. The constant theme was that Gavitt had been both an adviser and a friend, someone who always provided wise counsel, someone everyone both admired and respected.

"He was like a father to me," said former Friar coach Rick Barnes, now at Texas. "From the time he came into my life I never made a major decision in my life without talking to him."

Thursday had been the funeral Mass in the cathedral on a gray, drizzly morning, almost a snapshot of old Rhode Island and an era that's fading away. And maybe nothing said that better than DiGregorio, Barnes and Stacom being pallbearers, even if it's been nearly 40 years since they played for Gavitt. If that long ago winter gave those three players their Rhode Island immortality, it also gave Gavitt the season of his coaching life.

Since then, they always have stayed close, through all the years and all the changes. They were standing on the steps of the cathedral, the service over. It had been attended by John Thompson, the former Georgetown coach, Syracuse coach Jim Boeheim and UConn's Jim Calhoun, three men who went way back with Gavitt, three men who know they benefited greatly because once upon a time Dave Gavitt put together a basketball league that changed everything.

But in so many ways, Thursday morning was about Rhode Island and the huge footprint Gavitt left here. It also was the sense that something died with him, something as elusive and hard to define as an era.

"He always was the coach of us," said Marvin Barnes, whose past addiction problems have been well-chronicled. "And he always stuck by me. He came to see me when I was down and out. He never turned his back to me. We're like family. We are a family. We have a bond."

Barnes paused a beat, looked off in the general direction of the Dunk, almost as if running all those long ago memories through his head.

"And this bond goes all the way to the end."

CORKY TAYLOR

5/29/2011

"I don't think he's ever really gotten over it..."
—Chris Taylor

PROVIDENCE — Chris Taylor was in the third grade in a Minneapolis suburb when he first heard about it.

"My dad said your dad was in a big fight," another kid said to him.

A big fight?

Well, it was more than that. What Chris Taylor, who ended his Brown basketball career nearly three months ago, couldn't have understood back then was that it was one of the seminal fights in college basketball history, a product of both race and a certain time in America, the ramifications which linger to this day.

It happened in January 1972. It was between Minnesota, which was mostly an all-black team then, and Ohio State, which was mostly white. It had been a tense, chippy game, played in Minnesota between two of the best teams in the Big Ten, when Ohio State star Luke Witte drove for the basket with 34 seconds remaining and the Buckeyes up six. He was knocked down. Minnesota player Corky Taylor helped him up, then kneed him in the groin. While on the ground, Witte was kicked and stomped by Ron Behagan, another Minnesota player. A full-scale brawl developed, complete with fans rushing the court and another Minnesota player, future baseball Hall of Famer Dave Winfield, landing a few punches to an Ohio State player's head.

When it was all over, Witte was carried off the floor, then

hospitalized for several days, including 24 hours in intensive care. Corky Taylor and Behagan were suspended for the rest of the season.

Those are the facts. But they don't really tell the story. Nor do they tell the repercussions, like ripples in a quiet pond after someone throws rocks into it, ripples that take on a life of their own.

And to begin to understand it you have to be able to understand the times, a time when the country was going through both tremendous upheaval and change: Vietnam, the counterculture, black power, feminism, the entire sizzling stew that was America in the early 1970s. Sports were not exempt, and college basketball was on the front lines. By the early 1970s, the sport was beginning to be dominated by African-American players, and maybe the most surprising thing was that it had happened so very quickly. The not-surprising thing was that it caused all sorts of tensions.

Change always comes with a price tag.

Corky Taylor was in the epicenter of all that change.

He was from Detroit, and by the time he became one of the first black players at the University of Minnesota he already had been recruited by Tennessee. "Alabama's bringing in 'Nigras,' and we want to be ready for them," the assistant coach told him. Suffice it to say Taylor wasn't overly impressed by the recruiting pitch.

Then came the fight between Minnesota and Ohio State.

"I was created as a monster in the media," Corky Taylor says. "I was called ghetto, from a bad neighborhood in Detroit, even though it had been a nice middle-class neighborhood. They thought I hated Luke because he was white and I was black, but that wasn't it. In my mind, I was retaliating from other stuff that had happened earlier. I'm not proud of what I did, but the game had gotten out of hand."

In many ways, that one incident has haunted Corky Taylor ever since, the thing that's most remembered on his basketball résumé. Not that he was drafted by the Celtics in 1973. Or that he played overseas for a few years. But for the fact he was involved in the Luke Witte incident.

"I don't think he's ever really gotten over it," says his son, Chris. "I think it really impacted him. I think that he feels he got more blame than he deserved, that he was suspended longer, even though some of his teammates had done worse things. He's never hid from it, but I think it made him more sensitive to being unfairly treated."

It's now nearly 40 years later, in many ways a different world.

You can go on YouTube and see the fight, so Corky Taylor can't run from it even if he wanted to. An unfortunate incident in his youth is forever frozen in time. But time does heal, and it's helped heal Corky Taylor, who lives in a Minneapolis suburb and works for the city regarding civil rights issues. Four years later he wrote Witte a letter, saying that he always had respected Witte as a player and was sorry for what happened. Witte called him. Since then, they've kept in touch with each other, and about a decade ago, when Witte was coming to Minneapolis, Taylor met him at the airport and Witte stayed at his house.

In a sense, it's a great American story, two old players, one white and one black, two survivors of one of the worst racial fights in college basketball history, two men who have found a common ground.

And this weekend Corky Taylor is here for his son's graduation from Brown, another great American story.

For Chris Taylor is leaving with a 3.7 grade-point average and a finance job in Chicago, not to mention symbolically carrying a family so far away from a tragic night in January of 1972.

FENWAY MEMORIES

4/11/2012

"Remember this. Because this is a great moment."
—BILL REYNOLDS, SR.

BOSTON — It is freeze-framed in my memory forever.

I was in Fenway Park with my father and brother, and we were sitting in good seats between home plate and the Sox dugout, maybe 20 or so rows up, when Ted Williams came to the plate and the everyone in the ballpark stood up to cheer.

"Remember this," my father said. "Because this is a great moment."

It was late April 1952. I had just turned 7, and my brother was a year younger. It was afternoon, the sun was shining, and everyone around me was standing and cheering and I had no idea why. I knew who Ted Williams was, because everyone knew who Ted Williams was, even at 7 years old, but I had no clue that he'd been called up to fly airplanes in the Korean War, had no clue that this afternoon would be his last game in Fenway for nearly two years. I just knew that people were standing and cheering and my father was telling me to remember it.

That was my first time in Fenway, and I remember none of it except for that moment, and the ride from Barrington to Boston in those days. There was no Route 95 then, and to get to Boston you had to go up Route 1, through Attleboro, Wrentham, through Foxboro and into Dedham and Jamaica Way, until finally you were on Brookline Avenue and there were the light towers off in the distance, like some Emerald City.

There also were trips in Little League to Fenway, annual

pilgrimages in yellow school buses with everyone singing "100 Bottles of Beer on the Wall," and sitting deep in right field. Later, there would be trips with various girlfriends, and in those days there never was any trouble getting a ticket. And then there was the home opener in 1968. I was a senior in college, but blew off a test to go to the game, only to fail the course and not graduate with my class.

And there was the night in the fall of 1970 when my father was driving us to Fenway. It was the days of the counter-culture, when the generations seemed to stare at each over a distance as great as the Continental Divide, a time when something that could start out as the most casual of conversations could easily turn into nasty arguments full of anger and regret. So we hid in sports, hid in baseball.

In baseball we could find common ground.

It was just a few years after the '67 season, a time Fenway was more crowded, as if '67 had rekindled interest, the legacy of which exists to this day. I was no longer a kid. I was out of college, had an apartment on Providence's East Side, had been to basic training in the Army, was just old enough to know that nothing ever stays the same, not even families.

We were on Route 128 when he told me that he'd just come from the doctor's office and been told he had emphysema.

"What's that?" I asked.

He was dead nine months later.

The point is that long before I became a sports writer and going to Fenway became part of my job, I had been going to Fenway all my life. In a small way it always was one of life's constants; you changed, Fenway never did. That's different now, of course. Still, with all the cosmetic differences, it's still the same place, still a place where I can close my eyes and remember all the years and so many of the times. That's the beauty of it. So I hope it never closes. For this is where the memories are, and not just baseball ones.

Wasn't it old T.S. Eliot who once wrote that we measure out lives with coffee spoons? But old T.S. Eliot never could get around on the fastball anyway, right? Around here we measure our lives in trips to Fenway Park.

At least I do.

So there's not a time when I go to Fenway when I don't think of my father, don't think of that first time I ever went to Fenway Park, back there in some lost year of my childhood, back there in 1952 when I was just 7 years old and Ted Williams came to the plate on his last day before going off to the Korean War; and my father telling me to remember this moment, because it was an important one.

And remember it I have. That, and so many others.

Even the ones that have nothing to do with baseball.

PAUL GAINES

2/26/2012

"Nobody makes it on their own.
I stood on the shoulders of giants."
—PAUL GAINES

NEWPORT — This is about a coach, and a player.

It's also about a debt.

And even though it's a story that begins way back in such a different world and a different America, in many ways it's as relevant now as it was then, one more reminder that coaches matter, sometimes more than we can ever imagine.

It's a story that begins in Newport in 1949. The player was Paul Gaines, who would grow up to become the first black mayor of Newport, the first in Rhode Island for that matter. The coach was a man named Leo Crowe, who had come to Newport from Allentown, Pa., to be both a history teacher and the high school basketball coach. He had grown up in Lafayette, Ind., in a family of 11 boys, seven of whom played sports at Notre Dame from 1923 through the '30s. Crowe won three letters in football at Notre Dame, and also played basketball and baseball there.

"In the beginning I was afraid of him," Gaines says. "He was firm and he took no nonsense. He had a scar on his face, and when he was around you knew there was no fooling around."

Gaines, the youngest of six, lived in the black section of Newport called West Broadway. There was a black community in Newport then, for there always had been a black community in Newport, one that dated back to the 1600s, but as Gaines says, "It was never a ghetto. It was a neighborhood. Everyone knew everybody. It was a real community."

But he had grown up with discrimination. One of the ways it manifested itself then was that when you went to Rogers High School, which was on Broadway at the time, in what now is Thompson Middle School, the black kids were invariably put into the vocational building which was next door. It was 15 years or so before Martin Luther King and the start of the Civic Rights era, a time when black kids in Newport were put in the vocational school and that was just the way it was.

"All the black kids went into the trades then," Gaines says.

In fact, his father didn't even want him to play sports, wanted him to shine shoes after school, because that's what his older brothers had done.

But one day Crowe came over and took Gaines and his friend Ray Wilson, who one day would coach the famed basketball legend Julius Erving in high school, out of the vocational school and put them in college courses at Rogers.

"He just said, 'I'm moving you,'" Gaines says.

That changed everything.

Thanks to that move, Gaines and Wilson would eventually attend college.

Before that, though, Crowe also had his own little sociological statement, no small thing at the time. He started four black players one year in the early '50s, even sitting down some seniors to do that.

"That was something back then," Gaines says. "There was a lot of hullabaloo about that."

But Rogers went on to win the state championship that year. It was the first of four that Crowe would win in the '50s.

Crowe also arranged for Gaines and Wilson to go to Xavier, a black school in New Orleans, as they both had been named to the All-State team. They both left Rhode Island by train, then had to change to an all-black train in Washington, one that was headed to New Orleans.

"It was my first acquaintance with Jim Crow," Gaines says. "The sign said, 'For Colored People Only' and we sat behind the sign. There was no air conditioning. There was no food. It was always hot."

Ray Wilson lasted a year at Xavier. Gaines stayed.

Gaines played four years of basketball at Xavier, then came back home to Newport and became a history teacher. He was the assistant coach on the 1963 Rogers basketball team that won the state title.

Three years later, Crowe died at 54, having given up coaching seven years earlier following a heart attack. He was buried in Newport with Gaines as one of his pall bearers.

Gaines would go on to become a dean at Bridgewater State College. He also became the mayor of Newport, after having been on the City Council for four years. He served one term, a time when the city was in the international spotlight as host of the America's Cup. He came to believe that having a black mayor then was great for the city, a symbolic signal that Newport was a real place, not just sailing races and parties on Bellevue Avenue.

He is nearly 80 now, and he knows that none of his amazing life would have happened if Leo Crowe hadn't once walked into the vocational school at Rogers and taken him and Wilson out of it. Not the college. Not the teaching. Not being the first black mayor in Rhode Island. Not being a role model for generations of kids who have come behind him. None of it.

"Nobody makes it on their own," says Paul Gaines. "I stood on the shoulders of giants."

For he knows how far he's come from the Newport of his childhood, a time when a black kid from West Broadway was never supposed to go off to college and be a teacher and one day be a mayor, a time when all of that was as far away as some distant star in the nighttime sky.And he's come to know that it's all about passing things down, all about taking from someone and giving it to someone else, whether it's a hope, a dream, inspiration, or just an opportunity. All about what a coach named Leo Crowe once did for him.

CLEM LABINE

05/23/2013

*"One time Jackie wasn't allowed in a hotel
and he went out to sleep in the bus in the parking lot
so Clem went with him and they both went up
and slept in the luggage rack."*
—Barbara Levine

CUMBERLAND, R.I. — The picture dominates the room.

In a room full of pictures and memorabilia, a room full of base-ball history, this picture is also a statement. Of a certain time. Of a certain place in a country's psyche. And of the possibility of a better America.

It is a picture of two Brooklyn Dodgers baseball players embrac-ing in a locker room after a World Series win in October 1956, big smiles on their faces, one of the players white, the other black. Clem Labine and Jackie Robinson. And maybe most of all, it's a picture that speaks to both the promise of sports, and of America, too.

It's a theme that runs through the hit movie "42," the one about Robinson's first year with the Dodgers in 1946 and the overt racism he encountered as the man who broke baseball's color barrier. One of the most dramatic scenes is when popular shortstop Pee Wee Reese, a Southerner, walks over to Robinson in a game in Cincin-nati and puts his arm around him, an iconic moment.

Labine was not on the Dodgers in '47. It would be four years later before he made the Dodgers, the Woonsocket kid whose father had been a weaver in one of the city's old mills. But from the beginning, he spent time with Robinson at a time when racism was a much bigger opponent to Robinson than the opposing pitcher.

"They were very friendly," says Barbara Labine.

She is Labine's widow, and she lives in a condo off Mendon Road. She married Labine in 1981, after he was widowed, having met him at Kirkbrae Country Club in Lincoln. She had no idea who he was, didn't know anything about baseball, had no idea that he once had a big slice of Rhode Island sports immortality, the Woonsocket kid who had pitched in the World Series.

She is sitting upstairs in what she calls "Clem's room," where his career still lives on the walls.

There he is on a Sports Illustrated cover. There he is in innumerable pictures and plaques and magazine stories, as if his entire career is on the walls. There are three cartoons by Frank Lanning, the former Providence Journal sports cartoonist. There is a picture of the Dodgers' dugout. There is a picture of the Dodgers, all in shirts and ties, remnants of a different era. But there is no more dramatic picture of the one of him and Robinson embracing, big smiles on their faces.

"Clem was color-blind," she says.

He had been a paratrooper in World War II, had already traveled very far from the Woonsocket of his childhood. He also was one of the keys for the Dodgers of the 1950s, an integral part of their first world title in 1955, the guy out of the bullpen who put the punctuation mark on some of their biggest wins. When he retired in 1962, he was fourth in major-league history in saves.

But that was just the baseball. What he did for Robinson was more than just being able to get batters out in the late innings. The Dodgers often traveled by bus in those days, but it was the 1950s, and in so many ways, race was the serpent in America's Garden of Eden, especially during spring training in the South.

"One time Jackie wasn't allowed in a hotel and he went out to sleep in the bus in the parking lot," she says, "so Clem went with him and they both went up and slept in the luggage rack."

But it wasn't just Labine's sense of fairness and decency that linked him to Robinson.

"Clem was always a voracious reader and Jackie was very intelligent. He had been to UCLA; he read books," says Barbara Labine. "They were more than just teammates. They got along very well."

Not that this was always the norm. One of the themes that runs through "42" as forcefully as a fastball to the head is how difficult it was for Robinson in his own clubhouse. Racism was as omnipresent as spikes, and there were many teammates who were always treating him like a pariah, some outlier who had sneaked into their clubhouse. That attitude was still there in the 1950s, to the point that many of his teammates would shun him.

"That always bothered Clem," she says. "He could never understand it."

Throughout his career, Robinson was always getting death threats, to the point that one time reserve outfielder Gene Hermanski quipped, "Hey, Jackie. Why don't we all wear number 42 so they won't know where to shoot?"

In his later years, Labine and Barbara would often attend the Dodgers Fantasy Camp in Vero Beach, Fla., where she says he would put on the Dodgers' uniform and immediately get 10 years younger and two inches taller. Why not? He was the kid from Woonsocket who went all the way to the World Series, and who could have ever dreamed that up? He and Barbara were married for 26 years, until he died six years ago at 80, a boy of summer right to the end.

"Clem was a great baseball player," says Barbara Labine, "but he was an even better person."

The picture on the wall of him and Jackie Robinson embracing tells us that.

JALEN ROSE

11/6/2014

*"I used to have a negative feel about him
and now I don't."*
—JALEN ROSE

PROVIDENCE — He never knew his father. But Jalen Rose, who never met former Friar great Jimmy Walker, got to retrace his roots on the Providence College campus last month.

"I literally have goosebumps," Rose said.

Rose, the former member of the "Fab Five" at the University of Michigan and NBA star who now is an analyst for ABC and ESPN, was part of the symbolic start of this new Friar season that kicked off with "Late Night Madness" in Alumni Hall. Somehow that's only fitting. For Alumni Hall once was his father's own field of dreams, back there in the mid-1960s when Walker was as good as any player in the country.

But it was more than that, too.

To see Jimmy Walker was to have a sneak preview of the game's future. 1 remember seeing it looking into Alumni Hall in late November, way back in 1963.

"You have to see this new kid Walker," a former high school teammate, who was going to PC, told me.

"Why's that?" I asked.

"Because he does things you've never seen before," he said.

Yeah right, I thought. Then he got the ball and dribbled through his legs, something I had never seen before. Then he spun almost full circle, all the while keeping the ball in the same hand. Two things

I had never before seen, and I had seen a lot of basketball. So that's what I told Jalen Rose on the after hearing he was coming to Providence College and this small college gym that houses so many old ghosts that are all a part of who Rose is, whether he knows it or not.

So why now? Why did Rose agree to come see his father's school, this man he never knew, this man whose name always has hovered over Rose, whether he wanted it to or not?

"It's called maturity," Rose said.

And the circle of life, too.

One is the fact that Mike Jackson, one of Rose's old high school teammates, is an assistant with the Friars. Another is that he was once teammates on the Indiana Pacers with former Friar star Austin Croshere, who kept telling him he should see PC, see something that was a part of his history, whether he wanted to admit it or not. Still another is that Doris Burke, the former PC women's great who is an NBA sideline reporter, essentially kept telling him the same thing.

Still, he had to come to grips with the idea that he had never seen his father, never mind having any kind of relationship with him.

"I made a vow when I was just a kid that one of the main things I wanted to accomplish in my life was that one day he'd know my name," said Rose.

He was named after him — "Jalen" comprising the first two letters of his father's name (James), and three letters of his uncle's name. But his childhood seems like something out a Dickens novel, something far away from the fame and riches of the NBA.

"We had no electricity, no hot water, no heat," he once said in a magazine article, as his mother struggled to raise four kids as a single parent. "We'd wake up in the morning to wash with water heated on a hot plate. And we'd go to bed every night wearing skull caps, sweat shirts, and gloves."

But from the time he became part of the "Fab Five" at the University of Michigan in the early 1990s he was known in the basketball world as "Jimmy Walker's kid." As if his father had become some ghost who hovered over his life, even if his mother rarely spoke about him. I remember approaching Rose in the Michigan locker room in the Superdome at the 1993 Final Four. I said how I used to know his father, at least peripherally, had played against him several times. But it was apparent that day he had no interest in that, not then.

Their story was written about shortly afterward in Mitch Albom's 1993 book "The Fab Five."

"I didn't handle the situation well," Walker says in the book. "I remember Jeanne [Rose's mother] being angry."

In 2007 Rose went to Walker's funeral service. According to ESPN The Magazine, "He remained seated, his head partially bowed, his emotions visibly scrambled."

Later, he said that father and son had arranged to meet for the first time, but then Walker died of lung cancer, and Rose said, "I was hurt, saddened, and selfishly disappointed that we never had a chance to meet."

That was seven years ago.

In October, Rose was on the PC campus for the first time. He toured the campus. He walked down the hallway in Alumni Hall, where the pictures of the storied past stare out. One is of his father holding a trophy over his head in Madison Square Garden, back when his future was all ahead of him. Rose also addressed this year's Friars. He was the headliner of "Late Night Madness," the symbolic start of this new college basketball season.

"I'm glad I was able to make peace with my father," said Jalen Rose. "I used to have a negative feel about him and now I don't."

And he did it all in the same gym his father once turned into a personal shrine, the one where the echoes of all those past cheers still float around if you only listen hard enough, back when looking at Jimmy Walker was like looking at the game's future.

JEFFREY OSBORNE

8/11/2014

"…it's nice to come back to my hometown
and give something back."
—Jeffrey Osbourne

PAWTUCKET — This is a story about family. And about dreams, the ones that get passed down through the generations. It's also an American story, one that speaks to this country's great promise.

And it's a great Rhode Island story, no doubt about that, one that began almost a hundred years ago with a father who had his own musical dream, but had to wait to see his youngest son make it come true.

And it was all there on Sunday afternoon at McCoy Stadium.

The event was called the Jeffrey Osborne Celebrity Classic, and it was a softball game with a laundry list of celebrities, everyone from Magic Johnson to Pat Riley, from Kareem Abdul-Jabbar to Smokey Robinson, and more stars and celebrities from both sports and the world of music. It was part of a three-day event, one that switches to a golf tournament at Carnegie Abbey in Portsmouth the next two days, with all the proceeds going to local charities.

And what are all these celebrities doing here in Rhode Island for three days? That's the end of this story, one that began decades ago with a man named Clarence Osborne, whom everyone called "Legs." He was a musician, and he married his high school sweetheart from Pawtucket. He spent his nights playing in local bars and clubs, his dream out there in the future somewhere, maybe something only he could see.

Along the way, Clarence Osborne played with some of the great-est names in jazz. There were opportunities to leave his family and go out on the road with them, but he never did, the road not taken.

Jeffrey was the last of 12 kids. He grew up on Providence's East Side, in apartments that always were too small and where there never really was enough money. He grew up where music always was the soundtrack to his family's life, to the point that as a kid he often used to fall asleep outside his father's door, listening to him play.

At 13 years old, Jeffrey Osborne was playing in a club in New London, Conn., and after that he played the drums in some local groups. One night in 1969, he was playing in his family's small South Providence lounge when members of a Los Angeles group named Love Man Ltd. were playing. They were in town to play in a place called Mr. B's Joyland and they invited him to sit in on a couple of songs. As the story goes, their drummer got arrested on the street outside the club for smoking pot and Osborne had to sit in. When the night was over, the group invited him to go back to L.A. with them.

"Your father never went after his dream," his mother told him. "I want you to go after yours."

He was 20 years old, just a couple of years out of Hope High School. Thirteen years later he was Billboard magazine's top new male black vocalist, appearing on several national television shows. The next year he had a hit record. It was called "On the Wings of Love," and it was a great one. He also was singing the National Anthem at many of the Lakers' games at The Forum in Los Angeles.

"I began doing the anthem in L.A. in Magic's rookie season in 1979," he said, "and it seemed like every time I sang it the Lakers won," he said. "Then I sang at Magic's birthday party one year and that's where our relationship started."

Then Pat Riley began playing Osborne's songs at his practices. In short, it's been an amazing ride for Jeffrey Osborne, and maybe making it all the more meaningful is his understanding that his success has been his family's success, too. It takes a village? Sometimes it takes only a family. And a dream that got passed down through the generations.

Funds from his tournament go to a variety of things, one of which is the Clarence J. (Clay) Osborne FF

Foundation, which funds music scholarships for kids. Clay Osborne was a well-known Rhode Island musician who died in 2006 at 78, the oldest of the Osborne siblings. And, in many ways, this is his memorial to Osborne's late mother, Wanita.

"I watched her give back for her whole life," Jeffrey said. "Now it's nice to come back to my hometown and give something back."

Sunday night was the latest example, a celebrity softball game at McCoy Stadium. Or at least the preparation for it, as it was now 5 p.m., an hour before the game was supposed to start. There was Magic. There was Kareem. There was James Worthy. There were former Patriots. There was former Olympic star Michelle Kwan. There were the rumors that Riley, Doc Rivers, Smokey Robinson, and other celebs were on their way.

The field was mobbed by the media, and fans were beginning to fill up the stadium in the late afternoon sunshine, a sort of symbolic three-day homecoming for a Rhode Island kid who long ago made it big in L.A. but has never forgotten his roots.

"When he made it big, we all made it big," his brother, Terrell, said. "It was our vindication."

Vindication for his late father, who stayed at home when his dream went out on the road without him. Vindication. And the public capturing of a dream that a family had been chasing for generations.

DAN HURLEY

2/27/2015

"I wouldn't be involved with basketball without Coach B."
—DAN HURLEY

SOUTH KINGSTOWN — He quit the Seton Hall basketball team two games into his junior year.

It was December 1993.

"I was done," he said. "I was defeated."

He paused a beat.

"It was brutal," he continued.

He paused another beat.

"I hated basketball," he said.

Dan Hurley was sitting in the empty Ryan Center on the University of Rhode Island campus on a cold Tuesday afternoon. It was the day before his URI basketball team was scheduled to play Davidson in another crucial Atlantic 10 game in a season that has made Hurley one of the hottest young coaches in the country.

But he was not talking about that.

He was talking about a pivotal time in his young life, back when he was known as Danny and was coming of age in the basketball hothouse that was the Hurleys of Jersey City. Complete with the father, arguably the most celebrated high-school coach in the country, and his older brother, Bobby, the Duke All-American who was one of the glamorous college players of his era. He had talked about it recently in USA Today, but now he was talking about it in the Ryan Center.

"I was chasing ghosts," Dan Hurley said.

He also was all but wearing the pressure. To watch him play those first two years at Seton Hall was to watch a player who always seemed to be in some sort of psychic agony. The pained expressions. The bad body language. The frustration he always seemed to be carrying with him, right there on his skinny shoulders. To see him play then was to want to throw him a life raft.

"I had come to hate the game," he said.

This game that defined his family. This game he had grown up with. This game he had chased all his life. This game that obsessed him. Now, in the middle of his college career at Seton Hall, in the virtual shadow of his high school fame, it all had unraveled. To make it worse, his brother had just been in a very serious automobile accident in California, during his rookie season with the Sacramento Kings.

To Danny Hurley, it was as though his world had collapsed around him.

"I didn't want to even watch basketball," he said. "I had lost the game."

Enter George Blaney.

The same George Blaney who once was the longtime coach at Holy Cross, and whose son Brian is now an assistant coach at Providence College. George Blaney became the Seton Hall coach in 1994. One of the players he inherited was Hurley.

"Coach B saw a damaged young man," Hurley said.

He paused.

"I wouldn't be involved with basketball without Coach B."

This was said quietly, but the emotion was there, no question about, as if Hurley knows the debt he owes Blaney.

So began Hurley's rehabilitation. Both to restore his broken psyche, and his game, too. He was one of Seton Hall's leading scorers for the next two years, and afterward he had some opportunities to play in Europe. Instead, he got into coaching, first as an assistant for his father, then at Rutgers, then at St. Benedict's in New Jersey, a parochial school he quickly turned into a state power. That was the public statement that Danny Hurley had found a second act in basketball.

Now he's here, of course, where he has brought the crowds back to the Ryan Center, no insignificant thing in just his third year. It was supposed to take longer. Especially after he lost both Billy Baron and Jonathan Holton shortly after taking the job in 2012, not too long after the news conference announcing his hiring.

If nothing else, that shows Hurley's impact. This was supposed to be just another year of the Rams taking small, incremental steps, another year in the rebuilding process. Not this year that's seemingly come out of nowhere, full of young players who have been better more quickly than they were supposed to be.

The end result?

The short version is that Hurley's now one of the hottest young coaches in the country, delivering on all the promise of that introductory news conference nearly three years ago.

The longer, more important, version?

Dan Hurley has found a great second act in basketball, one that must have seemed as far away as a childhood dream back there in his third year at Seton Hall, back when the love was all gone and the game had become his own little prison. Back there when he had to walk away before he could walk back. Back when he had to find the love again.

Back before Dan Hurley found his own identity in this family game. A journey where this dream season is just the frosting.

POSTSCRIPT: After six years as head coach of the URI's men's basketball team, Hurley left for UConn, where he has been head coach of the Huskies since March, 2018. That same year, he received the A-10 Coach of the Year award.

BRUCE JENNER

4/28/2015

"Yes, for all intents and purposes, I am a woman."
—Caitlyn Jenner

PROVIDENCE — Maybe you have to be old enough to remember the 1976 Olympics, the one in Montreal. Maybe you have to remember when he was on the box of Wheaties, the ultimate symbol at the time of an American hero. Maybe you have to remember when he was the All-American boy, with his chiseled body and his longish hair.

Maybe you have to be old enough to remember when Bruce Jenner was this country's biggest sports hero.

But all that was long ago and far away.

It's a funny thing about Olympic heroes. They very seldom have a second act. At least Jenner never seemed to. Then again, what are you supposed to do after winning the decathlon in the Olympics? What are you supposed to do when you are 25 years old and you're being called the best athlete in the world, a national hero?

That's what Jenner was, no question about it. He visited President Gerald Ford in the White House. Sometimes it seemed as if he always was on a national celebrity tour. Or as Tony Kornheiser, then writing in the New York Times, said, "Jenner is twirling the nation like a baton, he and wife, Chrystie, are so high up on the pedestal of American heroism, it would take a crane to take them down."

But came down he did, for isn't that what fame so often is, the flame that burns out, a candle in the wind?

Yes, there was some acting. Yes, there were some TV commercials. Yes, there was a stint as a race-car driver. Yes, he lent his name for a while to a fleet of fitness centers.

But it's a funny thing about fame. Someone is always coming from behind you, pushing you further and further into the past tense, until in so many ways Jenner became a name that belonged to the past. To the point that in 2007, when he showed up on the television reality show "Keeping Up With the Kardashians," odds are that few in the audience knew who Kris Kardashian's husband once had been.

Back when I occasionally would stumble on the show, Jenner seemed like some guy on the periphery, floating in and out like some overgrown house boy. For a while he would occasionally be seen carrying a toy airplane, his hair longer, seemingly oblivious to the show's storyline, as loose and unstructured as that always seemed to be.

This was a former Olympic hero?

This was someone who once had been on a Wheaties box?

Then, one time on the TV show, he and Rob Kardashian, Kris Kardashian's son, were at a driving range, and Jenner was essentially telling the young Kardashian that he had to start to get his life together.

"What were you doing when you were my age?" Kardashian asked petulantly.

"Winning gold medals at the Olympics," Jenner shot back.

It was a vintage moment on "Keeping Up With the Kardashians," this TV show that take us inside this family that has become famous for being famous, arguably a peek inside celebrity's cheap heart. The irony was that Jenner always was the one with the real celebrity, one that was based on real accomplishments, the only one that wasn't famous for being famous.

Is it any wonder he seemed to become more and more marginalized on the TV show?

But now Jenner is back in the national spotlight, 39 years after that Olympic year. On Friday night he told Diane Sawyer on ABC that the rumors that have been all over the supermarket tabloids are indeed true: Bruce Jenner is in the process of becoming a woman.

In retrospect, there had been signs on the TV show: his longer hair, his increasingly feminized features, the tabloid rumors compete with a tabloid picture of him in a black and white striped dress. But Friday night was different. Friday night was national television. Friday night was the game-changer.

"Yes, for all intents and purposes, I am a woman," the 65-year-old Jenner said.

He said he's been a cross-dresser for years, and that he already had told the people closest to him before he went on television what he was going to say. If nothing else, it was a remarkable TV moment, one that took great courage, arguably more courage than he ever took in his athletic life.

This was a former Olympic hero saying he's had gender identity issues throughout his life, this former Olympic hero who has been married three times and has fathered six children. This was a former Olympic hero, who said that he's not gay, has never been with a man sexually, but has known for a long time that he's a woman in a man's body. This was a former Olympic hero who now has become a hero to transgender people everywhere, a man who had the courage to go on national television, look right into the camera, and say, "I am a woman."

Who knows where it leads? Who knows what the backlash is going to be? Who knows how the world will now look at Bruce Jenner, this person who once was as big a sports celebrity as there was in this country, someone who looked into the camera on national television last Friday night and spoke from the heart.

Good for her.

POSTSCRIPT: *Bruce Jenner changed his name to Caitlyn Marie Jenner after coming out as a trans woman in 2015. She starred in a reality TV show "I am Cait" about her transition. She is a registered Republican who ran unsuccessfully for governor of California in 2017, and has published a memoir entitled,* The Secrets of My Secret Life.

JERRY TARKANIAN

2/13/2015

*"You weren't getting any money from Coach Tark…
You were getting a second chance."*
—CHRIS HERREN

PROVIDENCE — I had two brief encounters with Jerry Tarkanian, the controversial Hall of Fame college basketball coach who died Wednesday in Las Vegas at 84.

The first was at the Marriott Marquis in New York City during the Big East Tournament in the late '90s. Someone had told him that I was the one who had written the book on Chris Herren's high school team. Herren was playing for him at Fresno State at the time.

"I love Chris," Tarkanian said in that soft raspy voice of his, looking at me with sad eyes that had seen so many things, both the good and the bad, in his long career.

"I love him, too," I said back.

He smiled and turned to walk away.

Then he turned back to me.

"He's crazy you know," he said in that soft voice.

"I know," I said.

He smiled again and walked away.

The second time was inside Madison Square Garden in March 1998. Fresno was in the N.I.T., and it was a couple of hours before the game was to begin. The team was on the court shooting around, and by chance I was in the second row right behind Tarkanian.

Then Mike Wallace walked in.

A week or two before he had profiled Tarkanian and Fresno State on "60 Minutes," a less than flattering look at a program in turmoil, full of campus incidents and drug suspensions and the growing theory that Tarkanian was coaching a circus disguised as a basketball team. That was the perception, anyway, his great UNLV teams with less success and more drama.

Wallace, in a dark suit, and his very recognizable face, sat down next to Tarkanian.

He began to talk to Tarkanian, part rationale for the story, part mea culpa.

"You [expletive deleted] me," Tarkanian said softly, staring straight ahead.

"Jerry," said Wallace, visibly upset, before trying to defend himself.

"You [expletive deleted] me," Tarkanian again, never looking at him.

Wallace got up and began to walk toward Herren, who turned away.

"Ah, Chris," Wallace said.

Herren had been another in Tarkanian's long list of reclamation projects after he had been thrown out of Boston College for too many failed drug tests in the spring of 2005. At the time, back in Fall River in his public shame, he had no idea what he was going to do. No matter that he didn't even know Tarkanian was still coaching, or didn't know where Fresno was. He knew who Tarkanian was, no doubt about that.

"I knew he was called 'Tark the Shark,'" he writes in his 2011 memoir "Basketball Junkie." "I knew some of his guys [at UNLV] had been caught in a hot tub with a gambler. I knew he was the guy always chewing the white towel, the guy who coached the "Runnin' Rebels," the guy who had been in the basketball movie "Blue Chips." I know he was the star of Gucci Row in Vegas, the unofficial name of all the money guys with the gold chains who sat courtside."

Tarkanian, who had won a national title at UNLV in 1990, said he was starting over.

To Herren, Tarkanian was a cross between the greatest salesman in the world and your grandfather.

"He had a shaved head and big hangdog eyes and this incredibly kind face, and he looked at you like he had seen it all and nothing was going to surprise him. It was very comforting. In all the time I was there, I never felt like a product. Tark was the best of the best. We had a different relationship. We were together a lot, and he always made me feel like I was his kid…Coach Tark was amazing. Here he was in his seventies and he was still getting after it. He was us in an old man's body. That was his gift."

Tarkanian forever seemed to be fighting the NCAA, forever seemed to be branded as the little guy with the shaved head, who always was trying to fast-break around NCAA rules. But it was his ability to relate to players as the decades changed that arguably was his greatest strength.

"He always adapted," Herren said Wednesday, minutes after he had learned Tarkanian had died. "You never got the sense that he was behind."

One day in Herren's first summer in Fresno he walked in Tarkanian's office and said he was 3,000 miles away from home, he was homesick, and he had no money.

"Chris, you have no money?" Tarkanian asked.

Then he put his hand in his pocket, took out seven rumpled dollars, and handed them over to Herren.

"Here, Chris, have some money," he said.

"You weren't getting any money from Coach Tark," Herren writes in "Basketball Junkie." "You were getting a second chance."

In many ways, that was at the heart of Tarkanian's reputation. He gave players second chances, only to see some of those decisions come back to haunt him. But he never changed, this man who always seemed to be fighting the NCAA, Tark against the world. This man who always seemed like some great fictional character.

"He was called 'Tark the Shark' for a reason," said Herren on Wednesday. "He was never a goldfish."

Mike Wallace would have confirmed that.

CHRIS BURNS

10/9/2015

"At this time in my life there is no holding back."
—CHRIS BURNS

SMITHFIELD — Thursday was the day that changed his life.

It was the day that Chris Burns, a onetime Bryant University basketball star who is now an assistant coach at the school, publicly said he was gay. The story was the centerpiece of the USA Today sports section, making Burns one of the biggest sports story in the country that day. And now, in the lobby of the Chase Athletic Center on the Bryant campus on a sun-splashed afternoon, Burns was talking about the long personal journey that led him to this day.

"I have a lot of different emotions," he said. "And it really doesn't feel like just a story."

He paused a beat.

"It's my life."

He knew he was gay when he was 14, but he didn't have a real identity at the time, to the point that he never said he was gay, never mind thinking of himself as a gay man. His life revolved around the game, and eventually becoming a high school basketball star in the small New Hampshire town of Merrimack.

"That was my identity back then," he said. "That was my story. All I cared about was playing basketball and being in the gym."

He went to Providence College for a year, where he was a non-scholarship player on the basketball team, before transferring to Bryant where he became a star, leading the Bulldogs to the Division II national championship in 2005. He is now 31. On this afternoon he is wearing a black T-shirt that says "Bryant Basketball" in big white letters, and he still looks young enough to be a player instead of a coach. About a year ago, he told his family. First, he told his brother, who hugged him. Then he finally got the courage to tell his mother.

"What?" she said. "You think I don't love you?"

He also told head coach Tim O'Shea about a year ago, and in the past few weeks, he told another assistant coach and a few other people at Bryant. Then he told the three Bryant captains. Then he told the rest of the team. And Thursday morning it was the lead story of the sports section in USA Today — Chris Burns out of the closet in the most public of ways.

But he hadn't told too many people in the game. And maybe that was just because he didn't feel comfortable, and maybe that was because he knows how macho sports can be, one of the last bastions of another time, at least on the surface. And there were times he thought that this was the day he was going to tell them, but he never did. But more and more, he came to dislike living in two very different worlds.

Until Chris Burns, according to USA Today, became the first openly gay assistant or head coach among the roughly 3,000 coaches in Division I men's and women's basketball. Until Chris Burns took the secret that he's been keeping for much of his life and told the world about it.

So why now?

"You just know," Burns said. "At this time in my life there is no holding back. That's gone. You know when the time is right."

And for him that's now, thanks in part to the support he has received. Famed Duke coach Mike Krzyzewski, who told USA Today about Burns, said "one act of courage produces another." And there's the support he's got from key staff people at Bryant. The support he's gotten from the Bryant players.

Or as Curtis Oakley, nephew of former NBA star Charles

Oakley, said, "…You feel like you can go to him for anything. Because he talked to us. He trusted us with his secret. He thought of us as family."

Family indeed.

An assistant college basketball coach took his secret and sent it out into the world, freeing himself in the process.

"I've waited 31 years for this moment," said Chris Burns.

Courage comes in many forms.

QUENTON MARROW

9/15/2015

"It was at night, and suddenly there was a big bang and my ear went deaf. I fell down..."
—QUENTON MARROW

PROVIDENCE — This city's ongoing gun violence now has a human face.

At least for me.

His name is Quenton Marrow, and he was one of the kids on the 2013 Hope High School basketball team I shadowed for a book scheduled to come out in January. He was shot three times the other night in what appears to be a random act of violence, shot while playing a video game in a second floor apartment, the bullets coming through the ceiling from the apartment above.

The year I knew him he was a kid who always seemed to have a big smile on his face, and always wore glasses with big black frames. He was a junior that year, and didn't get a lot of playing time. But after the first league game of the season, a loss at Hendricken when Hope had been flat out awful, Hope coach Dave Nyblom had addressed the team in the locker room, the smell of defeat hanging in the air.

"You didn't play one minute tonight," he said pointing at Marrow, as the team sat slumped in front of him. "But you were cheering on your teammates all night long. You were always enthusiastic and engaged. You were in every huddle, getting guys pumped up. You were tremendous."

Yes, he was.

From the way he always was first in the after-practice runs in Hope's old second floor gym, to his infectious energy, he always was one of the team's unsung heroes.

A couple of weeks later the Hope team was on a bus to play a team from Charlestown, Massachusetts, a school in the shadow of the Bunker Hill Monument, one of Hope's few games outside of the Rhode Island Interscholastic League that year. By chance, I sat next to Marrow on the ride from Providence.

It was already apparent that there was something a little different about Marrow. He always dressed well. He always was open, friendly in ways some of the other kids were not. He also seemed more grounded than many of the other kids, in that he had no desire to be a professional athlete, the stereotypical fantasy of so many inner-city kids.

"I want to be an electrician," he said, as the bus went up Route 95.

He lived in South Providence, which meant that he had to walk to the East Side and Hope every day because he lived just a little too close to qualify for free bus passes, and couldn't afford to buy one. For his father lived in Boston, and his mother recently had lost her job.

The bus went through Boston that day in the winter sunshine, and passed the Boston Garden, where the Celtics and Bruins play.

"Have you ever been to the Garden?" I asked.

"No," he said.

Off in the distance, on the other side of the Charles River, was Harvard, visible in all its splendor.

"What's the most prestigious college in the country?" I asked Marrow.

"Harvard?" he asked, the question in his voice.

"Do you know where it is?"

"Not really," he said.

"It's right there," I said, pointing out the window.

"Really," said Quenton Marrow, a big smile on his face.

But now he was on the phone talking about having been shot.

"There were five of us and we were watching TV on the first floor, with about 10 more out in the backyard," he said. "It was at night, and suddenly there was a big bang and my ear went deaf. I fell down in the kitchen."

The shots had come from the second floor, but he didn't know who lived there. There was blood and there was fear, and maybe most of all, there was a sense of unreality about it, as if suddenly he was in the middle of some violent video game. One bullet pierced his lung and just missed his liver. It is still lodged in his body. The second bullet cut his forearm. The third went through his right shoulder and came out his back. He was in Rhode Island Hospital for four days.

And now?

His right hand is still numb, and he has a bullet still in his body.

That's the physical part. The psychological part? Well, that may take a little longer.

For all this was happening in his own neighborhood, the place he grew up in, the place that is home. He says he's never been in a gang, never had a beef with anyone. He just graduated from a one-year course at a technical school in Norwood, Massachusetts. He still wants to one day be an electrician. He still has his dreams.

But now?

It's as if the bullets took more than their little pound of flesh. They also took a part of Quenton Marrow's innocence, too.

One more of the human faces in this city's ongoing gun violence.

JACK NICKLAUS

3/10/2016

"I wish you well and I hope you get healthy, hope you get to play, hope you get out there as soon as you feel like you can play and I hope you play well."
—JACK NICKLAUS

PROVIDENCE — It was a small story in the New York Post the other day, one that quickly went out on the wire.

It's a story about Jack Nicklaus and Tiger Woods, and it should be read by anyone who either plays sports or follows them, for that matter. It was datelined Palm Beach Gardens, Fla., where Nicklaus saw Tiger for the first time in a long time. The setting was Nicklaus' home, where he had invited a group of prospective Ryder Cup players and captains for dinner.

One was Tiger, the same Tiger Woods who has won 14 majors and has made no secret of his desire to break Nicklaus' all-time record of 18 major golf championships. And Nicklaus' message?

"You know you and I have talked about it and nobody wants their records broken," Nicklaus told Woods. "But I don't want you not to have the ability to have that opportunity to do so by your health. So I wish you well and I hope you get healthy, hope you get to play, hope you get out there as soon as you feel like you can play and I hope you play well."

Read those last two sentences again. Because they fly in the face of what so much of contemporary sports culture has morphed into in this age of win at all costs, winning as everything. Maybe it's always been there, one part of the American ethos, maybe best described in the old Vince Lombardi line, "Winning isn't everything, it's the only thing." It's certainly the theme that runs through sports like a river going downhill. From youth sports, to high school sports, to college sports, to the pros: if you don't win enough games odds are you're not going to have your job all that long. It's all the same.

The lessons that can be learned through sports? Lifelong lessons that transcend the final score? What we, as a society, like to think sports are really about? Yeah, that's all fine and dandy, but did you WIN?

This always has been the battle within youth sports, one that's played out in every city and town in the country, the subtext behind so many of the good intentions. In a sense it's always the elephant in the middle of the field, the one that nobody ever really wants to deal with, never mind admit it's actually there.

And if that's the case in youth sports, what do you think the reality is in professional sports, a business as cold as a loan shark's heart? It's about winning, and if you win enough of the tournaments that truly matter, it becomes where you are on the game's all-time leaderboard. That's what gets some guys remembered forever, and the rest just seem to slip further away as the years go by, names receding more and more into the past tense.

But Nicklaus was telling Woods that he didn't really want to be golf's all-time winner if it came with some unwritten asterisk, the fact that Tiger Woods' quest to surpass him has been hindered by his back injuries.

Would anyone else have said it?

Who knows? What matters is Jack Nicklaus said it. For this is Nicklaus' athletic immortality we're talking about here, no insignificant thing when you're Jack Nicklaus and everyone who follows golf knows that Nicklaus has won the most majors, and fewer know who is second and who is third. So he certainly could have simply held his party and that would have been it. Tiger would have gone his own way. Nicklaus would have gone his own way. Life would have gone on.

Isn't that the way it usually is in sports, each superstar spinning in their own orbit, often oblivious to what is swirling around them?

But Nicklaus was sensitive to what Woods has been going through, as if it takes one of the game's all-time greats to understand what another all-time great is going through. The doubt. The uncertainty. The fear his body is betraying him, as if he somehow has betrayed the golfing gods, and this is some kind of karmic payback.

That is what is so admirable about Nicklaus' statement to Woods. Because he didn't have to do it. He easily could have said nothing, and no one would have thought any less of him for doing so. He could have said nothing, and the golf world would have gone on, and no doubt the party at his house would have gone on, too. There's also no doubt that Woods didn't expect him to say it. How could he have expected that?

It wasn't Nicklaus' finest moment in golf, that's for sure. His career tells us that. But it was a wonderful moment, nonetheless.

RHODE ISLAND COUNTRY CLUB

7/2/2017

"Who said things don't get better?"
—BILL REYNOLDS

BARRINGTON — Once upon a time, back when I was a kid in the late 1950s and early '60s, I used to caddy at Rhode Island Country Club on Nayatt Road, a beautiful old course full of history and tradition whose last four holes stare out at Narragansett Bay.

The overwhelming majority of the kids who caddied then were of Italian heritage, living in the Maple Avenue and Middle Highway section of town, the working class area of Barrington then that never made the real estate brochures. It was the area that didn't live up to the town's perception throughout the state as the place where all the rich people lived, even if it were always more complicated than that, and even if the people of Italian heritage had built the town.

The caddies would sit under a big tree that stared out over the first fairway. About 50 yards to the left was a pool area with a snack bar. They weren't allowed to go there, even if I could, as a member's son. They were treated as second-class citizens, and I hated it, for many of them were my friends.

It was a different era, of course.

How different? Every September the club's member-guest tournament was held and on Thursday and Friday the Italian kids were excused from school to caddy in the tournament, because many of their families needed the money. That's how different.

But as the years went by, I began to realize the huge debt I owed to that particular time and place. How it gave me a certain social conscience, even if I had no clue what the phrase meant at the time. How it taught me to judge people by who they were, not by their ethnicity, not by their color, not by their religion, not by all those things that can get in the way if you let them.

That's the great lesson of sports, of course. It was only 70 years ago when Jackie Robinson first integrated major league baseball, a mere flick of time in the universe. And what are sports today if not a springboard to the American Dream? Maybe more important, what are sports if not some big social laboratory for people of different races and different ethnic groups, to meet on common ground?

These were the lessons I took away from my childhood, the important ones anyway. They were about valuing what someone brought to a team, about judging people by who they were and what they did, not by what their last name was. Sports did that for me, the debt I owe them. And the lessons are all still around us in so many ways, if only we take the time to look.

I recently received an email from Gary L'Europa, the president of Rhode Island Country Club and a neurologist by trade. He had read a column I wrote about an 86-year-old African-American named Bill Allison, who couldn't play on white courses when he was young, and he wanted to invite him to play golf at the Rhode Island Country Club. L'Europa said that he had grown up in Johnston, the Italian son of a blue-collar worker. He learned to play golf at Triggs, the longtime public course in Providence. He said he's not the first club president of Italian descent — just one more example that times change.

Rhode Island Country Club certainly has. For it's easy to see places locked in a certain time, a certain place. But society is always changing, always evolving, always moving forward. Doesn't history tell us that life is like a river, never standing still, but always flowing somewhere, whether we like it or not?

We see it all around us, in so many ways, some in our collective face, some in much more subtle ways.

So to visit Rhode Island Country Club on Saturday afternoon was a little like taking a trip through a time tunnel. At least for me. The caddy benches that used to stare out at the course are long gone. The little shed that used to be off the first fairway, where the older kids used to shoot craps on slow days, all the while swearing and yelling? That's gone, too. The word is the club is more family-oriented now, a sign of the times. All that, and some members of Italian heritage, too.

Who said things don't get better?

FAREWELL YAWKEY WAY

5/2/2018

*"I am still haunted by what went on here
a long time before we arrived."*
—JOHN HENRY

BOSTON — He has been dead for 42 years now, this South Carolina plantation owner, this South Carolina man who once owned the Red Sox for 43 years.

But he's still one of the biggest stories hovering over the Red Sox in this soon to be summer of 2018, due to the small street that runs alongside the third-base side of Fenway Park in Boston, the small street that was named for him in 1977.

Jersey Street had been renamed Yawkey Way in homage to the man who owned the Red Sox from 1933 to 1976. But his name has become a constant reminder of the Red Sox' haunted past, the obvious symbol of the Red Sox being the last team in Major League Baseball to integrate, the unfortunate past that's always seemed to follow them around like an afternoon shadow that never goes anyway, the baseball version of Original Sin?

Or, as William Faulkner once famously wrote, "The past is never over. In fact, it's not even past."

So the question for some time was: What to do with Yawkey Way? At the bequest of John Henry, the current Red Sox owner, the City of Boston announced on April 26 that it would be changing the name of Yawkey Way back to Jersey Street.

But who was Tom Yawkey?

This is the question Bill Nowlin, who has been the vice president for the Society of Baseball Research since 2004, and has written roughly 35 related books on the Red Sox, sets out to answer in his new book "Tom Yawkey: Patriarch of the Boston Red Sox," a wonderful portrait of Yawkey, who was so shaped both by the time and place he came of age in, and crippled by them, too.

Was he racist, or just a product of the times he lived in?

Or was it both?

These are the questions, and they are complicated. The Yawkey name is all over Boston if you know where to look. Massachusetts General Hospital has a 10-story Yawkey Center for Outpatient Care. Boston Medical Center has the Yawkey Ambulatory Care Center. There is the Yawkey Center for Children and Learning.

And that's just the tip of the iceberg.

But in the summer of 2015, Adrian Walker, an African-American columnist for the Boston Globe, wrote a column in which he suggested Yawkey Way should be renamed.

"It's past time for that ill-fitting tribute to go," he wrote.

So began the discussion for a new era.

For by that time Yawkey had been dead for nearly 40 years. You all but had to be a baseball historian to know the Red Sox' sad history, but now the issue was front and center again, what with Yawkey Way being back in the news. The issue came to the forefront again last summer, back when one of the big stories was the removal of some of the confederate monuments in the South. That was when Henry said that the Red Sox would lead the charge to change the name of Yawkey Way.

"I am still haunted by what went on here a long time before we arrived," he said.

So what did go on?

Nowlin's book has an entire chapter on race, one in which he writes: "It seems unavoidable that we revisit the question of Yawkey and race."

No doubt.

What emerges is a man of the South whose attitudes about race were, no doubt, shaped by that experience. Call it racism. Call it growing up in the moneyed white world of the southern aristocracy in the first half of the 20th century. Call it indifference. Call it anything you want. But as late as 1958 the Red Sox didn't have any black employees, never mind players, the kind of legacy that never goes away. The kind of history that never goes away.

That always has been the franchise's Original Sin, of course, even now, so many years later. Especially in these rigid, black and white times we now live in, where everything is seen as either right or wrong, no gray, and we often judge the past like jurors who can't wait to go home for the day. Or as Glenn Stout, who has written extensively on the Red Sox throughout the years, says in "Tom Yawkey," "Yawkey took pains to avoid addressing the question at all...at every opportunity, Yawkey foisted the issue off on a collection of sycophants, yes-men, and cronies he employed."

And, ultimately, to the great detriment of the Red Sox, the franchise's enduring badge of shame.

And, ultimately, Yawkey's too, fair or not.

So farewell Yawkey Way.

The past has been officially exorcised.

GORDIE ERNST

3/18/2019

"…I hope Gordie Ernst is innocent. For old times' sake."
—BILL REYNOLDS

PROVIDENCE — Once upon a time he was our local version of Chip Hilton, the great sports hero of the Clair Bee novels that were written in the 1950s about the kid who glided through the seasons as if always on smooth ice.

All-State in hockey.

All-State in tennis.

And more important?

He was The Providence Journal's Honor Roll boy back there in the spring of 1985, the newspaper's annual award for the most well-rounded student-athlete in the state, the crème de la crème of all the boys who played sports in the Rhode Island Interscholastic League. And, as former Journal sports writer Mike Szostak once wrote, Ernst was "the golden boy of Rhode Island high school sports in the '80s."

High praise indeed.

And making it seem all the better at the time was that he was the son of Dick Ernst, the longtime coach of both hockey and tennis, mostly at Cranston East, one of those iconic figures in the insular world of Rhode Island high school sports. Someone who was playing in local and regional tennis tournaments throughout his life, a name everyone in Rhode Island sports knew. Someone who had both the poise and the presence to be in the spotlight in those tender years.

For the longest while it all seemed like a great Rhode Island story, one of those you couldn't make up, almost as if the Ernsts had become the first family of Rhode Island sports. Dick Ernst. Gordie Ernst. Bobby Ernst. Andy Ernst — Gordie's brothers, who also played both hockey and tennis very well.

That is the back story, at least part of it.

Gordie went to Brown, where he played both hockey and tennis, an amazing success story by all accounts, this kid who grew up in middle-class Cranston, the son of a teacher.

And after that?

After that, Gordie Ernst didn't seem to be around here much anymore.

I knew him back then, once did a Sunday magazine story on him and his amazing tennis family, back there in the late '70s when The Journal had a Sunday magazine and I used to freelance for it. Through the years I would hear this and that about him, like the times he used to give Michelle Obama tennis lessons at the White House, and nothing would really surprise me.He always seemed to have the kind of down-home Rhode Island personality that could get along with anyone, as if "pretentious" was just another word in a dictionary.

Giving Michelle Obama tennis lessons?

Why not?

But now the game has gotten more complicated, as Ernst, who last summer became the new women's tennis coach at URI, was arrested and charged last week with racketeering conspiracy in the sweeping national college admissions scandal. A disgrace, at least around here.

And that's the sad part.

At least for me.

Ernst is one of dozens of people indicted in the scandal by federal agents for allegedly accepting $2.7 million in bribes that were masqueraded as "consulting fees" during his time as the Georgetown tennis coach. Whatever it is, it's a mess. To the point that URI placed him on paid leave, while this now very public scandal sorts itself out. To the point that this is a serious charge, one that's handled on the front page of newspapers, not the sports page. One that has consequences far beyond just losing a game.

And maybe most important, it's a big-time public body blow to someone who once was held in very high esteem around here. Gordie Ernst has been in the spotlight for a long time now, almost as though he's never really been out of it. One of those names you came to know if you read the sports page through the years.

But this is no longer about sports that little kids play for nothing.

This is about an alleged grown-up crime, numbers with a lot of zeroes behind them. This is about real life.

And I hope Gordie Ernst is innocent.

For old times' sake.

POSTSCRIPT: After pleading guilty to multiple fraud charges, Gordie Ernst was sentenced to 30 months in prison in July 2022.

PHOTOGRAPHY CREDITS

PART ONE

Rick Pitino — 1987 (Providence Journal files)
Dennis 'Oil Can' Boyd — 2007 (Journal files, Providence Journal)
Vinny Pazienza — 1986 (Scott Robinson, Providence Journal)
Billy Donovan — 1987 (Kathy Borchers, Providence Journal)

PART TWO

Marvin Barnes — 2008 (Connie Grosch, Providence Journal)
Joe Mullaney — 1981 (Providence Journal files)
Ed Cooley — (Kris Craig, Providence Journal)
Armand Batastini — 1998 (Rachel Ritchie, Providence Journal)

PART THREE

Billy Perry — (Providence Journal files)
Yudeweh Gbaa — 2008 (Glenn Osmundson, Providence Journal)
Lamar Odom — 2013 (Bob Breidenbach, Providence Journal)
Peter Manfredo, Jr. — 2010 (Kris Craig, Providence Journal)

PART FOUR

Dave Gavitt — 2011 (Bob Thayer, Providence Journal)
Dan Hurley — 2017 (Bob Breidenbach, Providence Journal)
Quenton Marrow — 2015 (Kris Craig, Providence Journal)

Made in United States
North Haven, CT
23 July 2023

39383797R00182